The Philosophy of Art

Stephen Davies

BLACKWELL PUBLISHING
350 Main Street, Malden, MA 02148-5020, USA
9600 Garsington Road, Oxford OX4 2DQ, UK
550 Swanston Street, Carlton, Victoria 3053, Australia

First published 2006 by Blackwell Publishing Ltd

1   2006

Library of Congress Cataloging-in-Publication Data

Davies, Stephen, 1950–
    The philosophy of art / Stephen Davies.
       p. cm.——(Foundations of the philosophy of the arts)
    Includes index.
    ISBN-13: 978-1-4051-2022-7 (alk. paper)
    ISBN-10: 1-4051-2022-3 (alk. paper)
    ISBN-13: 978-1-4051-2023-4 (pbk. : alk. paper)
    ISBN-10: 1-4051-2023-1 (pbk. : alk. paper) 1. Art—Philosophy. 2. Aesthetics. I.
Title. II. Series.

N66 D32 2006
701—dc22

                                                                                2005010994

A catalogue record for this title is available from the British Library.

Set in 11.5pt Perpetua
by SPI Publisher Services, Pondicherry, India

The publisher's policy is to use permanent paper from mills that operate a sustainable forestry policy, and which has been manufactured from pulp processed using acid-free and elementary chlorine-free practices. Furthermore, the publisher ensures that the text paper and cover board used have met acceptable environmental accreditation standards.

For further information on
Blackwell Publishing, visit our website:
www.blackwellpublishing.com

Contents

Figures

Preface

Why Study the Philosophy of Art?

It is widely thought that the arts provide social and personal goods of the highest value. One measure of a society's maturity, sensitivity, and sophistication is the quality of its greatest artists and, more generally, the extent to which its government and public support the arts. Meanwhile, a person who has no interest in any of the arts can be thought to be not fully rounded. On all but the most elitist construal of what art is, almost everyone draws on one or other form of art in ways that are significant to their sense of themselves and their perspective on others. Participation in or exposure to the arts is supposed to contribute to the individual's psychological, emotional, and moral development along with their well-being.

Yet such claims about art's importance can seem puzzling. The production and consumption of art does not directly enhance our survival. Indeed, much art stands conspicuously apart from ordinary, practical concerns. It lacks the immediate, functional value of science and technology. Besides, art usually offers its rewards more to the person who engages with it on its own terms for the sake of appreciating its individuality than to one who treats it merely as a means to pre-specified, extrinsic ends. And even if art is a source of knowledge and experience, it often provides such an indirect and complicated route to these that we should wonder what they have to do with its importance. Though we might accept that art contributes valuably to human self-realization and fulfillment, the kind of nourishment it supplies and how it delivers this are not immediately obvious.

These are not the only respects in which art is perplexing. It comes in a bewildering variety of kinds. Individual works often are interpreted in different, even conflicting, ways. Some art is difficult to comprehend and may be provocative or just plain weird. People differ in their tastes and judgments. Despite all this, we expect a degree of uniformity and objectivity in aesthetic assessments. People are much more bothered if others fault their artistic preferences and evaluations than they would be if it were their liking for blue M&Ms, say, that is challenged. This suggests that, despite their wide-ranging diversity, aesthetic preferences are not regarded as purely subjective.

The study of philosophy refines invaluable skills and techniques. For example, students learn how to analyze and evaluate arguments critically, fairly, and constructively. Also, they are trained to express their understandings of complex or abstract ideas in terms that are clear and precise.

The philosophy of art provides, as well as these general benefits, specific ones that come from addressing the puzzles mentioned above. We can deeply enrich our insight into our practices and ourselves by reflecting on what appears odd or intriguing about them and by attempting to explain art's significance to our lives. After all, the production and appreciation of art is among the most distinctive of the traits that make us uniquely human.

In thinking about art, here are some of the questions a philosopher might raise: When and why did art originate? What theories best illuminate why people make and consume art? What kinds of things are art and what makes them art? What is the purpose of interpreting art and what constraints, if any, govern its interpretation? What kinds of content and meaning do artworks possess? How do they express emotions? How does art represent what lies beyond its boundaries? Are artworks valuable because they convey insight about the world that cannot be easily obtained in other ways, or does their value lie in their separation from the demands of ordinary life? Is there a connection between aesthetic and moral value?

These and other questions are considered in the following chapters.

Applications and Questions

The chapters of this book fall into two parts. The first, covered in chapters 1–4, is largely theoretical. To bring things back to earth, I close each of these chapters by discussing concrete applications of ideas they contain. The second part, chapters 5–8, deals with more practical (though still general) topics. The issue of how these arguments are to be applied arises inevitably in conjunction with their exposition, so I consider relevant examples and treatments within the body of the chapter. All chapters close with questions intended to provoke consideration of how the ideas that are outlined might be extended or developed.

References and Readings

I have avoided burdening the main text with citations of previously published material, which otherwise might overwhelm it.

Some general references are invaluable and cover all the topics discussed in this book, and much else besides. Also, the material they contain is often more digestible than that found in scholarly journals and monographs. They should be the first resource consulted by any student. To avoid repetition, I list them now.

Aesthetics: Critical Concepts in Philosophy, ed. J. O. Young, 4 vols. (London: Routledge, 2005).

Aesthetics and the Philosophy of Art: The Analytic Tradition, ed. P. Lamarque and S. H. Olsen (Oxford: Blackwell, 2004).

Blackwell Companion to Aesthetics, ed. D. Cooper (Oxford: Blackwell, 1992).

Contemporary Debates in Aesthetics and the Philosophy of Art, ed. M. Kieran (Oxford: Blackwell, 2006).

Blackwell Guide to Aesthetics, ed. P. Kivy (Oxford: Blackwell, 2003).

Macmillan Encyclopedia of Philosophy, editor-in-chief Donald M. Borchert (2nd edn., New York: Macmillan Reference USA, 2005)

Oxford Encyclopedia of Aesthetics, ed. M. Kelly, 4 vols. (Oxford: Oxford University Press, 1998).

Oxford Handbook of Aesthetics, ed. J. Levinson (Oxford: Oxford University Press, 2003).

Routledge Encyclopedia of Philosophy, editor-in-chief E. Craig, 10 vols. (London: Routledge, 1998).

Routledge Companion to Aesthetics, ed. B. Gaut and D. McIver Lopes (2nd edn., London: Routledge, 2005).

An annotated selection of readings is appended to each chapter. Note that most of the works indicated are *not* intended by their authors for introductory students. Readings are listed either where their authors are named in the chapter or where they provide relevant ancillary arguments. Students who wish to follow up particular issues at a philosophically sophisticated and detailed level should consult these references.

Among the journals devoted specifically to aesthetics and the philosophy of art are *British Journal of Aesthetics*, *Journal of Aesthetics and Art Criticism*, *Journal of Aesthetic Education*, and *Philosophy and Literature*. In the readings at the end of each chapter I abbreviate these as *BJA*, *JAAC*, *JAE*, and *PL*.

Acknowledgments

I am grateful for the feedback I have received from students who have studied the philosophy of art with me, and for the comments of Philip Alperson, the series editor, John Brown, John Dilworth, Jonathan Farrell, Ted Gracyk, Jonathan McKeown-Green, Justine Kingsbury, Stephanie Ross, and Dabney Townsend. Jeff Dean and Danielle Descoteaux, of Blackwell Publishing, my project manager Janet Moth, and anonymous reviewers provided invaluable advice, assistance, and criticism.

Chapter One

Evolution and Culture

One way of working our way into the kinds of questions that are central in the philosophy of art – what is art? what is the significance of art? how is art to be understood? – is by asking about art's origins. In this chapter, I explore the contrasts between two divergent stories, one biological and the other cultural, about art's foundations. According to the first, the activities involved in making and appreciating art are products of human evolution. As such, they are universal and old. The second view sees art as the product of a particular time and culture, that of eighteenth-century Europe. It maintains that the concept familiar to us today first emerged then and there. According to this account, the appearance of art was comparatively recent and initially localized.

1.1 A Biological Basis for Art

Here is a story that might be told about the biological basis of art's creation and appreciation by an evolutionary theorist:

> Art is universal. All over the world, mothers sing and hum their babies to sleep. Storytelling, rhyming, and dramatized enactments are present in all cultures. The same is true of music and dance, as well as of depictions of people and animals, along with designs and patterns, which are drawn in pigment or charcoal, molded from clay, and carved or whittled from wood, bone, or stone. Humans everywhere decorate and beautify their environments, possessions, and bodies.
>
> Art also is ancient in its origins. European cave paintings date back more than 50,000 years, while some rock paintings of the Australian

aborigines are 20,000 years old. Carvings and molded figurines appear in the late Pleistocene, some 10,000 years ago, and artifacts decorated with patterns and motifs are far older. While much art is perishable or non-material, its former existence can be deduced from traces that survive. For example, musical instruments made from bones date to at least 45,000–60,000 years ago.

As well, art is a source of pleasure and value. Even if artworks serve practical functions, such as appeasing the gods in ritual ceremonies, their production, use, and contemplation usually provide enjoyment to those involved. Though the pleasure art engenders can come as a momentary thrill or chill, much art is a source of abiding satisfaction and deep fulfillment. It warms and adds meaning to our lives. Indeed, we often regard it as helping to define our very identities: a man might be the kind of person who has a passion for rhythm and blues and who despises country & western; a woman might regard Sylvia Plath's poetry as central to her existence, so that she could become indifferent to it only if she underwent some dramatic change in personality or circumstances.

These three features — universality, historical age, and intrinsic pleasure or value — are indicative of the biological adaptiveness of the behaviors with which they are associated. In other words, these characteristics are symptomatic of underlying genetic dispositions passed from generation to generation because they enhance the reproductive success of the people who have them. The behaviors in question are universal because they reflect a genetic inheritance that is common to humankind. They are old because humans reached their current biological form some 20,000 years ago as hunter-gatherers on the savannahs of the late Pleistocene. And they are a source of pleasure (like food, sex, and healthy exercise) in order to motivate people to pursue them and thereby to pass on their genes to future generations who will be successful breeders in their turn.

It is plausible, then, that the impulse to make and consume art is a product of biological evolution. It is important to be clear about what this means. The thought is not that there is some single gene for art, or that our biology determines behaviors with respect to art that operate as inflexible reflexes. The genetic bases of the production of art are undoubtedly complicated. They require the realization of complex systems and circumstances, both personal and social, for their activation, and the behaviors to which they give rise are plastic, being subject to learning, influence, development, refinement, and the like. There can be no denying that art includes a huge, conventionalized, socio-historical component. The idea, then, is not that the making and consumption of art can be analyzed reductively as mechanical reactions blindly programmed by our genetic inheritance, but rather that they stem from and are channeled by biologic-ally rooted inclinations and proclivities that are then actively and intelli-gently taken up in ways depending on each person's individual, social, and historical environment. In other words, art behaviors draw on biological agendas and energies that direct and constrain, but only in fairly general terms, the forms of their cultural expression. The view with which this one is to be contrasted maintains that the behaviors associated with art are *purely* cultural and *entirely* contingent.

The evolutionary biologist can choose between two positions about the relation between human biological endowments and the production of art. The first maintains that the making and consumption of art are directly adaptive; that is, they are responsible for reproductive success, which is why they were selected. According to the second, these propensities were not directly targeted by evolution, but they are a happy and inevitable byproduct of other behaviors that were.

A common version of the first approach notes that reproductive success depends on our attracting mates, which we do by advertising our fitness as a potential partner and parent. One way of doing so is by demonstrating that we can apply relevant skills and talents to the activities that will be involved. Or, and this might be more successful, we might display in a general way that we have intelligence, originality, creativity, flexibility, and virtuosity in thought and action. And finally, we can dramatize and emphasize our fitness by showing that we can afford the luxury of "wasting" our talents on activities that have no survival value. Art-making and artistic performance, which so often require extraordinary skill and dedication in their conception, planning, and execution, while not being directed to survival in an obvious way, are among the ulti-mate tools for sexual advertisement and seduction. In this view, art behavior, like the peacock's tail, has evolved through the process of sexual selection.

A different account takes a broader and (to my mind) more plausible view of art's evolutionary significance. Art plays a crucial role in intensifying and enriching our lives in general, both as individuals and communities.

It brings us together as producers or performers and consumers or audiences and thereby engenders cooperation, mutuality, and a shared identity. When coupled with other socially important events, such as rituals and ceremonies, it heightens their already special powers. As such, it plays a vital role in transmitting and affirming the community's knowledge, lore, history, and values. It enhances the reproductive success of the members of communities not by making copulation more likely, but instead by contributing vitally to the creation of an environment in which individuals and their children can flourish, this being one in which there is mutual support and respect, a shared sense of belonging and caring, stability, self-confirmation, a feeling of control of or accommodation with nature, and so on.

It could be objected that the first of these accounts seems to undervalue the far-reaching significance of art within human affairs, and that the second does not distinguish a role specific to art as such, while both make the tie between art and reproductive success closer than is believable. If such criticisms prove strong, evolutionary theorists could fall back to the more modest alternative, according to which art is an indirect but important spin-off from other behaviors for which there has been evolutionary selection. It is not difficult to imagine what these behaviors are. Curiosity, adaptability, intelligence, the ability to plan and reason, imagination, improvisatory facility, and patience are all characteristics that promote the survival of people and their heirs. And what is likely to pay off is that these capacities are general and rewarding for their own sakes, not tied in their application only to addressing a limited set of short-term, obvious problems for survival. But once such a creature has evolved and finds itself with some spare time, it continues to employ its talents. It can busy itself with inventing new weapons or a more effective mousetrap, but it is as likely to make up stories, paint evocative pictures of the animals it hunts, decorate its hair with pretty flowers, test what interesting sounds it can make by flexing its hunting bow against its body and plucking the string, and so on. No less important to it will be emotions and their expression, the communication of thoughts, and the development of manipulative and other technical skills. These too can find expression in the production of art; for example, in musical invocations by instruments of the tones of the human voice, in the versification of utterance along with the use of metaphor, assonance, irony, and the like, and in developing pictorial and other forms of representation.

1.2   The Cultural Invention of Art

Here is a second story about art's origins, as it might be told by a cultural historian.

> We think of the arts as a loose but natural collection – literature, drama, painting, poetry, sculpture, music, dance – unified by the fact that their products are to be contemplated for their own sake. As such, the arts are to be contrasted with the crafts, such as saddle-making, boat-building, and plumbing. The crafts are directed at the useful functions that their products can serve. By contrast, works of art are not mere means to ends but are ends in themselves. Their value lies within them, not in benefits and applications that come with their effects.
>
> Other differences between the artist and the artisan (or crafts-person) indicate differences in their respective activities and products. The artisan is not expected to be original and he is good at his job to the extent that he can successfully follow the relevant rules, models, or recipes. A work of craft is good if it matches the appropriate template and performs its desired function. By contrast, the artist must be creative and original. Good art cannot be produced by slavish rule-following and imitation. In fact, artists are often rebellious or eccentric in their personalities and their methods of production. Great artists are geniuses whose works transcend the rules and conventions of their time. Meanwhile, the best art is often unique in its value and, in any case, all art is to be judged and appreciated only for the experience its aesthetic qualities produce in a suitably placed observer. This spectator must distance herself from "interested" concerns – that is, from practical uses the artwork could be given, either for her personally or more generally – in order to make herself available to the appropriate experience, which involves the pleasurable contemplation of the work's beauty and other aesthetic properties viewed only for the sake of their contribution to its overall aesthetic effect.

If our conception of art is the one just described, then art is a product of a specific culture and history, not of biology. This conception is local and comparatively recent, not universal and old, because it emerged gradually in Europe over the Enlightenment and the modern age – that is, from the mid-eighteenth century to the early twentieth – under the influence of specific socio-economic conditions that did not obtain elsewhere or in earlier times. Historians of ideas dispute when particular elements of this way of thinking emerged. They also argue about whether nineteenth- and early twentieth-century developments in aesthetic theorizing misrepresent the views that first appeared in the eighteenth century. These scholarly debates will not detain us here. Despite significant differences between the view's variants, and despite the long period over which it emerged, by the early twentieth century the doctrines associated with this conception of art had become dominant in Anglo-American philosophy of art.

The story continues:

> Because art can be such only when made and appreciated as falling under the concept that identifies it, it follows that non-Western cultures do not have art in our sense, and that art as we now understand the notion was not produced in the West prior to, say, the early eighteenth century. Pieces from outside the ambit of recent Western cultures can become art through appropriation to the Western *artworld*, which is the constellation of traditions, practices, institutions, roles, writings, and theories relevant to making and appreciating the repository of accepted artworks. And to the extent that Western culture has become thoroughly globalized, people from other societies can make art now. But those who have never shared the modern age Western concept have not been creators of art, though they may have had their own, functionally similar practices.

(As a concession to her opponent, our story-teller might allow that biologically based urges and interests would tend to encourage the flowering of some correlate to the Western notion of art in other, sufficiently stable, cultures.)

In ancient times, the various artforms were not recognized as comprising a unified group. Music, for example, was classed with mathematics and astronomy, while poetry was grouped with grammar and rhetoric. The first to link the artforms together explicitly and to separate them from other disciplines and activities were the authors of encyclopedias and books in the 1740s and 1750s. Also, when the term *art* (*ars* in Latin, *techne* in Greek) was used in earlier times, this was in order to distinguish works of *art* from works of *nature*; that is, *all* humanly made things were works of *art*. The term attained its current usage, in which it marks a special subset of humanly created items and opposes these to the products of human crafts, only in the late Enlightenment and modern age. As this implies, artists were not previously differentiated from artisans, which was appropriate given that almost everyone worked by copying or borrowing, that individuality was not expected or highly valued, and that many members of a workshop might cooperate on the production of any given work. The job of an artist was that of a servant, usually either of the church or court. He – most were men – was often directed in what to do and when to do it. J. S. Bach, for example, was a church composer who had to produce new music on a weekly basis. Between 1704 and 1744 he composed 300 church cantatas, only one of which was published in his lifetime. Similarly, Domenico Scarlatti wrote more than 600 harpsichord sonatas for Maria Barbara, who became the queen of Spain. Only 30 were published during his lifetime. Such composers had to produce a constant supply of music to fill the needs of the church, state, or court. Though the individuality and skill of supreme creators like Shakespeare, Michelangelo, or Dante was acknowledged in earlier times, it was not until the nineteenth century in Europe that large numbers of artists established their independence, and with this came the cult of authorship, signed as opposed to anonymous works, emphasis on originality, and the idea that the artist is inspired and creative in ways that mere artisans are not.

Changes in the social status of artists of the time were a consequence of far wider alterations within society. There was a gradual swing of economic power toward the emerging merchant middle class. As a group, they had the wealth to patronize the arts and the desire to confirm themselves as equal in discernment to serious and refined members of the upper classes. This new market for art made it possible for an exceptional few "free-lance" artists to survive precariously at the close of the eighteenth century.

This shift of art from the private to the public sphere coincided with the arrival of institutions and practices that are now considered fundamental to the artworld. The late eighteenth century saw the appearance of public concert halls (along with the introduction of subscriptions for series of performances of new works), the art gallery and public exhibitions, the art academy and salon, art criticism and reviews, art history and biography, art theory, and a transfer of copyright for literary works from publishers to authors. In previously established theaters and opera houses, rearrangement of the seating and lighting focused the audience's attention on the stage, not their fellows.

Meanwhile, philosophers of the eighteenth and the nineteenth centuries, including giants such as Immanuel Kant and Arthur Schopenhauer, set down the foundational principles of the new science of aesthetics. Art is concerned with the beautiful and the sublime, these being the cardinal aesthetic properties. (Later philosophers list a greater variety of properties – balance, harshness, serenity, power, elegance, clumsiness, and so on – but these can be regarded as species of beauty and sublimity or their opposites.) Beauty is a source of immediate delight, as when we find a rose attractive. An example of the sublime is the vastness of the night sky, with its countless number of stars. The experience of the sublime includes negative feelings of awe and insignificance in the face of nature's indifference, power, and magnitude, but it has a positive aspect also, to the extent that we become aware of ourselves as capable of grasping and comprehending such matters. Where the beauty of a thing is not judged in terms of its kind or function, but instead, in terms of its formal and perceptible properties as given directly to the senses, that judgment concerns what Kant calls *free* beauty. Some later philosophers offer such judgments as their primary examples of the truly aesthetic reaction. A concern with something's kind, function, or practical usefulness can interfere with a proper aesthetic response, because it selectively structures what is perceived in the object, rather than allowing the object's features to announce their own significance, as it were. To explain why not everyone who is prepared to encounter a thing's aesthetic properties can recognize them, even when their ordinary perceptual faculties are in order, eighteenth-century theorists posited the existence of a special faculty of aesthetic perception, that of taste. Only those with taste can truly experience an item's aesthetic properties and arrive at an objective judgment of their worth. Aesthetic experience of an item's formal beauty or sublimity tends toward the ineffable. Aesthetic experience is not solely perceptual. It is infused by a cognitive but non-conceptual process described by Kant as involving the free play of the imagination and the understanding.

It was not part of the agenda of these philosophers to disenfranchise art made prior to the eighteenth century or in sophisticated non-Western cultures. Indeed, they took their paradigms of art from ancient Greece and Rome, from the works of Homer and Sophocles. For example, the nineteenth-century German philosopher G. W. F. Hegel argued that Western art had been in decline from the early Christian era. Others made reference to art from Egypt, India, and China. Schopenhauer, for instance, discussed Islamic and Indian art. Nevertheless, the story according to which art is an invention of eighteenth-century, Western culture proposes that the conception of art that these philosophers were the first to articulate and analyze does not pre-date the eighteenth century. Their theories captured and described this new concept, which they went on, anachronistically and inappropriately, to apply more widely.

In summary, the second tale argues that the modern concept of the arts — which is our current concept and the one we are trying to analyze — crystallized out of the changing ideas and practices of eighteenth- and nineteenth-century Europe. People who do not distinguish art from craft do not share the same concept and do not make art in terms of that concept. The concept was not possessed prior to the eighteenth century nor was it possessed outside the West before the globalization of Western culture. So, art is not ancient and universal. It is a comparatively recent and origin‹ localized socio-philosophical creation.

1.3 The Big and the Small Picture

I call the previous presentations *stories* and do not attribute them to particular authors. This is because each is a simplified composite assembled from a family of related positions. Individual theorists sometimes develop distinctive variants and often disagree with others who fall roughly in the same camp, as well as with those who do not share their basic premises. (See the readings section at this chapter's close for more information about who holds what view.) A more careful and sophisticated analysis would explore the detail of these differences.

Notice also that the stories have been presented uncritically. If they were to be cross-examined, we might raise issues such as the following: Can we reliably infer the biological origins and significance of complex cultural practices from their modern manifestations, as the biological theory seems to suppose? Or, can people make and appreciate art only if they possess and self-consciously apply the relevant concepts, terms, and theories, as is perhaps implied by the view that art is a recent cultural invention? Meanwhile, the plausibility of each of the competing strands within the broader theories should also be interrogated.

Instead of taking those directions, I consider the apparent tension between the two theories and the attitude appropriate to that. Both the biological and cultural views tap into important assumptions underlying our intuitive understanding of art. We are inclined to think art is grounded in and reflects our common humanity. The evolutionary story starts from there and proposes that there is a biological underpinning to the art-related interests and predilections we share. We also tend to think that art's local expressions are largely shaped by historical and social contingencies. The view that art is a cultural invention begins there and argues that art-related behaviors are not constrained by biology or evolution (except insofar as these fix our basic structure and physiology). There is a genuine opposition between the positions, since the one concludes that the making and appreciation of art has a universal, biological basis, even if these behaviors are directed and refined by the local cultural setting, while the other describes the same practices as purely cultural in a way that escapes or transcends the influence of biology. Yet there is the prospect of reconciling them, since the widely held intuitions from which each begins are not strictly opposed.

There are two frequent responses to conflicts such as this. The first proposes that the truth lies somewhere in the middle and that we should reconcile the two views by seeking their common ground. That is not an easy option in this case, as it might be if the difference were one about the *extent* to which nature and nurture each contributes to how we behave in society. The disagreement in this case is not about the relative strengths of these two inputs, but about whether our biology constrains or directs the nature of art *at all* once it has shaped our most basic physical and mental endowments. Moreover, there is no obvious middle ground between the proposal that art is very old and universal and the counterclaim that art is recent and local in its origins. The second way of responding to such disputes is by suggesting the disagreement between the positions is more apparent than real. This would be the case, for example, if it turned out that they are not talking about the same thing. In what follows I argue against this option.

1.4 "It all depends what you mean by the word *art*"

As was just observed, it might be thought that it is easy to resolve the appearance of conflict between the claim that there is a biological basis to art and the alternative that treats art as a cultural invention by noting that proponents of the two stories obviously do not mean the same by the term *art*. Since they are not discussing the same thing, differences in what they say do not indicate a disagreement. If various people say of a mole that it is a burrowing mammal of the family *Talpidae*, a spy who remains dormant for a time before becoming active, a concentration of melanin on the skin, a pier or breakwater, and a unit of chemistry, they do not disagree because each is referring to a different meaning of the English word *mole*. And if one person says a mole has dark velvety fur and another apparently denies this, saying that a mole is typically constructed of stone, wood, metal, or concrete, their disagreement is more apparent than real, because they have different meanings of the word *mole* in mind. According to this view, something similar is true of art when one theorist says it is universal and ancient and the other appears to deny this.

This seemingly simple solution needs to be carefully considered, however. It cannot amount to the claim that each theorist can give the term any
meaning she chooses. Both aim to provide a true tale about what *art* refers
to in its ordinary, common use, so their accounts must be answerable to
the term's ordinary meaning or meanings. The proposed solution could
work only if the English word *art* has various publicly accepted but
different meanings, including ones assumed by the two stories. So far so
good, but the proposed solution requires more: there must be no basis for
regarding the one meaning as more conceptually foundational than, and
thereby as subsuming and explaining, the other. Because, even if it were
true that the word *art* has both meanings, the competing theorists might
disagree about which is more conceptually central. In fact, this seems to
be what is happening. So, the task of reconciling their theories may not be
simple after all.

Here is a more sophisticated approach allowing that the two theorists
differ in what they mean by *art* but acknowledging that a disagreement of
substance remains. The person who argues that art is universal because
it reflects behaviors and tastes conditioned in part by our biological
inheritance might see the disagreement in these terms:

> The term *art* can be applied in a restricted way to Western "high" art, as it
> was developed in Enlightenment Europe and later. Equally, it can be
> applied in a restricted way to the aesthetically pleasing ritual artifacts of
> small-scale, pre-industrial societies, or to ancient Greek tragedies, and so
> on. But these specific, narrow applications of the term identify species
> falling under the umbrella of a single genus. Other species within this
> genus include folk, popular, domestic, and religious art. These differ
> while falling under the same genus, just as domestic cats differ from tigers
> though both share membership in the genus *Felix*. The theory describing
> art's biological basis aims to characterize the evolutionary forces shaping
> the behaviors that produced the *genus*, not the local concerns that led to
> its differentiation into *species*. It therefore can claim conceptual priority
> because it provides the most general and overarching account if our
> concern is to understand what art — all art, in its various species — is

The person who argues that art is comparatively recent and local, being
restricted to post-seventeenth-century Europe (until Western culture
went on to colonize and overcome all others), conceives of the conflict
differently:

The term *art* or its equivalent has a history of use dating back millennia in which it identified anything that was made by humans, as opposed to works of God or nature. Gradually, it came to acquire a more specific application in Europe, in which it refers to works of art as opposed to works of craft. There is a historical thread between these different uses — the later one emerged over time from the former. No conceptual or meaning tie was preserved, however. In its post-seventeenth-century use, the term took on meanings and associations quite distinct from its earlier ones. (Compare it with a word like *plumber*, which has a modern meaning historically continuous but otherwise quite distinct from its ancient one, in which it designated someone who worked in the metal lead.) Because the task at hand is to analyze our current idea of art, which cut its ties with past meanings when it was forged in the philosophical and social upheavals of the Enlightenment, the concept that must take priority is the comparatively recent, Western one, since that has super-seded all others and there is no broader category for art under which it can be subsumed.

Our two imaginary theorists do mean different things when they talk about art, but that does not mean their disagreement is empty or merely "semantic." Each can acknowledge the meaning emphasized by the other, but they differ about which of these is central to the analysis. Can their dispute be settled without begging the question in favor of one side or the other, as would happen if we simply assumed that there is non-Western, pre-Enlightenment art in the relevantly current sense of that term, or if we assumed that Leonardo could not have produced art just because he probably did not distinguish his painting from the practical products of artisans as sharply as we do? I am not sure I know the answer to this question, though I incline to the conviction that art is old and universal in ways that suggest no single culture or period can claim exclusive ownership of the concept.

What will become clear in following chapters, I hope, is that how we approach many of the puzzles that arise when we think about art's nature and its place in human affairs is likely be affected by whether we lean to the view that assigns a biological role for human nature in art or, instead, to the idea that art as we understand it is purely and arbitrarily cultural. That means also that we may be able to look back with new insight on this opening puzzle after we consider these further issues, taking them on their own terms.

Applications and Connections — The Museum, Tourist Art,
Popular Art, and Ancient Art

It is useful to connect the previous discussion with current debate about the status of the art museum.

One perspective regards the art museum negatively. It maintains that, when art is separated from the context of its creation and from its role in the life of the community, it is bled of its relevance and power. The job of art is to intensify and add significance to people's lives through its immediate involvement in things that affect them directly, such as religion and rites, courtship and domestic life, work and entertainment. When altarpieces are ripped from churches and displayed together in a museum, or when J. S. Bach's cantatas are performed apart from the eighteenth-century Lutheran church services to which they were integral, they can no longer engage with the daily existence of the community. To fill that void, something else, usually of lesser quality, replaces it. To display art in a warehouse, where it is pinned and labeled, is to kill it, to alienate it from the setting in which it matters to ordinary folk, thereby impoverishing their lives.

A different point of view is more positive. Art museums provide, as other settings do not, for the undisturbed contemplation of art, which is how it should be approached. Contextualizing artworks by presenting them together and ordering them by artist, period, and style is the way to optimize their appreciation. (By contrast, sitting through long sermons and Bible readings in order to hear Bach's music would be a boring distraction, and the gloomy interiors of churches offer conditions for viewing carvings and paintings that are far from ideal.) Besides, Western high art over the past several hundred years was created for contemplation under the special conditions art museums and concert halls make available. The museum and concert hall are its natural home. Rather than removing art from the wider community, art museums and concert venues are publicly accessible institutions integrated into and catering for the societies in which they are housed. They bring art to people who otherwise might lack the opportunity to see and hear it. (Previously, much art was the preserve of private wealth and not for public display.) In addition, museums play important curatorial, preservative, scholarly, and restorative functions. They guard and treasure art that otherwise would have been lost as the social contexts in which it was produced were overtaken by the advancing tide of modern life.

The first view, with its emphasis on the functional role of art within the community, echoes many of the sentiments associated above with the evolutionary theory of art. Ellen Dissanayake – an American who studies human behavior cross-culturally and who regards the making and consumption of art as an evolved behavior with the function of creating a community within which individuals can flourish – clearly advocates some such position. She argues that humankind is not adapted to the alienating conditions of modern, industrialized, urban life, and that Western high art has lost its way over the past century, becoming increasingly esoteric, unrewarding, and irrelevant. Her paradigms for healthy, artful societies are small-scale, pre-industrial, non-Western ones. Meanwhile, the second account, which stresses the thought that art should be contemplated in a manner that extracts it from its social backdrop and which regards institutions like the art museum as admirably suited to serving this purpose, harmonizes with aspects of the art-as-cultural-invention position.

In fact, the links just proposed as holding between the two pairs of opposed positions are extremely weak. Whether a person adopts the biological or the cultural account of art need not determine whether she goes along with the positive or negative account of the museum. Explaining why this is the case can help us understand more about the two debates: art as nature versus art as culture and museum-based art versus community-based art.

Not all advocates of the idea that art belongs in and serves the community and not all critics of the museum take their stances because they believe that art is an evolved behavior. For example, the American pragmatist philosopher John Dewey wrote early in the twentieth century that art should be organically integrated with life's more quotidian aspects, and he criticized the estrangement of art from the community when it is housed in museums, but he was not committed to an evolutionary account of art's origins or universality. Also, even theorists who are prepared to affirm the special value of Western high art can be disparaging of some of the museum's activities and policies. For example, some reject the acquisitive imperialism that has seen the global harvest of statues and other pieces from cultures across the world. To mention a notorious case, ancient marble statues were removed from Athens in the early eighteenth century by the seventh earl of Elgin. Despite repeated requests from the Greek government, the statues have not yet been returned from the British Museum. These critics of the museum desire the repatriation of works such as the "Elgin marbles," so that other societies can reclaim and more effectively preserve the integrity of their cultural heritage.

Similarly, advocates for the museum do not always suppose that art is a recent invention of Western culture, which is why museums usually include statues from Greek and Roman antiquity, medieval religious carvings and paintings, and so on. Nor do they necessarily reject the credentials of non-Western and domestic candidates for art-status. In recent decades, materials originating in other cultures have been transferred from natural history to art museums, along with displays of the products of domestic skills such as weaving, quilting, and sewing. The spirit of this trend seemingly is one of belated recognition and acknowledgment. As well, the practices of the museum are more embracing and community-directed than formerly. For example, there is a move to new styles of display, including theme rooms that bring together paintings, sculptures, rugs, screens, furniture, and the rest, as they might have coexisted outside the museum. These show how art is or was integrated with its social context.

Turning now to evolutionary accounts, it is clear that their proponents need not be automatically committed to denigrating the museum and praising community-based art practices. Not all such theorists regard art's evolutionary function as shoring up and affirming the community's values, or value the celebration of cultural difference. Those who hold that art should have a universal appeal that transcends local, cultural differences could welcome the way in which museums insulate artworks from the particular social environments in which they happen to be created.

A yet more interesting observation draws attention to the fact that not all advocates of the theory of art as a cultural invention take a positive attitude to what was allegedly created. Some see the European creation of art as motivated by unacknowledged desires to insidiously promote elitist ideologies, often with patriarchal overtones. Accordingly, they condemn the art museum as an institutional embodiment of reactionary forces for cultural suppression. When the art museum takes in folk and non-Western artifacts, this is decried as appropriation and cultural colonization. And when it updates its styles of display, the new forms are challenged for being no less artificial and contrived than were the earlier fashions in presentation that are replaced. Theorists of this persuasion argue that, if art can be invented, it can also be reinvented or replaced, and this is what is needed. They decry the art museum for serving as a tool of an artworld regime that should be overhauled or overthrown.

Ideologies of elitism are not the only dogmas to be wary of, though. Those who despise them sometimes seem guilty of their own distortions when it comes to the discussion of community-based art, especially that of small-scale, pre-industrial societies. It is widely assumed by Westerners that "primitive" cultures have art traditions that are old, simple, and stable. Because they have these features, it is reasoned, these traditions tap deep into the spiritual ethos and fundamental values of their home societies and of humanity more widely. Cultural tourists seek out such communities, expecting to find special nourishment through contact with what are identified by the tourists as these cultures' arts. In doing so, they apply standards for authenticity they would never dream of imposing on Western art. No one would criticize an American composer for having been influenced by the music of foreign (European or Asian) cultures, or for challenging the conventions used by his predecessors. Neither would they condemn the performer for playing an instrument that was manufactured in Japan, or the performance because it is staged for a fee-paying audience many of whom are tourists. Yet performances of non-Western music in indigenous contexts are liable to be dismissed as inauthentic if there is any taint of Western influence or commercialism about what is done. This double standard perhaps indicates that a Romantic ideology is responsible for shaping an inappropriate image in Western thought of what art is and how it functions within small-scale communities.

As Larry Shiner, a contemporary American philosopher, has objected, there is no basis for supposing the so-called art of small-scale, pre-industrial societies is less eclectic, innovative, fusion-oriented, or financially motivated than our own varieties. (The evidence usually suggests that it is and always was so.) In that case, there is also no ground for believing that community-based art is more real, rich, or "authentic" than the sophisticated, complex, recent, quickly evolving art movements of modern, industrial Western societies. Shiner takes this line not in order to validate Western high art but for the sake of debunking the mythologies Westerners weave around the products of other cultures, which he thinks are best not regarded as art.

I turn now to another strand in the debate between advocates of the biological account of art's basis and the art-as-cultural-invention theory. This subplot concerns the products of popular culture. Defenders of the view that art is old and universal are inclined to be inclusive, regarding modern, popular entertainments as art, if not always of the best kind, while some of those who claim that art is an invention of eighteenth-century Europe are more conservative. They put art on a higher pedestal than ordinary occupations and functional artifacts. But as before, there is not a neat match between these various stances. The evolutionary theorist can be conservative and elitist about what is to count as art, especially if she thinks that only a few people at any given time are able to derive selective advantage from their skills in making or appreciating art. Meanwhile, those who argue that art practices are arbitrarily cultural as a step to advocating their reform or rejection often include on the agenda a more liberal, democratic franchise for the "art" of the future. They would have us reinvent art to make it more encompassing and broad-based, less ideologically driven and politically slanted, and so on.

Modern-day cultural theorists tend to be critics of the art establishment and its practices, as was indicated above. Nevertheless, there is a long history of conservatism that equates art with the highest achievements of Western civilization and distinguishes art from works of popular entertainment, which are despised along with the crafts. A common charge holds that entertainments, because they aim to be accessible, inevitably target the lowest common level of taste by relying on stereotypes and formulas that inhibit the audience's imaginative and critical engagement with the ideas and values they promote. (The truth of these various allegations should be questioned, of course. When tested against actual examples, they often appear to be false, as the contemporary American philosopher Noël Carroll has shown. For example, much popular fiction is replete with distinctive characters, while genres like the thriller demand from their audience imaginative engagement and critical analysis.)

Not all critics of the products of popular culture embrace the position that art belongs exclusively to post-Enlightenment Western culture, though. Some oppose, not folk or popular art as such, but what might be called "mass" art, which is the product of technologies of mass dissemination. Handcrafted works and others bearing the mark of individuality and authorship might be accepted as art, even if they come from outside the European high art tradition of recent centuries. For others, the goal is to distinguish the good from the bad, without assuming that this will automatically sort all works of fine art from all other cultural products designed to amuse or entertain.

Though the approaches just described do not attempt to confine art to post-eighteenth-century high European culture, neither do they lend support to the theory that art is universal and old. The art establishment often accepts as art the outstanding examples of photography, popular music, movies, and the like, but does so not in recognition of art's humble ubiquity but, instead, to distinguish these particular pieces from the mainstream remainder. In other words, a few works from popular and folk culture, from beyond the West, and from much earlier periods are promoted to the status of art because they are identified as exceptions that transcend their origins. This is not an attempt to democratize the concept of art. Instead, it represents an attempt to brace art's ramparts against some possible counterexamples.

It might be thought that the claims of the conservative can be defeated by drawing attention to facts testifying to art's wide existence. For instance, very old rock and cave paintings, such as those at Chauvet and Lascaux, are said to prove that humankind had art from its earliest beginnings. And the presence of indigenous forms of music and dancing in non-Western cultures is offered as showing that art occurs beyond the West. The problem with these counterclaims is that the empirical data can be interpreted in other ways. Here is the worry: we often have no idea of the intentions of the makers of these ancient pictures, or of how the pictures were regarded and used in their cultures of origin, yet we consider such matters crucial to the recognition and interpretation of contemporary art as art. Similarly, given familiar problems of language translation and of interpreting the practices of other cultures, when we believe art is found in them we might be arrogantly imposing our own conception where it has no place. So, claiming that the rock paintings or non-Western dances are art simply begs, rather than answers, the question at issue. Where the available information fits more than one theory and the disagreement is about which, if any, can be proved, analysis of the issues, not more data of the same kind, is needed.

If the debate cannot be settled by uncovering further evidence of the same sort, how can it be pursued? Here is how the defender of art's universality might continue the discussion:

> We share a common biology with the people of the late Pleistocene and of other cultures. As fellow humans, we have many desires, fears, emotions, and needs in common with them. Their worlds should not be completely impenetrable, therefore. After all, both anthropology and history are credible academic disciplines. There is no barrier of principle that separates their worlds from ours, so the enterprise of understanding what they do and of discovering concepts and practices they share in common with us is a legitimate and potentially successful one.

A second point concedes that, where we do not know the purposes for which the (possible) art of earlier times and other cultures was made, our understanding of that art is bound to be incomplete. In particular, we will lack the knowledge necessary to appreciate its symbolic, metaphoric, and religious import, to name a few of the ways in which artworks can have significance. All that is necessary, however, is that we be able to *identify* such pieces as art, not that we are able to *appreciate* the subtleties and complexities they undoubtedly possessed for their makers. That we are not well placed to appreciate the art of other times and places does not entail that we cannot correctly identify that art as such.

How do we make this initial recognition, though? Perhaps we do not need knowledge of a piece's origins to detect within it properties of formal beauty, such as grace, elegance, and balance – more will be said about aesthetic properties like these in chapter 3 – and perhaps it is not difficult also to observe their apparent centrality to the design of the item in question. Where it is obvious that someone has gone to a great deal of trouble to create them, we can be sure such properties were regarded either as contributing to the thing's primary function or as of value in their own right, and the case has been made for regarding the item as art. If such properties are absent or only marginal, either the piece is not a work of art or, anyway, we cannot tell that it was one.

One objection to the argument that we recognize cave painting and non-Western dancing as art on the basis of their humanly contrived beauty denies that beauty is the hallmark in terms of which we recognize art as such. Much contemporary Western art could not be correctly identified as art on this basis. Here is the reply:

> The argument about cave art does not rely on the strong claim that all art displays formal beauty. The objection is right to reject this strong claim. Instead, the argument about cave art makes a weaker assumption: that the prominence of humanly created beauty in artifacts is, where present, a reliable indicator of the item's art-status. It proposes a thesis about art's history, not a definition for art: historically, the production of art was likely to start with and give prominence to the universal appeal of properties that will unreflectively strike the audience as beautiful.

This is not to deny that complex semantic or semiotic properties are not also significant in art, even at its outset. Neither is it to say that a focus on formal beauty had to remain central as art-making traditions unfolded. Indeed, such traditions could in time give rise to non-aesthetic and anti-aesthetic art – art that sets out deliberately to eliminate aesthetic aspects in favor of other features, such as symbolic complexity, or, alternatively, that sets out to be ugly. So the argument claims only that some art, almost certainly including art's earliest forms, can be identified as such on the basis of the prominence it gives to beauty, where this result seems to be a consequence of deliberate human design.

There is a second, stronger objection to the argument that we can recognize old and non-Western art as such because of its humanly designed beauty. It denies that humans from different eras and cultures agree in their judgments about the beauty of realistic depictions of animals and natural landscapes. In that case, the beauties we find in cave paintings and non-Western dancing reflect our own culture's tastes, and tell us nothing about how the paintings and dances were intended by their makers or perceived by their original audiences. The denial that there are trans-cultural standards for aesthetic beauty is rejected by some evolutionary psychologists, who claim to have demonstrated a universal preference in children for savannah landscapes. In addition, surveys of people in many different countries by the Russian émigré artists Alexander Melamid and Vitaly Komar have revealed a surprisingly high level of homogeneity in aesthetic preferences for landscape features, content, balance, and color. Such views, and the proper interpretation of the data, are disputed by cultural relativists, however. Either they deny that the aesthetic judgments of people from different eras and cultures truly agree, or they explain the agreement across contemporary cultures as due to the unconscious influence of the West and its values.

In this section I have drawn attention to applications and connections that reveal ways in which the division between the two theories discussed in this chapter could ramify into other areas. At the same time, the discussion serves as a warning. The debates that have been highlighted – about the role of the museum and the status of popular entertainments, for example – could be motivated by commitments and might arrive at their conclusions by routes unlike those involved in either of the two stories with which we began. Sometimes polar contrasts admit of intermediate and subtly graduated alternatives, and similar conclusions sometimes follow from divergent sets of premises. So, even if the cases here might help us better understand and articulate what is at issue between the views with which we started, they should also alert us to other ways by which outwardly similar issues could come to the fore.

Questions

1.1 The inhabitants of a tropical island perform religious ceremonies in their temples each month at the full moon. To attract their gods to and entertain them at these rites, they make elaborate floral and fruit offerings and perform exquisite dances and dramas. Tourists who come to the island find these ceremonies fascinating, though they do not understand or do not care about their religious significance. So popular are the ceremonies with tourists that the natives begin to stage temple ceremonies also at the new moon, though they know none of their gods will attend at that time. Later still, they export their dances and dramas to purpose-built performance venues where the tourists, who now pay a fee for entry, can watch them in comfort. The dances and dramas are shortened and simplified somewhat, to suit the tastes of the tourists. Eventually, the natives are converted by missionaries and abandon their former religion. The temples stand derelict, but the dance and drama traditions are preserved for performance to tourists. The natives now view the dances and dramas not as religious in function but "for their own sake," which is how the tourists have always appreciated them.

Is this a story about the progressive degradation and ultimate loss of an indigenous art tradition or, instead, one about how a local practice evolved to produce art where there was none before? Are the tourist performances an authentic expression of the indigenous culture?

1.2 The people of all cultures and times sing to their babies, sketch animals and humans, decorate their pots, tell and enact stories, and so on. Can we accept this yet deny they have music, painting, and drama? Can we allow they have music, painting, and drama, yet deny they have art?

1.3 Can a person make art if he or she does not have the concept of art?

1.4 Are there artforms found in other cultures that are not also found in the West? Do Asian shadow puppet plays and Japanese origami qualify as artforms, for example?

1.5 Could a facemask that is worn once for a religious ceremony and then discarded be art? Could a ritual artifact that is only used in the dark, and cannot therefore be seen, be art?

1.6 Suppose cups once used in the Japanese tea ceremony are put on display in cabinets in a museum. Does their separation from the ritual in which they have cultural significance and utility promote their status as art, or, instead, does it deprive them of artistic value?

1.7 Rhythmic songs have always been used to accompany repetitive labor. Sailors sang sea shanties, for example, as they hauled up the anchor. Modern devices can make such activities unnecessary. A powered winch raises the anchor; mills grind rice that was previously pounded by hand-held poles; woven materials are stretched by machines rather than between groups of weavers. Imagine that someone tries to keep the old work songs of her community alive by forming a choral group. Are their performances authentic? Can the result count as art only if the performances are authentic? Would you argue the same way about songs in the same styles but newly composed by members of the group?

Readings

Among those who have argued that art is a practice evolved in the service of sexual selection are Steven Pinker, in *How the Mind Works* (New York: W. W. Norton, 1997), 521–6, and Geoffrey Miller, in *The Mating Mind: How Sexual Choice Shaped the Evolution of Human Nature* (New York: Doubleday, 2000), ch. 8. For a critical evaluation, see Denis Dutton's "Art and Sexual Selection," *PL* 24 (2000), 512–21.

A more developed and appealing account is offered by the ethologist Ellen Dissanayake, in books published by the University of Washington Press in Seattle: *What Is Art For?* (1988), *Homo Aestheticus: Where Art Comes From and Why* (1995), and *Art and Intimacy: How the Arts Began* (2000). She argues that art is a form of "making special" that enhances individuals' reproductive success by enriching and sustaining the kinds of cooperative communities in which they can flourish. Dissanayake is a critic of theories that see art as evolutionarily valuable merely as a tool for seduction. Nevertheless, her approach is not without problems of its own; see Stephen Davies's "Ellen Dissanayake's Evolutionary Aesthetic," *Biology and Philosophy* 19 (2004), 1–14. A broader philosophical discussion of the issues involved in providing an evolutionary account of art's production is offered by Ronald De Sousa in "Is Art an Adaptation? Prospects for an Evolutionary Perspective on Beauty," *JAAC* 62 (2004), 109–18.

Some philosophers have suggested that the units of cultural evolution are "memes" – that is, ideas, along with the mechanisms by which they are replicated and propagated – rather than genes. For an example, see *The Meme Machine* (Oxford: Oxford University Press, 1999) by Susan Blackmore. Daniel C. Dennett is one philosopher who has applied this view to art in "Memes and the Exploitation of Imagination," *JAAC* 48 (1990), 127–35.

The claim that there are universal habitat and landscape preferences is defended by Gordon H. Orians and Judith H. Heerwagen in "Evolved Responses to Landscapes," in *The Adapted Mind: Evolutionary Psychology and the Generation of Culture*, edited by J. H. Barkow, L. Cosmides, and J. Tooby (New York: Oxford University Press, 1992), 555–79. Also relevant is *Painting by Numbers: Komar and Melamid's Scientific Guide to Art*, edited by J. Wypijewski (New York: Farrar, Straus & Giroux, 1997), and for critical discussion, Ellen Dissanayake's "Komar and Melamid Discover Pleistocene Taste," *PL* 22 (1998), 486–96.

For a famous account of the emergence in the eighteenth century of taxonomies grouping the fine arts together for the first time, see Paul O. Kristeller's "The Modern System of the Arts: A Study in the History of Aesthetics," *Journal of the History of Ideas* 12 (1951), 496–527, and 13 (1952), 17–46. In *The Invention of Art: A Cultural History* (Chicago: University of Chicago Press, 2001), Larry Shiner develops the idea that art is an invention of eighteenth-century Europe and accepts the corollary that art is not found in earlier times or other societies. Rather than defending the special value of Western fine art, Shiner is inclined to reject it as elitist and patriarchal. A similar theme is presented in Paul Mattick's *Art in its Time: Theories and Practices of Modern Aesthetics* (London: Routledge, 2003).

Of course, many histories of aesthetics take it for granted that art was created in Homer's Greece, Michelangelo's Italy, Shakespeare's England, and so on, though they acknowledge changes in the concept and the way in which it came to be applied. For an example, see Wladyslaw Tatarkiewicz's *History of Aesthetics*, edited by C. Barrett and D. Pesch and translated by A. and A. Czerniawski, and R. M. Montgomery, 3 vols. (The Hague: Mouton, 1970–4). For a historian's account of appreciation, collecting, and connoisseurship of the kinds associated with art but occurring prior to the eighteenth century as well as afterwards, see Joseph Alsop's *The Rare Art Traditions: The History of Art Collecting and its Linked Phenomena Wherever These Have Appeared* (New York: Harper & Row, 1982). Alsop identifies five cultures additional to that of Enlightenment Europe – ancient Greece, ancient Rome, Islam, China, and Japan – that independently developed traditions of collecting fine art and what he calls art "by-products," that is, museums, art historians, connoisseurs, forgers, dealers, etc.

Among the eighteenth- and nineteenth-century thinkers who were important in developing philosophical theses and concepts concerning the aesthetic in nature and art were the earl of Shaftesbury, Jean-Baptiste Du Bos, Joseph Addison, Francis Hutcheson, Edmund Burke, Charles Batteux, Alexander Baumgarten, David Hume, Denis Diderot, K. W. F. von Schlegel, Jean-Jacques Rousseau, Friedrich von Schiller, and Friedrich Nietzsche. Of special importance are: Immanuel Kant's *The Critique of Judgment*, first published 1790, translated by J. C. Meredith (Oxford: Clarendon Press, 1928); Arthur Schopenhauer's *The World as Will and Representation*, first published 1819 and expanded 1844, translated by E. F. J. Payne, 2 vols. (New York, Dover, 1969); and G. W. F. Hegel's *Aesthetics: Lectures on Fine Arts*, first published 1835–8, translated by M. Knox, 2 vols. (Oxford: Oxford University Press, 1975). For a historical overview, see Monroe C. Beardsley's *Aesthetics from Classical Greece to the Present* (Alabama: University of Alabama Press, 1966), chs. 8–10, and, for a more polemical account, George Dickie's *The Century of Taste* (Oxford: Oxford University Press, 1996).

Defenses of the view that non-Western cultures make art are offered by Richard L. Anderson in *Calliope's Sisters: A Comparative Study of Philosophies of Art* (Englewood Cliffs, NJ: Prentice Hall, 1990) and H. Gene Blocker in "Is Primitive Art Art?" *JAE* 25:4 (1991), 87–97. In "Why Philosophy of Art in Cross-Cultural Perspectives?," *JAAC* 51 (1993), 425–36, Julius M. Moravcsik argues that art can be made by people who do not share with us exactly the same word or concept. Denis Dutton criticizes the assumption made by many anthropologists that cultural differences prohibit the judgment that art occurs in non-Western societies in " 'But They Don't Have Our Concept of Art,' " in *Theories of Art Today*, edited by N. Carroll (Madison: University of Wisconsin Press, 2000), 217–38. But for a philosophically sophisticated critique of some of these arguments, see Larry Shiner's "Western and Non-Western Concepts of Art: Universality and Authenticity," in *Art and Essence*, edited by S. Davies and A. C. Sukla (Westport, CT: Praeger, 2003), 143–56. Shiner's discussion of tourist art is in " 'Primitive Fakes', 'Tourist Art', and the Ideology of Authenticity," *JAAC* 52 (1994), 225–34.

Two useful collections discussing the role and function of the museum are *The Museum in Transition: A Philosophical Perspective*, edited by H. Hein (Washington, DC: Smithsonian Institute Press, 2000) and *The Idea of the*

Museum: Philosophical, Artistic and Political Questions, edited by Lars Aagaard-Mogensen (Lewiston, NY: Edwin Mellen Press, 1988). John Dewey's defense of community-based art is in *Art as Experience*, first published 1934 (New York: Perigee Books, 1980), especially 1–13. Dewey's position is criticized by Albert William Levi, an American philosopher, who defends the museum in "The Art Museum as an Agency of Culture," *JAE* 19:2 (1985), 23–40.

The distinction between art and craft is emphasized by, among others, the English philosopher R. G. Collingwood in *The Principles of Art* (London: Oxford University Press, 1938), ch. 2. Critics of the contemporary culture of their time go back to Plato and are too numerous to list. Two well-known twentieth-century attacks are by the German philosopher Theodor W. Adorno in "On Popular Music," *Studies in Philosophy and Social Science* 9 (1941), 17–48, and by the social commentator and educator Allan Bloom in *The Closing of the American Mind* (New York: Simon & Schuster, 1987). Critics of the application of technology and procedures for mass production to art include the twentieth-century German philosophers Martin Heidegger in the title essay of *The Question Concerning Technology*, translated by William Lovitt (New York: Garland, 1977), 3–35 and Walter Benjamin, "The Work of Art in the Age of Mechanical Reproduction," in *Illuminations: Essays and Reflections*, edited by H. Arendt and translated by H. Zohn (New York: Harcourt Brace & World, 1970), 253–64. In the long first chapter of *Philosophy of Mass Art* (Oxford: Oxford University Press, 1998), Noël Carroll demonstrates that many criticisms leveled at the mass produced art-cum-entertainment of today either misconceive its function or underestimate its artistic variety and interest.

Chapter Two

Defining Art

2.1 Necessary Conditions and Sufficient Conditions

Students of philosophy often begin their essays with dictionary definitions, until they realize that these are of little help to people who are competent masters of the language but who are puzzled about the nature or coherence of familiar concepts. Nevertheless, it might be hoped that a philosophically informed approach to art's definition will clarify issues relevant to our understanding of what art is or is not. In this chapter we consider if art can be defined, and review some of the definitions that have been offered.

To help us on our way, here is a definition of a definition of art:

> A definition of art should indicate what all and only art has in common and in virtue of which it is art. In other words, a definition should identify the elements that all art must have, such that anything possessing them thereby is art.

This definition can be expressed in more technical terms, which I now introduce. A *necessary* condition for something's being an X is a condition that *all* Xs must satisfy. The presence of oxygen is a necessary condition for the occurrence of fire, and being male is a necessary condition for being an uncle. All fires involve the presence of oxygen and all uncles are male. Notice that things other than Xs might satisfy the same condition, however. Not all males are uncles and not all oxygenated environments contain fires. A *sufficient* condition for something's being an X is a condition that, when satisfied, guarantees that what satisfies it is an X. Being a bear is a sufficient condition for being a mammal and being in the United States is a sufficient condition for being in the northern hemisphere. Notice that, though everything meeting a given sufficient condition for being an X thereby is an X, there can be other ways in which different things get to become Xs. Elephants are mammals but not as a result of being bears, and people in Norway are in the northern hemisphere though they are not in the United States. Now, if we specify the *necessary* condition (or the set of necessary conditions) that is *sufficient* for something's being an X, we have indicated a combination of conditions such that *all* and *only* Xs meet them, which is the hallmark of a definition of X-hood. Monotremes can be defined as members of species of *egg-laying mammals*, since it is both a necessary and sufficient condition for being a monotreme that something belongs to a species with this combination of characteristics.

Having explained the notion of necessary and sufficient conditions and how an appropriate combination of them can be used to select the features that all and only the instances or members of a given kind display, we can now express the earlier definition of a definition of art as follows: a definition of art should identify the *necessary* condition (or the set of necessary conditions) that is *sufficient* for something's being art.

Definitions deal with the *nature* of the concept in question. For example, monotremes are mammals in which the females lay eggs rather than giving birth to live young. Arriving at a definition of art involves considering if it is crucial to art's nature that it must display originality, be created within an institutional context, be pleasurable when contemplated, be expressive of emotion, be perceptually similar to other artworks, and so on. By contrast, the *extension* of a concept is the class of things that fall under it. All and only spiny anteaters and platypuses are monotremes. Art's extension includes at least some paintings, novels, plays, musical pieces, and sculptures. (Whether quilts and African ceremonial masks qualify for inclusion depends on how the debate outlined in chapter 1 is resolved.) An adequate definition of art must cover everything that falls within art's extension and exclude all that does not. This test is not always easy to apply, however, because we are sometimes uncertain or disagree about whether some particular piece is to be counted as art. At least we can be sure that a proposed definition fails if it excludes paradigm artworks, such as Beethoven's Ninth Symphony or Picasso's painting *Guernica*, or if it includes paradigm non-artworks, such as the shock absorbers at the back left of my car. (Even if anything could *become* art, not everything *is* art at any given time. Among the things that are not art currently are the shock absorbers.)

As just explained, we can be interested in determining art's *extension* – that is, the list of things that are or have been artworks – in order to test the adequacy of a proposed definition. We can also be interested in mapping what the concept encompasses for other reasons. Indeed, a person can want to get a sense of art's extension, and perhaps to debate the status of controversial borderline cases, even if she holds that art cannot be defined.

2.2   Essentialism and Anti-Essentialism

The enterprise of definition is commonly thought to have the goal of describing the essence – the fundamental, distinguishing nature – of what is defined. On this view, an interest in definition involves a commitment to *essentialism*. Essentialism regards the members of kinds as characterized by an underlying principle or pattern. In the case of natural kinds, the fundamental essence might be structural: gold is the element with an atomic number of 79. When the kinds are organic, the fundamental essence is likely to be bio-historical: the gorilla is a species marked by a particular genetic pattern and a particular history of descent from evolutionarily earlier organisms. Bio-historical essences tend to be less clearcut than the structural essences displayed by inorganic natural kinds. Such essences involve micro-structural components, for example in terms of the species' DNA signature, but this structure "tolerates" a wider spread of deviations than is customary in inorganic natural kinds. Yet messier are many cultural kinds – such as parking tickets – which often lack a distinctive micro-structural essence and are better characterized in terms of some combination of the intentions with which they are created, the functions they are commonly used to fulfill, their status or location within institutions and practices, and so on. Parking tickets around the world might be made from many different materials and take a wide variety of shapes. What collects them into a kind is an officially designated role they are supposed to play in the distribution of opportunities for access to parking.

One way of thinking about the debate outlined in chapter 1 is as a disagreement about art's essence. According to the view that art is a local invention of eighteenth-century Europe, its essence is purely cultural. According to the alternative, which sees a biological component as shaping and constraining the cultural expressions that art can be given, art has a complex, bio-cultural essence. In this view, art is in part a natural kind, though the forms it takes are more plastic and culturally conditioned than is so for more biologically basic behaviors such as eating, crying, laughing, and sleeping. As such, it is perhaps similar to marriage, cooperation, or language.

About the middle of the twentieth century, a number of philosophers suggested that there is no point in trying to define art. Some denied that art can be defined at all, while others argued that it cannot be defined usefully or informatively. These were not, as one might suppose, reactions to a rash of new but inadequate definitions. Rather, they reflected a general move against the philosophical project of essentialism. The first group denied that art has an essence in terms of which it can be defined. They are anti-essentialists. The second denied that its essence could be hidden from us, and hence denied also that an account of this essence could be helpful in addressing the philosophical puzzles art and its appreciation seem to prompt. This second group, like the first, opposes the attempt to define art.

Why have philosophers been attracted to anti-essentialism in respect of art? There are several possible reasons. A general opposition to essentialism might follow from a person's rejection of accounts of essences proposed within metaphysics more broadly. And she might be particularly wary of the idea that culturally constructed "natures" have the stability and clarity that talk of essences sometimes is taken to imply. With particular reference to art, the bewildering variety of artworks and their revolutionary and provocative character can also undermine her faith in the idea that all share a common nature. The avant-garde art of the twentieth century played a significant role in defeating definitions that had prevailed in earlier times, such as ones maintaining that art is representation, expression, or significant form. As well, feminist writers have rightly revealed one motivation for anti-essentialism as coming out of skepticism about the agendas and commitments of proponents of the project of definition. Feminists have rejected essentialism, both in biology and as it is presented in art theory, as attempting spuriously to justify the hegemony of male thought and power. According to the feminist critique, ideologies that operate as tools of political repression are falsely represented as definitions possessing a timeless, natural, asocial, universal objectivity. Some other anti-essentialists are also doubtful of what they regard as linear and reductive modes of thought employed by those who propose definitions, and of the assumption that everything under heaven can be explained by cold logic and hard science.

2.3 Arguments against Art's Definition

As noted, a first possibility is that art is not definable. In the 1950s, the American philosopher Morris Weitz argued that no conditions are necessary for something's being art. In particular, artifactuality (the property of having been humanly made) is the best candidate for a necessary condition for art, but not all art is artifactual since driftwood can become art without being physically modified. If there are no necessary conditions for a thing's being art, there cannot be a definition of art of the kind indicated above; that is, in terms of jointly necessary and sufficient conditions.

As regards the point about artifactuality, one might deny that driftwood can become art merely by being picked out and called such. Either the driftwood is not art or it is artifactualized in the process by which it becomes successfully presented as art. Alternatively, one might find some other necessary condition for art that the driftwood case satisfies. A possibility is that it is necessary for something's being art that it is subject to human creative acts with certain aesthetic or other appropriate intentions.

More generally, the objection is misconceived when it concludes that there is no necessary property as a result of observing that there is no single property all artworks share in common. There might be more than one way something can become art, in which case the necessary condition might be *disjunctive*, that is, expressed as an *either–or*. To take a non-art example, it might be a necessary condition for being a parent that one be a biological father, *or* a biological mother, *or* that one legally adopt a child, without there being a single relevant element common to all these methods. Similarly, what might be necessary for something's being art could be that it is either *thus* or *so*, where *thus* and *so* possess no properties in common. A number of ways of filling out this kind of schema will be indicated later in this chapter, but here are some of the possible alternatives in such a definition – that the piece succeeds as an artwork, or is intended to be an artwork, or falls within an established artwork category, or possesses a significant number from a cluster of art-relevant properties.

Here is a second argument for art's non-definability that was also presented by Weitz: its creative, rebellious, transgressive nature prevents its definition. Much art is concerned with repudiating what was thought essential to the art-status of its precursors. As soon as a candidate definition is proposed, some artist will set out and succeed in defeating it.

This new argument is no more convincing than the first. It proposes that art has a certain *nature*, and claims of that sort are already first cousins to definitions. If it is true that art must be creative and rebellious, then these look like necessary conditions that could feature in a potential definition. There is no reason to suppose that a definition must insist that art has a particular kind of content or style, or that it is unchanging, or that new kinds cannot be created. If art is often or distinctively self-referential and transgressive, such qualities could be listed in a definition, and that definition will not be easily defeated by reactions in the future against what is important in the art of the present.

As mentioned earlier, an alternative way of rejecting the project of art's definition suggests that, though it is possible to define art, the result cannot be useful or revealing. One way the point is made is in terms of the observation that people are usually successful in identifying artworks as such by relying on their "folk" – that is, their ordinary, non-theoretic – intuitions, whereas they would not necessarily know how to apply a philosopher's technical definition. The American philosopher W. E. Kennick dramatized this idea by arguing that, if a warehouse were on fire, an ordinary person would succeed if told to rescue the artworks but might not know what to save if instructed in terms of philosophers' definitions (such as that she should collect the items with significant form, or that fit into a true and coherent narrative tying them to past art, or that provide intrinsic pleasure when their aesthetic properties are contemplated for their own sakes). In explaining the reliability of our folk intuitions, it might be suggested that, since art is a cultural creation, and as such is the result of our decisions, no adequate definition could reveal anything new or interesting about it. A plausible definition is bound to be uninformative and redundant.

Kennick's argument faces some obvious objections. Artworks now are not as easy to identify as Kennick implies, and our intuitions prove fallible more often than he seems to accept. (These observations are discussed further in the "Applications" section that closes this chapter.) And even if philosophers' definitions do not help us pass the warehouse test, it does not follow that they are inadequate or lacking in interest. Most people would do fairly well in locating the gold items in a shopping mall, yet would have no idea how to identify items with an atomic number of 79, but that does not show that gold cannot be usefully defined in terms of its atomic number. It demonstrates only that we often successfully use methods of identification that pay no heed to definitions. This is where the second move is supposed to come in: if art could not have a hidden or unfamiliar essence, then the definition should more or less coincide with the folk understanding, and therefore must be both obvious and unnecessary. But is it plausible to maintain that no social practice or other human creation could have a hidden or surprising nature? Sociology and anthropology often assume otherwise when they study religious sacrifices, witchcraft, divination, astrology, and the like. Accounts of these offered by their practitioners are bound to be fundamentally misguided if, as is likely, gods are not affected by offerings, there are no witches, the future cannot be predicted from tea leaves, and it is false that the disposition of the constellations influences human character and action. Yet these customs and activities often have distinctive structures or important social functions and can be characterized in terms of these. Because the people who invented and participate in these practices fail to understand their true nature, they are likely to be surprised by the definitions that are proposed by social scientists.

Anyway, we can question the assumption that art is purely a construction of human culture, because it begs the question against the alternative according to which art partly involves the expression of our biological nature. Once this possibility is allowed, it is easy to see how we might be ignorant and mistaken about its nature, just as we have often been ignorant and mistaken about the role played by biological factors in many other human behaviors, such as the emotions. A *theory* of art's value would have to explain its place and significance in human affairs, and perhaps we could not be deeply mistaken about that sort of thing, but art might be *defined* in terms that could be surprising, at least in their implications for difficult, vague, or borderline cases.

2.4   If Not an Essence, What Unifies the Concept of Art?

Anti-essentialists need to explain the apparent coherence of the concept of art, but without appealing to some underlying essence.

A number of philosophers, including Weitz, take up an observation of the Austrian philosopher Ludwig Wittgenstein: games are not related via an essence each shares with the others; instead, there are *family resemblances* between games. These philosophers suggest that artworks are united by a network of criss-crossing resemblances, though there is no one respect in which all artworks resemble each other.

This account is at best incomplete, because it cannot explain how the first artworks – that is, the historically earliest examples of art, whatever they were – became such. They had no artistic predecessors to resemble. And the position has difficulty accommodating *readymade art*. (The readymades were ordinary, functional objects acquired by the artist, Marcel Duchamp, titled by him, and presented as art.) Duchamp turned a snow shovel into a work of art by titling it *In Advance of the Broken Arm* and presenting it in the context of the artworld. That artwork surely resembles other non-artwork snow shovels more than it resembles any other artwork. But the major objection to this view is that resemblance is too cheap a relation to perform the job assigned to it, because every thing resembles every other thing. (There are a zillion ways in which the Eiffel Tower resembles the battle of Little Bighorn. For a start, they are both mentioned in large encyclopedias, neither is sold in the cheese section of my local supermarket . . .) If talk of resemblance is to have explanatory power, it must indicate what kinds and degrees of resemblance count toward something's being an artwork. To do so, however, would be to move in the direction of supplying a definition.

The same difficulty – that it can be plausible only if it takes on the form of a definition – besets another approach, according to which it is sufficient for something's being art that it possesses a certain number or combination of art-relevant properties, though no one art-relevant property is common to all artworks. The most recent version of this approach is by the British philosopher Berys Gaut, who calls it the *cluster theory*. He offers the cluster theory as an improvement on Weitz's anti-essentialism. Here is a representative list of the cluster of properties that might be identified as art-relevant: the item is intended to be art; it falls squarely within what is an established art category; it possesses aesthetic, expressive, formal, or representational properties; it has the capacity to communicate complex meanings; its production requires skill; its production requires creative imagination; it is a source of pleasure in itself; and it invites the cognitive and emotional involvement of its audience. (Advocates of the cluster theory can disagree about what properties and how many belong to the art-relevant set, but let us skip past such debates.)

It is difficult to see why the cluster theory is supposed to be at odds with the project of defining art, however, because it can easily be reformulated as a disjunctive definition. For example, the definition might go as follows: something is art if it has any nine of the ten art-relevant properties, or if it has property 5 and any other six properties, or if it has properties 2 and 4 and any other five properties . . . The list of alternatives might be long, especially if the degree to which a property is possessed is also relevant, but provided the list can be completed and is considerably shorter than the list of all possible artworks, the result is a complex yet otherwise respectable definition. By this definition, it is both necessary and sufficient for something's being art that it satisfies at least one of the listed combinations of art-relevant properties. The cluster theory might better be interpreted as indicating the level of disjunctive complexity that an adequate definition will require, not as supporting the view that art cannot be defined.

Is there any account of what falls under the concept of art that can resist the gravitational pull of essentialism? One position that does so can be introduced via the following analogy. You wonder of a pile of items what makes them a unified collection. The answer, as it happens, is that they were all on my shopping list. The list covers all sorts of things. Perhaps some of the things listed are there purely on my whim. Even in cases where I give reasons, such as *I need it* or *I have run out*, there are other things that I also need or have run out of that I decide not to add to the list on this occasion. In other words, the "reasons" I give for what is on the list are not reliable in their predictive power because I am not bound to be consistent or even rational. My "reasons" come into play only retrospectively, though they do draw attention to factors I counted when making each individual decision. The list is capricious to the extent that I am. What unifies the pile is nothing above the fact that I listed the items together. There is no underlying essence. There is only a series of arbitrary decisions (including, perhaps, the decision about when to begin and when to stop). I call this view *radical stipulativism*. When applied to art, radical stipulativism comes to this: the *only* thing artworks have in common is that they have been listed as art by the relevant experts, who have no conclusive or compelling (though they may have intelligible but insufficient) reasons to back up their decisions. A view along these lines has been offered by the British philosopher, Kathleen Stock.

Radical stipulativism should be distinguished from an outwardly similar position, usually called *particularism*, adopted by some theorists in ethics. When applied to art, the particularist would argue that there are good reasons in each individual case for something's being art or not, but it is not possible to organize these reasons systematically into principles or rules. What makes each artwork an artwork are factors that are specific to it, and properties that might make one piece art could count against the arthood of another, different piece. The difficulty particularism faces is that of explaining how reasons could be good, determinative, and non-arbitrary on the one hand, yet unruly and unprincipled on the other. By contrast with the particularist, the radical stipulativist holds there are no compelling reasons, not even ones unique to each case, prior to the experts' choice. Once the verdict is reached, "reasons" can be pointed to, but they take their power from the authority of the decision, not the other way round.

Radical stipulativism is not without some appeal. What goes on in the artworld sometimes seems to depend on who says what and on judgments that are driven more by the contingencies of fashion and subjective taste than by considered reasons applied consistently. But radical stipulativism faces some obvious objections. It cannot readily explain how the earliest artworks qualified as art, because the presence of experts seems to presuppose the existence of a tradition or practice on which they are expert. Radical stipulativism also owes us an explanation of how the experts – who are typically identified as gallery directors, art historians, and distinguished critics – merit this status if they are not subject to common, public standards of consistency and reasonableness in the exercise of their authority. In general, we might doubt that there are experts on taste as there are on more straightforwardly factual matters. More importantly, radical stipulativism comes at a high price. It holds that, ultimately, there is no rationally decisive basis for drawing the border between art and non-art where we do. Most anti-essentialists think it is one thing to reject the possibility or usefulness of a formal definition for art, but quite another to claim that the demarcation of art from non-art is arbitrary, which is probably why most anti-essentialists stop short of embracing radical stipulativism.

2.5   Some Definitions of Art

Even if the arguments of anti-essentialists are not successful in showing the impossibility of art's definition, they do indicate some of the pitfalls to be avoided. Art's complex variety and rebellious nature count against definitions identifying art with a given structure or content. It remains to be seen, however, whether what distinguishes artworks is their *relational properties* – properties resulting from their connections to things beyond their boundaries – as opposed to *intrinsic properties* – properties inherent in the work regarded in isolation from all else, including the history and context of its production. Perhaps art can be defined relationally, i.e. by reference to the way its works stand in relation to art institutions or traditions, for instance. As for objections to the political agendas and commitments of definers, we can accept that unwarranted biases should be guarded against without also agreeing that the attempt at definition is doomed to falsifying distortion and failure. The lesson to be learned is that a definition of art must have the plasticity and complexity needed to accommodate the historical variability and cultural volatility that undeniably are among art's most distinctive features.

Most of the definitions proposed in recent decades – and there have been many – accept this challenge. Generic versions of the representative theories are outlined and critically discussed below.

2.5.1   Aesthetic functionalism

The first view defines art in terms of its intended purpose or function and characterizes this as the delivery of an aesthetic experience. Accordingly, I call this view *aesthetic functionalism*. Aesthetic functionalism maintains that something is an artwork if it is intended to provide the person who contemplates it for its own sake with an aesthetic experience of a significant magnitude on the basis of an appreciation of its aesthetic features, provided the percipient is in an appropriate frame of mind. (With its emphasis on the pleasurable contemplation of aesthetic properties, aesthetic functionalism is related to the eighteenth- and nineteenth-century aesthetic theories mentioned in chapter 1.) A representative exponent of aesthetic functionalism is Monroe C. Beardsley, an American philosopher of the twentieth century. He defines art as an arrangement either of conditions intended to be capable of affording an aesthetic experience with marked aesthetic character, or of a kind that is typically intended to have this capacity. A recent variant, proposed by the British philosopher Nick Zangwill, holds that something is art if an artist had a creative insight into the possibility of generating aesthetic properties – the elegant balance of forms within a painting, say, or the wistful sadness of a melody – through an appropriate organization of non-aesthetic properties – such as patches of paint, or sequences of tones – and the aesthetic properties were intentionally generated through the application of the artist's insight. (The nature of aesthetic properties is described further in chapter 3.) Though this variant of aesthetic functionalism does not go on to mention the experience to which appreciation of a thing's aesthetic properties is supposed to give rise, it implies that it is the value of this experience that gives significance to the artist's insightful activity.

Aesthetic functionalism is well suited to account for the earliest art and for the introduction into the canon – the set of acknowledged and great works – of new artforms, new genres, and singular artworks that do not appear to belong to any pre-established category, because the art-defining intention does not require reference to an established art practice or tradition of works.

Aesthetic functionalism does face problems, though. It may have difficulty avoiding circularity. A *circular* definition is uninformative because it defines what is in question by saying, in effect, that it is itself. If art is to be defined in terms of the experience it engenders, it has to be possible to characterize aesthetic experience and the kinds of properties to which it is a reaction independently of describing them as the experience and properties that result from successful art-making intentions. Doing so may not be easy.

Another difficulty for the theory is presented by artworks apparently lacking in, or even rejecting, aesthetic properties. Examples can include conceptual pieces (along the lines of *Everything ever thought by the seventeenth person to parachute from a plane*) that present no sensual, straightforwardly perceptual features. Also, some of Duchamp's readymades were chosen deliberately for their non-aesthetic character. One example, the snow shovel that became *In Advance of the Broken Arm*, was mentioned earlier. Others included a comb, a bottlerack, and a urinal. This last, titled *Fountain*, was purchased by Duchamp and signed by him with the manufacturer's name. As with many of Duchamp's works, *Fountain* was issued in repeat "editions" in later years. To save the theory by denying that these are art (as Beardsley does) would put aesthetic functionalism at odds with prevailing contemporary opinions that accept the credentials of such works. Alternatively, allowing that such pieces become art in some other, non-aesthetic way (as Zangwill does) concedes that the definition offered by the aesthetic functionalist is incomplete, for it identifies (at best) only one of the routes by which something can become art.

A further problem for aesthetic functionalism is that of accounting for bad art. The theory can allow that something might fail to have interesting aesthetic properties or to produce a rewarding aesthetic experience because the artist failed to give it the features she intended. It can also account for works that fall short in delivering the appropriate experience because they have become damaged so that their aesthetic properties are lost or no longer accessible. It might even cover the possibility that changes in the taste of succeeding generations blind them to the work's aesthetic merits, with the result that no one later can experience the work as was intended. But when all such cases are taken into account, there remains a residue of bad works that functional definitions cannot accommodate. These bad works were made just as the artist intended, and the audience is fully prepared and qualified to receive from them the intended experience, but, nevertheless, they do not deliver what art should. At the same time, they undoubtedly are artworks, because they were intended to be art and they belong squarely to established genres or kinds of art. In other words, their makers succeeded in what they intended and the audience recognizes what was intended, but what was intended turned out either not to be aesthetically worthwhile or not to be of the kind the aesthetic functionalist identifies as art-defining. A great deal of art is without aesthetic or other merit, though there was no failure in the execution of the artist's intentions, no lack on the part of the audience, and no other intervention to prevent the aesthetic results or uptake that the aesthetic functionalist regards as crucial within art.

2.5.2 The institutional theory

A second definition is that of the *institutional theory*, according to which an artwork is an artifact of a kind created by an artist to be presented to an artworld public. To be an artwork, an artifact must be appropriately placed within a web of practices, roles, and frameworks that comprise an informally organized institution, the artworld. Instead of defining art in terms of its intended primary function, the institutional theory highlights the social *procedures* by which something attains arthood.

Radical stipulativism, which was mentioned earlier, might be consistent with the institutional theory. This would be the case if the people who make things art as a result of declaring them to be such attain that authority by getting to occupy particular positions within the artworld, namely, the role of expert. However, the American philosopher George Dickie, who is the institutional theory's developer and main proponent, does not offer it in order to promote stipulativism. He thinks that it is the artist who creates the artwork, not independent experts, and that the status of art is something achieved, not merely conferred. The point of emphasizing that the artworld institution underpins this process is not to confirm that art is arbitrary and lacking in any unifying essence but, rather, is to draw attention to the fact that art-making actions qualify as such only within the context of artworld practices. Just as knocking a ball into a hole can count as making a par only against the background of the practices, conventions, and rules of golf, so the act, for example, of applying pigments to canvas counts as creating art only against the background of the practices of the artworld. What makes something art is the decisions made by the artist. (These decisions frequently are preceded by the artist's creative actions in applying paint to canvas and the like, but this prior stage is not necessary if ordinary objects can be appropriated by artists who turn them into artworks without modifying them.) There is no reason at all to suppose art-making choices could be arbitrary. The artist's decisions require an appropriate institutional setting if they are to be successful in art's creation and, to that extent, art is institutional.

The institutional theory is well placed to explain how something could be art even though it is poor in aesthetic value and in other respects. The theory faces these potential difficulties, however: to define art as what is made by artists for presentation to an artworld public may lead to an objectionable circularity if we cannot in turn define artists and artworld publics without reference to artworks. In addition, the artworld looks less like an institution than a practice – a way of doing things regulated by social conventions, such as greeting people by shaking their hand – because it is not structured in terms of roles defined by the specific duties and rights they confer on their occupants. If art-making does not depend on institutional controls, established either formally or informally, the institutional theory fails. Also, the institutional theory seems unable to account for the earliest artworks. It can allow that art institutions gradually evolved from an individualist background, and that the first artworks, which emerged only with the institutions they depend on, had precursors that resembled them. But either it must deny that paintings and sculptures of 10,000 years ago count as art or it must argue that the appropriate institutions already were in place by then, and neither option looks attractive. It seems more likely that the first artworks pre-dated the practices and institutions that later grew up around acts of art-creation. In other words, institutions imply the existence of established traditions, and none were in place when the first artworks were created.

2.5.3   Historicism

A third class of theories is *historicist*: something is art if it stands in the appropriate historical relation to its artistic predecessors. Historicists differ in their characterizations of the relation that must hold between an aspirant to the status of art and its established artwork predecessors if its candidacy is to be successful. In other words, they disagree about what the art-defining relation is. James D. Carney proposes that something becomes art if and only if it is stylistically similar to prior artworks. Jerrold Levinson maintains that the new artwork must be intended for a regard typical of the regards invited for past art. Noël Carroll advocates that something is an artwork if and only if it can be fitted into a true and coherent narrative tying it to past art. Each of these variants of historicism faces objections peculiar to it, but our concern here is with the general approach.

By acknowledging the role of tradition within art, historicist theories can explain why not everything can be made to be art at every time. And by making art's self-referential nature central – that is, by insisting that each new work of art must be appropriately related to already established works of art, even as it departs from them – historicism is well situated to make clear how art changes and develops over time, so that what is artistically possible at any given moment depends in part on the artworld's previous history. But the theory faces an objection that, by now, should be predictable. It does not account for the earliest art, which by definition lacked artwork predecessors. Additionally, it may have difficulty in explaining how historically unprecedented genres – photography, jazz, interactive computer creations – merit inclusion within the artworld. And above all, revolutionary art is hard to include without also letting in items with no credible claim to the status of art. The problem here is that, instead of following, amplifying, or extending the previous tradition, some artworks set out to invert, reject, or repudiate it, and it then becomes difficult to maintain that such pieces qualify as art by virtue of the relation they hold to the prior tradition while at the same time excluding many non-artworks that also differ and depart from what was previously counted as art. Also, feminist theoreticians have been suspicious of the historicists' approach because it legitimizes the present in terms of past traditions that were shaped in part by sexist prejudices that excluded women and their art contributions from art's "official" realm.

One way of dodging some of the objections raised against the theories discussed above is by amalgamating them into a *hybrid* definition, as Robert Stecker, a contemporary American philosopher, does. In effect, this approach recognizes an element of truth in each of the attempts at definition so far considered, but faults them all for accounting for only some art. What they cannot do alone, however, they might accomplish in combination. The hybrid definition makes clear that there are several ways something can become an artwork; that is, the definition it proposes is disjunctive in form. To allow for the earliest art and additions to the tradition from outside, it finds a place for functionalism. To accommodate art's changing functions and conventions, it embraces historicism. To explain how something might be art simply by falling within an established genre (even if it is not functionally successful or is not self-consciously brought under the concept of art by its maker), it resorts to a version of the institutional theory. An example of a hybrid definition of the kind just envisaged might take this form: something is a work of art if and only if it is in one of the central artforms of the time and is intended to fulfill a function art has at that time, or it achieves excellence in fulfilling a function central to art.

Although some of the objections applying to particular theories of art's definition can be handled when these theories are subsumed as complementary parts of a hybrid definition, a difficulty remains. The institutional and historicist theories make art relative to an artworld, an organized practice that has established a tradition. But if there is the possibility that there are artworlds other than the Western one, and nothing in these approaches has demonstrated otherwise, these theories are incomplete, because they do not explain what makes an artworld an *art*world.

2.6 Definitions and Non-Western Art

The possibility just identified as a problem for hybrid and some other definitions – that there might be artworlds other than the Western one – draws us back to the central question of chapter 1: is art universal in its occurrence, or solely a product of European culture that now occurs globally only because that culture has come to dominate others? If the latter is the case, there is no artworld relativity problem, but if art is indigenous to many different cultures, the definitions mentioned above may be inadequate. Can they accommodate the existence of non-Western art?

If non-Western cultures have art institutions that parallel those of the West, the institutional theory could provide for the existence of non-Western art. So too, could historicist theories of art's nature, provided other cultures have self-conscious art-making traditions. Some may do so. Those of Japan, China, India, Iran, Iraq, and Indonesia, to name a few, appear to have the relevant institutions and traditions, along with indigenous theoretical, philosophical, critical, and historical study of these, plus structures established with the goals of patronizing, training, and preserving these various practices. By contrast, the art-like activities of small-scale, pre-industrial, non-Western cultures tend to be much less institutionalized than in the Western artworld, and members of the culture might not identify or theorize these traditions and the roles that go with them as comprising an artworld. Institutional and historicist theories could recognize the status as art of Chinese paintings, say, but not of African masks used in religious ceremonies. This failure to be inclusive would make them vulnerable to the artworld relativity problem. They cannot explain how the religious and like practices of non-Western cultures comprise artworlds by identifying the products of these as artworks, because that would be circular given that they analyze something's being an artwork in terms of its being the product of artworld institutions or traditions. So their account is incomplete until more is said about the nature of artworlds. And the prospects for that account are unpromising because it is doubtful that all artworlds share the same kinds of formal or historical structures.

Because aesthetic functionalism does not tie art-status to artworld traditions, practices, or institutions, it avoids the artworld relativity issue. And it can allow that items made in non-Western cultures are art so long as these are made with the primary purpose of engendering worthwhile aesthetic experiences via the contemplation of their aesthetic qualities. In this way, it too might enfranchise much of the sophisticated art of the Middle and Far East. But it also seems ill equipped to recognize as art items intended primarily to have educative, ritual, or other instrumental functions, which rules out most of what might count as art in small-scale societies, as well as popular and domestic art more generally. In other words, aesthetic functionalism begs the question against the possibility of artworlds in which art is not primarily intended for aesthetic contemplation apart from any practical function it may have.

For the most part, it is not clear if the theorists who develop these definitions intend to exclude the possibility of all non-Western art, or to include only high non-Western art, or to take within art's ambit a broad and humble range of artifacts. And perhaps some of them see the task as defining only Western fine art, without intending thereby to prejudge the possibility that art has a wider constituency. (Some do seem to assume that art occurs in other cultures and extends to ancient times, even when they focus mainly on Western fine art of the past 200 years.) Their attempted definitions are not prompted by the issues raised in chapter 1. More often, they are motivated by the question *Can and should avant-garde Western (so-called) art be accepted as art, and if so, what are its credentials?*

2.7   Taking Stock

The discussion of art's definition has not helped us settle the controversy with which we began, which concerns the disagreement between those who maintain that art has a universal, ancient basis in our evolved biology and those who claim, to the contrary, that art is an invention, unconstrained by biological directives, of the Enlightenment and modern age of

European culture. In fact, we will need to know how to resolve that disagreement before we can properly evaluate the adequacy or otherwise of most definitions, because the definers tend to assume that we already know the concept's extension.

Moreover, I have criticized the arguments not only of those who think art cannot be defined, or cannot be defined usefully, but also the definitions offered by their opponents. There is no clear winner here. Among the advocates of definitions, there is perhaps a growing consensus in favor of hybrid formulations. Functional accounts might be needed to accommodate the earliest artworks and the introduction of novel artforms. And it may be necessary to invoke institutions and historical traditions to explain how items qualify as art when they are intended to be non-aesthetic or anti-aesthetic. This much is clear: if it is accepted that small-scale non-Western cultures possess art and their own artworlds, and that art can often be intended more for ritual use, educative enlightenment, and entertainment than for contemplation for its own sake alone, a rich account of art's functions will be needed, along with acknowledgment of art's institutional variety, if an adequate definition is to be found.

Though we have not settled how art is to be defined, or if it can be at all, and while we are no nearer to answering the puzzle raised in chapter 1, we have considered issues that are important to understanding the nature of much art. Art sometimes can have an aesthetic purpose and perhaps this was characteristic in its historically early forms. Art sometimes relies for its creation, presentation, recognition, acceptance, and proper appreciation on a background of informally institutionalized practices and conventions. Art sometimes is shaped by its own history, with the result that its functions and forms can be modified over time through bootstrapping processes relying on self-reflection, self-reference, and self-repudiation.

Applications and Connections — Intuition versus Definition, Art's Value and Definition, Euthyphro *and Experts*

Earlier there was mention of the claim that a person can rely more on her intuitions than on philosophers' definitions when it comes to identifying art as such. Kennick's "warehouse test," recall, is meant to demonstrate that the attempt to define art is redundant and that any forthcoming definitions will be worthless or uninformative.

In reply, it was observed that we can have a faulty grasp of the underlying purposes of our social practices, with the result that definitions of these may surprise us. Here is an additional objection to Kennick's argument: our intuitions are not as clear or trustworthy as he claims. The rescuer might easily identify as art nineteenth-century European art paintings, books of poetry, musical scores, and sculptures when she enters the warehouse, but what of the modern artworks that often resemble ordinary, non-art objects? Carl Andre's *Equivalent VIII* is comprised of 120 firebricks arranged two-deep in a pattern of 10 by 6. If the rescuer has never heard of Andre's work, is she likely to recognize it as art? And if she has heard of it, yet the warehouse also contains building sites with stacked bricks, is the rescuer's intuition alone sufficient to guide her to the artwork? Probably not.

To examples of this sort it might be replied that many people thought Andre's work was controversial in its claim to art status. They deny that piles of bricks, or Duchamp's *Fountain*, or Andy Warhol's *Brillo Boxes* of 1964 – which, though they were made of painted plywood, look, as Warhol intended, almost the same as the cardboard cartons in which Brillo scouring pads were delivered to supermarkets – are works of art. According to this response, it is appropriate that such pieces are not identified as art by the rescuer because they are not art.

Yet this answer draws attention to another problem with the position it hopes to defend. People differ, sometimes strongly, in their intuitions about what is or is not art, and that is why the status of some works is controversial. Some people think it obvious that *Fountain* and *Brillo Boxes* are art – indeed, that they are important artworks – while other people are no less sure that they are not art. (The latter group might agree, however, that such pieces provide an interesting commentary on art even if they are not art.) Moreover, no individual person is guided inevitably by her intuitions. After consulting them, she might feel uncertain and unresolved. She might recognize that a putative artwork is a borderline or hard case and be unsure whether it should be ruled in, out, or as falling into an irresolvable category. These considerations suggest that Kennick's claims for the reliability and decisiveness of our intuitions are exaggerated.

Opponents of attempts to define art often draw attention to the challenge posed to the definitional project by the diversity and inventiveness of avant-garde art. What is less often remarked is the manner in which opponents of the enterprise of definition are similarly vulnerable. People differ in their intuitions about what is art, and the individual's intuitions sometimes provide little assistance because she knows them to be manifestly unclear or untrustworthy. The folk understanding of art is partial and fragile. It does not have the robust certainty that is required to establish that the pursuit of a definition could never be relevant to educating and refining our understanding of what art is.

Here is another topic: there can be theories of art that are not also definitions. There is, after all, the theory that art cannot be defined. A different kind of theory, presented by the nineteenth-century German philosopher, G. W. F. Hegel, and more recently by the American philosopher and art critic Arthur Danto, maintains that art had a historical destiny or agenda that it has now fulfilled. According to Hegel, the goal of art was to serve as a phase in a process by which Spirit would come to understand its own nature, and art discharged this role in the classical Greek period, two millennia ago. In contrast, Danto maintains that art's historical purpose was to develop to a stage at which it could pose a philosophical question about its own nature – *What distinguishes art from ordinary things?* – which it did in the 1960s. Neither of these theories is offered as a definition of art.

Nevertheless, it might be felt that a condition for any definition's adequacy is that it accounts for art's worth and importance. In other words, a definition should provide a theory of artistic value. Institutional and historicist definitions have been criticized for failing to provide any such story. They do not explain why it matters to us whether or not something is art. Aesthetic functionalism fares better in this regard because it reflects on art's power and import. It defines art in terms of its function of producing an aesthetic experience and often characterizes that experience as valuable in and for itself. To qualify as art, something must either meet a threshold of functional effectiveness or at least be intended to do so. In other words, to qualify as art, something must be intended to afford an appropriately attentive percipient with an aesthetic experience of significant magnitude, and all art thereby must be intended to be valuable, assuming that its value is measured by its functional success.

Before we give the nod to aesthetic functionalism, however, we should ask if there are respects in which the project of supplying a theory of art's *value* might be distinct from that of offering a *definition* of art. A theory of art's value should tell us why the production and consumption of art are significant in human affairs. It can do this by concentrating only on the better artworks. Indeed, this is the most promising strategy if only the better artworks achieve the kind or degree of value that gives the enterprise of making and consuming art its point. And it is not surprising that the better works are left to carry this burden if, as seems likely, art-making is a difficult and challenging activity in which hard work and the best intentions are not sufficient to guarantee the value of what is produced. By contrast, a definition must be exhaustive of all art and exclusive of all that is not art. It must cover art that is poor or mediocre, as well as that which is excellent. For that reason, what it says might tell us little about artistic merit and its sources.

This division – between defining something and accounting for its value – is not uncommon, even in relation to matters we regard as of the utmost consequence and seriousness. Adequate definitions of parenthood, justice, murder, honesty, and so on typically do not explain their importance within human life. What could be more significant than truth? Yet one philosophical definition of it – a proposition is true if and only if what it asserts is the case, so *snow is white* is true if and only if snow is white – looks bland and trivial. Plainly it does not tell us why the truth is so important that some people can be willing to sacrifice their lives to preserve it.

It is undeniable that we should consider the source of art's value and importance to us (chapter 8, where there is discussion of what we gain from art and of the various ties between art and morality, takes on that task). It is less obvious that definitions of art can be faulted for neglecting that value, however. Criticisms of that sort might easily reflect unreasonable and inappropriate expectations about what an adequate definition of art must deliver.

As a change of topic, now consider a point that may be significant in assessing the role of experts in the determination of a thing's status as art. In a dialog on the nature of piety – that is, religious devotion – the ancient Greek philosopher and arch-essentialist Socrates famously queries the proposal that what makes an act pious is that the gods love it. He suggests that the gods love pious acts because they recognize and value them as such, in which case those acts are already pious before they receive the approval of the gods. In a similar tone, we might question the view that something is art because it is declared to be so by experts, supposing there are some. Being experts about what is art they are liable to be right, but this does not mean that it is their decision that makes the item in question art. More plausible is the idea that their expertise lies in recognizing what is already art when they come across it. Their pronouncement reports what is true independently of their having discovered it.

A defender of radical stipulativism can make two objections to this conclusion. The first notes that, on this view, something could be art though no one in fact recognizes this. Now, we might allow this, say, for a completed painting that is destroyed in a fire before it is publicly displayed, but it is not plausible that something brought to the public and offered as art for a long time, yet that is always rejected by the experts, might be art after all. After some time, rejection defeats a candidate's claim to art status.

If the accidentally destroyed piece is art, it is obvious that the endorsement of experts is *not* a necessary condition for something's being art, unless the suggestion is that the artist is the expert in this case. That claim would be implausible, however. The artist's creative role and her intentions seem much more relevant to what she achieves than does the level of her wider art knowledge and experience. Also, if something is art if it is accepted as such over time by the wider art community, despite its rejection by the experts, then validation by experts is again *not* a necessary condition for something's being art. Is the approval of experts *sufficient* for something's being art? Not if their judgment is fallible, because then more than their endorsement would be needed before the object of their approval qualifies as art. And even if their support does play a role in the conferral of art-status, it may be insufficient to do this on its own. For example, perhaps the artist must also have the relevant kinds of intentions, or perhaps the artworld public must agree. The first objection fails, therefore, to demonstrate that it is the ruling of the experts that settles what is art.

The second defense of the view that something becomes art only on the say-so of the relevant experts registers the extent to which what succeeds as art, and subsequently goes on to direct the course of the unfolding tradition, depends on contingencies and quirks of the artworld and art market. Feminists and other social analysts have raised doubts about the integrity of the canon when it is viewed as a repository of masterpieces (that this epithet indicates they are works created by masters betrays a bias at the outset against women artists). They argue that gender inequality in the artworld is evident in the social, economic, and institutional barriers that have limited and still do limit women's opportunities for making art, in the undervaluation of women's efforts as artists, and also in the relegation of the kinds of artifacts traditionally produced by women – for example, quilts, needlework, weaving, and pottery – to the diminished categories of crafts or "decorative arts." In other words, they accept that arbiters decide what is art, but they attack the ideological and other biases lying behind the decisions made by these "experts."

Now, if the claim is that there are arbitrary socio-political elements of power and fashion that skew the conduct of the artworld, which is often misrepresented as governed only by universal standards of objective aesthetic value, we can surely agree. I think we should be more reluctant to go along with the claim that the difference between the English playwrights William Shakespeare and Ben Jonson lies solely in the fact that the former had a better press agent, so to speak. But however the point in question is

developed, its implications for the task of defining art can be accommodated. Drawing attention to the prejudiced influence of the artworld's
powerbrokers does not entail denying that art has a nature. We can
certainly allow that potential definitions should be scrutinized for unjusti-
fied political assumptions that might distort them, while maintaining that
the activity of working toward a philosophically based definition is a useful
and plausible one.

Questions

2.1 Suppose I protest against the latest piece of avant-garde art by
standing beside it with a placard on which I have painted *This is
rubbish, not art!* How can revolutionary art qualify as art on the basis
of its referring to and repudiating earlier art without my placard also
qualifying as art?

2.2 What claims do firework displays, figure skating, flower arranging,
laser light shows, cake decorating, crafting pop song videos, gardening, scrimshaw carving, quilting, and painting racing and rally cars
with logos and advertisements have to be artforms?

2.3 Must artworks be artifacts – that is, made by humans – or could they
be found readymade in nature?

2.4 Some artists have modified their bodies and presented the process or
result as art. For example, the American artist Chris Burden crawled
over broken glass, was crucified, and was shot in various artworks.
The French performance artist Orlan exhibits as art videos of
surgery performed on her face to give it the features of art-historical
beauties, such as the forehead of Leonardo's Mona Lisa. Does Orlan's
work suggest that cosmetic surgery should be regarded as an artform? Are beauticians correct in their advertisements when they call
themselves *aestheticians*? Many forms of personal decoration involve
alteration of the body – plucking, cutting, filing, piercing, tanning,
tattooing, stamping, binding, scarring, and incising. Under what
circumstances could such practices become artforms, or an individual claim to be a work of art by virtue of her bodily alterations?

2.5 Many definitions imply that art must be *humanly* produced. Is it
unreasonable to assume that non-human animals, such as birds and

apes, cannot make art? Should a definition take account of the possibility that Martians made art long before humans evolved?

2.6 Consider this list of art-relevant features: the item is intended to be art; it falls squarely within what is an established art category; it possesses aesthetic, expressive, formal, or representational properties; it has the capacity to communicate complex meanings; its production requires skill; its production requires creative imagination; it is a source of pleasure in itself; and it invites the cognitive and emotional involvement of its audience. Are any of these more relevant than the others to something's potential status as art? Are any of these features possessed by all artworks necessarily? Are any of them sufficient alone for something's being art? What combinations from the list are sufficient for something's being art?

Readings

For critical reviews of anti-essentialism and of many proposed definitions of art, see Stephen Davies's *Definitions of Art* (Ithaca: Cornell University Press, 1991), Robert Stecker's *Artworks: Definition, Meaning, Value* (University Park: Pennsylvania State University Press, 1997), and the collections *Theories of Art Today*, edited by N. Carroll (Madison: University of Wisconsin Press, 2000), and *Art and Essence*, edited by S. Davies and A. C. Sukla (Westport: Praeger, 2003). Most of the writings listed below not only advocate one or other position but also criticize the rival alternatives.

Morris Weitz's influential arguments against the possibility of defining art appear in "The Role of Theory in Aesthetics," *JAAC* 15 (1956), 27–35. One of the earliest and strongest challenges to Weitz's anti-essentialism is Maurice Mandelbaum's "Family Resemblances and Generalization Concerning the Arts," *American Philosophical Quarterly* 2 (1965), 219–28. William E. Kennick outlines the warehouse test in "Does Traditional Aesthetics Rest on a Mistake?" *Mind* 67 (1958), 317–34. Ludwig Wittgenstein's discussion of family resemblance is in *Philosophical Investigations*, translated by G. E. M. Anscombe (3rd edn., Oxford: Blackwell, 1968), 32–4. B. R. Tilghman applies Wittgensteinian ideas to art and criticizes essentialists in *But Is It Art?* (Oxford: Blackwell, 1984). A version of the cluster theory is offered in " 'Art' as a Cluster Concept," in *Theories of Art Today*, 25–44, by Berys Gaut. Kathleen Stock's radical stipulativism is presented in "Historical Definitions of Art," in *Art and Essence*, 159–76. General doubts about the likelihood of art's being successfully defined are outlined by Thomas Leddy in "The Socratic Quest in Art and Philosophy," *JAAC* 51 (1993), 399–410, and in David Novitz's "Disputes About Art," *JAAC* 54 (1996), 153–63.

Feminist skepticism about the project of definition is considered by Peggy Zeglin Brand in "Glaring Omissions in Traditional Theories of Art," in *Theories of Art Today*, 175–98. For a famous essay on inequalities in the treatment of women artists and what they produce, see Linda Nochlin's "Why Have There Been No Great Women Artists?" *ARTnews* 69 (1971), 22–39.

Definitions of the aesthetic functionalist variety are proposed by Monroe C. Beardsley in "Redefining Art," in *The Aesthetic Point of View*, edited by M. J. Wreen and D. M. Callen (Ithaca: Cornell University Press, 1982), 298–315, and Nick Zangwill in "The Creative Theory of Art," *American Philosophical Quarterly* 32 (1995), 307–23. George Dickie first presented a developed account of the institutional theory in 1974, but he revised the theory significantly in *The Art Circle: A Theory of Art* (New York: Haven, 1984). In "Art: Function or Procedure – Nature or Culture?" *JAAC* 55 (1997), 19–28, he considers if art is a natural-kind activity, as opposed to a cultural-kind activity. Varieties of historicist definitions are provided by James D. Carney, in "The Style Theory of Art," *Pacific Philosophical Quarterly* 72 (1991), 273–89, Jerrold Levinson, in "The Irreducible Historicality of the Concept of Art," *BJA* 42 (2002), 367–79, and Noël Carroll, in "Historical Narratives and the Philosophy of Art," *JAAC* 51 (1993), 313–26. Robert Stecker defends a hybrid definition in *Artworks: Definition, Meaning, Value*, and offers a useful overview in "Is it Reasonable to Attempt to Define Art?," in *Theories of Art Today*, 45–64.

The artworld relativity problem – that most definitions presuppose the Western artworld context, either without arguing that no other artworlds exist or without analyzing what makes the many artworlds *art*worlds – is discussed in Stephen Davies's "Non-Western Art and Art's Definition," in *Theories of Art Today*, 199–216.

The thesis that art has a historical destiny that it has fulfilled, thereby bringing its historical progress to an end, was presented in the 1820s by Hegel in *Aesthetics: Lectures on Fine Arts*, first published 1835–8, translated by M. Knox, 2 vols. (Oxford: Oxford University Press, 1975) and by Arthur C. Danto, "The End of Art," in *The Death of Art*, edited by B. Lang (New York: Haven, 1984), 5–35.

For debate about whether questions of art's value must be answered by any adequate definition of art, see Nick Zangwill's "Groundrules in the Philosophy of Art," *Philosophy* 70 (1995), 533–44 and Stephen Davies's "Essential Distinctions for Art Theorists," in *Art and Essence*, 3–16. Also relevant is *But Is It Art?* (Oxford: Oxford University Press, 2001) by Cynthia Freeland.

Chapter Three

Aesthetics and the Philosophy of Art

This chapter draws attention to a shift that took place about the middle of the twentieth century in the way Anglo-American philosophers began to think about art. Earlier in the century, philosophers took inspiration from theories first developed in the eighteenth century that emphasized formal beauty and the separation of art, which is to be appreciated for its own sake alone, from craft, which is practically useful. To these ideas, they added the suggestion that there is a distinctive frame of mind, one of "distanced" contemplation, that should be adopted in appreciating the aesthetic character both of nature and art, the *aesthetic attitude*. Developments and controversies within the arts prompted other philosophers later in the century to reject these ideas as inadequate for explaining the identity and content of artworks. They argued that aesthetic theories of art cannot account for the kinds of properties that make an artwork the work that it is, or even for the meaning it possesses. The identity and content of an artwork, they said, emerge only in relation to aspects of the situation in which that work is created. The aesthetic theory of the first half of the twentieth century disregarded such matters, and even described consideration of them as antithetical to aesthetic perception and enjoyment. It focused on the inner psychology of the percipient, instead of on the art-historical setting and the social practices, conventions, and institutions within which art is made and consumed. The new philosophy that emerged later in the century challenged and rejected the old theory. It targeted art specifically, not the broader category of the aesthetic.

We have already met with theories that indirectly reflect the division between these two, competing approaches to the discussion of art. The style of definition labeled *aesthetic functionalism* in chapter 2 fits generally with the aesthetic view of art, whereas the *institutional theory* and *historicist* definitions regard socio-historical aspects of the context of creation as crucial to art's nature. Moreover, themes central to the debate in this chapter, such as those about the determinants of the identity and content of artworks, return later. Chapter 4, on art's varieties, is partly concerned with characterizing the kinds of features that fix an artwork's identity, while chapter 5, on art's interpretation, considers the content of artworks and what is required for recognizing and appreciating it.

As well, the discussion here provides a serious challenge to the suggestion mooted in chapter 1, that art is an invention of eighteenth-century Europe. The philosophical aestheticians of that time did not develop their theories to show that no art pre-existed their era. Indeed, they all assumed the Greeks and Romans had art. Nevertheless, the claim that art is an eighteenth-century invention accords the philosophers of the Enlightenment and early modern age a central role by holding that the *concept* of art, not just the formal institutions of the artworld, emerged during the period, and that philosophers' theories played an important part in publicly articulating and analyzing that concept. Our current philosophical understanding of what is art was inherited from this source, it is alleged. So, the argument concluding that art is a cultural invention rests on the claim that our current concept of art is adequately represented by aesthetic theories of the nature both of art and of aesthetic experience that faithfully preserve at their core ideas and concepts that were developed by important eighteenth-century theorists, such as Kant, and their nineteenth-century heirs, such as Schopenhauer. If the mid-twentieth-century repudiation of earlier aesthetic theories is well founded, as is argued in this chapter and subsequently, it is not true, after all, that our current concept of art was revealed through the tradition of aesthetic philosophizing that began in the European Enlightenment.

3.1   Aesthetic and Artistic Properties

To help understand the following discussion of the experience and nature of art, it will be useful to clarify the notion of an *aesthetic property*. (Recall that such properties were singled out in chapter 2 when *aesthetic functionalism* was discussed.)

Aesthetic properties are usually characterized as objective features perceived in the object of appreciation when it is approached for its own sake. Such properties are internal to the object of appreciation. They are directly available for perception in that their recognition does not require knowledge of matters external to the object of appreciation. In particular, their recognition does not depend on information about the circumstances under which the item was made or about its intended or possible functions. These properties announce their significance, as it were, through the experience they provide. To quote a list drawn up by the British philosopher Frank Sibley, the following adjectives describe examples of aesthetic properties: unified, balanced, integrated, lifeless, serene, somber, dynamic, powerful, vivid, delicate, moving, trite, sentimental, tragic, graceful, delicate, dainty, handsome, comely, elegant, garish, and beautiful. Obviously many aesthetic properties have an evaluative component, and this may be negative (dumpy) or positive (dainty).

Typically, aesthetic properties are described as *second-order* or *higher-order* properties, because they are based on (or are supervenient on) other, simpler, non-aesthetic properties of the aesthetic object. Philosophers disagree about how the relevant kind of supervenience is to be analyzed, but they do not dispute that there is *some* connection between the item's aesthetic properties and details of its structure and content. The unity of a painting will depend somehow on the disposition of base elements, such as shapes, color fields, and textures; if it is garish, this will be because of the colors it uses and how it displays and combines them. Generally speaking, two things that are otherwise identical should share the same aesthetic properties, while a change to a thing's structure or content is likely to affect its aesthetic character.

Many of the properties of artworks do not meet the specification just given for aesthetic properties. In a painting, it may be appropriate to interpret a dove carrying an olive branch as symbolizing peace, or an old man with a lion in a desert as St Jerome, though such things are apparent only to someone who views the works in terms of the conventions of religious iconography. These conventions are used by artists, but they are not among their paintings' perceptible content. Also, one work may quote from, refer to, or allude to another and, again, this takes us beyond consideration solely of its internal features. It can be original, influenced by some earlier work, the first of its artist's middle phase, the swansong of a tired genre, or unusual for its treatment of shadows. It can be intended to emulate, subvert, reject, or redirect the default art traditions, genres, and practices of its time. Some works belong to kinds with specific functions – they are elegies, portraits, or hymns, for example – and this is not apparent from their aesthetic properties alone. For the sake of the contrast, let us refer to art-relevant, non-aesthetic properties of the kinds just indicated as *artistic*.

Are expressive, representational, and narrational features *aesthetic* or *artistic*? In some cases they surely are artistic. Judgments about the realism or verisimilitude of a representation require comparisons that take one beyond the work's immediate boundaries, as does consideration of the idea that a musical work expresses its composer's feelings. But what of those cases in which the focus is on the work's expressive character, or on the appearance of what it represents, or on the content of the story that is being told? On the one hand, these belong to the work, but on the other, their perception presupposes a wealth of experience and knowledge brought to the work from the outside world. Are these better regarded as aesthetic or artistic features of the work?

The answer is likely to depend on how such things are to be analyzed. (Expressiveness is discussed in chapter 6 and representation in chapter 7.) For instance, if a work is expressive of X, or represents Y, or describes the story of Z only if it is intended to, and this is not always infallibly and immediately perceptible within the work, it looks as if no such aspects of works of art could count as aesthetic. In that case, theories that focus exclusively on aesthetic properties will be plainly incapable of accounting for the identity and character of most artworks. This would be a cheap victory against aestheticism, though. So let us concede that the autonomy of the aesthetic is not endangered when the spectator brings her knowledge of English to her reading of the novel, her familiarity with the appearance of common things or events to her viewing of pictorial representations, and her educated sensitivies to emotions and the contexts in which they arise as she listens to the music. Accept, if only for the sake of the argument, that modes of expression, representation, and narration falling squarely within the work come under the ambit of the aesthetic.

We are now in a position to characterize the clash between aesthetic theory and the philosophy of art. The former maintains that consideration of the aesthetic in art is adequate for art's appreciation as art. Reflection on a work's artistic properties is not relevant to its proper reception. The latter view denies this. Indeed, it maintains that awareness of a work's artistic properties is crucial not only to understanding it but also to identifying it as the artwork it is.

I should add this warning: not everyone makes the *terminological* distinction adopted above. The term *aesthetic* is often used in a broad way, to include what I have called the artistic. (That does not mean those who follow this use are unaware of the distinctions I have drawn here.) Also, I allow that it is far from clear where we should draw the line between the two, as I explain further below. Nevertheless, I prefer to formalize the separation between the kinds of properties that are in question because this should help us keep clear about where the crux of the disagreement falls.

3.1.1 An illustration

The distinction between aesthetic and artistic properties can be made clearer and more vivid through the study of a concrete example. I have chosen a Balinese painting for the reason that, for most Westerners, the piece's artistic properties are not as readily apparent as they would be had I chosen an artwork from a more familiar tradition. Please carefully examine the reproduction in figure 3.1.

The painting's aesthetic properties should be visible in its appearance, even to those who know little of the work's origins or functions. We can see that the picture shows men and a woman, including a man with four arms and another with an elephant's head. As well, there is a character with the appearance of a monster. The depiction divides into five parts, each of which is likely to be a scene in a narrative, since some characters appear in more than one scene. The story that is referred to is not part of the work's aesthetic character, however, because it can be followed only by someone who knows which individuals are depicted and the conventions dictating how the scenes are to be read. Without that specific knowledge, it is not even clear that the goodies can be sorted from the baddies.

Let us concentrate on the form. The central, seated couple are at the focal point. The scenes flanking them to left and right have a satisfying symmetry. The painting splits horizontally into more or less equal upper and lower parts. What is more, the upper scenes have a calm quiet compared to the dynamism apparent in the actions shown in the lower ones. As a result, the disposition of energies neatly maps on to the vertical distribution of shapes, creating a balanced tension between the picture's upper and lower portions. This helps the whole to cohere, and does so without making the overall form static and rigid.

We could examine the piece's aesthetic characteristics further, but enough has been said, I hope, to leave that further analysis up to the reader. When that task is complete, what has been left out? What is lost to the person who is blind to the work's artistic properties? To make this apparent, I now consider the painting's narrative subject, its style, and its symbolic content.

The narrative adapts an ancient poem with sources in India and Java. It begins with the seated pair, Sanghyang Semara and Dewi Ratih, who are man and wife. They are very much in love. Semara is sent to arouse the god Siwa from his meditations – he is pictured in the painting's top left – so that Siwa can father a non-human child who will be able to defeat the evil monster, Rudraka. When disturbed, Siwa is in a blind rage and destroys Semara with fire. Siwa, disguised as a man and riding an elephant, startles Ratih (in the picture's bottom right). She gives birth to the elephant-headed Ganesa (as shown in the top right scene). When grown, Ganesa joins Siwa, again in human form, to fight Rudraka. (This event is shown in the painting's bottom left.) In the conflict, Ganesa's left tusk is broken. He stabs and kills the monster with the fragment of tusk. Meanwhile, whenever human couples make love, Semara lives again and is reunited with Ratih.

Though it is a recent work and uses modern media (watercolors, ink, and acrylics on cloth), the painter adopts a very old, traditional style for this work. The two-dimensionality of the depiction and the fixed facial profiles are typical, because the style is based on the shadow puppet theater, with which it shares its iconography. For example, whenever the forces of good and evil meet or fight on the shadow screen, the goodies are on the viewer's left and the baddies on the right, and this arrangement is displayed in the bottom left scene of the painting. As well, the dress and headdresses of the characters show their social status, and Siwa is unmistakable in his godly form not least because of the number of his arms. The monster Rudraka shows features associated with creatures of a beastly, coarse character: round, protuberant eyes, large nose, and prominent fangs. By comparison, the gods and Balinese characters are fine-featured and restrained in their poses. The eyes of male characters always are above the lid-line, whereas those of females are always below.

The painting's contents clearly have symbolic import. The work serves as a visual metaphor for the cycle of death and creation, destruction and renewal, acknowledged by the Balinese as a central tenet of their Hinduism. Siwa is the god of destruction and return. He is the dissolver and recycler of the spirit. At death, all Balinese undergo cremation, which is followed later (so they believe) by reincarnation, and to that extent Semara's fate represents the general pattern of human existence and non-existence.

The artistic significance of this work is more particular and penetrates further, however, than this rather general symbolism. The Balinese identify six passions that must be tamed if the individual is to attain maturity: lust, anger, greed, confusion, drunkenness, and envy. A solemn ceremony, usually held after puberty and before marriage, is devoted to the individual's entry into adulthood. (This is one of five rites of passage Balinese undergo, the last being cremation.) In effect, this ceremony signals the individual's commitment to achieving the self-control needed to master the six demons she harbors within. As part of the ceremony, the individual's teeth, especially the canines (or fangs, as the Balinese call them), are filed down so they are smooth. This act symbolizes the renunciation of animal inclinations and appetites, which the Balinese despise in humans. The painting's story includes an indirect but unmistakable reference to these beliefs about human nature – as Ganesa demonstrates, broken teeth kill demons.

The tooth-filing ceremony has a further implication. It signals the individual's newfound orientation toward adulthood and with it a growing preparedness for love and marriage. Also, tooth-filing is regarded as a beautifying process, making the person's face more refined and attractive and thereby readying him or her for love. Accordingly, the ceremony is presided over by the goddess of beauty, Dewa Kama (also known as Sanghyang Semara Ratih), who is represented, among other ways, through depictions including Semara and Ratih. The characters portrayed in this Balinese painting are, therefore, potent symbols of sexual maturity and partnership, as well as reminders of the importance of self-control and calm wisdom. Their images are intimately linked to the tooth-filing ceremony, being painted on fabrics the participant lies on during this ceremony.

The Balinese picture has many aesthetic qualities, and there is no denying their interest, but the greater part of its importance resides in its artistic properties, as is immediately apparent to those for whom it is intended. The viewer who concerns herself solely with the picture's aesthetic qualities would not begin to suspect its true (which is its artistic) import: it is a tooth-filing picture full of powerful symbols. It makes a connection deep into the heart of Balinese metaphysics and cosmology. It is not merely a cartoon-styled narrative; it is a religious icon. This is apparent, of course, only to the person who has the relevant knowledge of painting traditions, as well as of Balinese custom, lore, and belief, and who brings the work's immediate contents into an appropriate relation with these external considerations. In this, the Balinese picture is no different from many pictures of other cultures. Indeed, the significance of *art* pictures typically lies more in their artistic content and qualities than in their aesthetic ones.

Already I am anticipating conclusions that will come later. Before jumping to embrace them, we need to return to the beginning by examining arguments offered for and against the competing positions.

3.2   The Aesthetic Attitude and Art for Art's Sake

Here are some of the key elements claimed within aesthetic theory, as it was developed in the early twentieth century, to comprise our concept of art.

The appreciation of art targets the aesthetic properties artworks possess. To be fully prepared to receive a work's aesthetic properties, the percipient should adopt a particular mental attitude, the aesthetic attitude, which is one of distanced or disinterested contemplation. To achieve this frame of mind, she needs to bracket out her natural or typical concerns with respect to the object's usefulness, value, history, and classification in order to prevent these from distracting or inhibiting the proper experience of the object of attention. In other words, an aesthetic interest in something as an end in itself excludes all thought or knowledge of it as a means to the perceiver's or anyone's ends.

In 1912 Edward Bullough, a British aesthetician, summed up the view when he argued that aesthetic experience involves the adoption of *psychical distance*. As he described it, psychological distancing *has a negative, inhibitory aspect – the cutting out of the practical side of things and of our practical attitude to them – and a positive side – the elaboration of the experience on the new basis created by the inhibitory action of distance*. Bullough focused more on an explanation of the negative aspect. A man who doubts his wife's faithfulness needs distance in order not to muddle his appreciation of Shakespeare's *Othello* with thoughts of his own situation. Meanwhile, the interest of the critic puts him in danger of achieving too little distance. Jerome Stolnitz also rejects as non-aesthetic any focus that has the purpose of passing judgment, with the consequence that the art critic, who cannot be indifferent to the fact that she is paid for her work and who views what she does in order to write the reviews that are expected, will have difficulty in adopting the aesthetic attitude and thereby achieving an aesthetic experience, as will anyone whose interest in art has a practical motivation. Other non-aesthetic motivations for engaging with art, according to Stolnitz, include any cognitive concern that pays heed to a piece's historical or sociological context, or that studies or classifies it.

Stolnitz believes his views correspond with those of aesthetic theorists of the eighteenth century. It certainly is true that similar views were propounded before the twentieth century. Indeed, they had wide currency among artists and critics, as well as philosophers. In the nineteenth century the French writer Charles Baudelaire stressed the distinctive psychology of the aesthetic attitude, and the Irish author Oscar Wilde was an advocate of art's independence from practical matters. The idea that aesthetic interests and practical concerns are mutually exclusive is promoted by Mark Twain, the American novelist. In *Life on the Mississippi* (1883), he tells how experience taught him to "read" the river, so he saw ripples on the surface as indicating the presence of sandbars, the sun and clouds as predictors of the weather, and distinctive trees as landmarks. He claims that this knowledge led him to lose something that could never be restored to him while he lived: *All the grace, the beauty, the poetry had gone out of the majestic river.* (Despite what he writes, the reader cannot help but notice that, when Twain goes on to describe his former experience, he is able to capture in loving detail the romance and beauty of the scene.) Twain then observes that he pities doctors, because they must see the lovely flush on a woman's cheek not as beautiful but as a symptom of some disease. He continues rhetorically: *Does he ever see her beauty at all, or doesn't he simply comment upon her unwholesome condition all to himself? And doesn't he sometimes wonder whether he has gained most or lost most by learning his trade?*

3.3 Aesthetic Theory Criticized

The mid-twentieth-century challenge to these ideas can be introduced by drawing attention to the fact that aesthetic theories often exemplify the notion of the aesthetic by reference to natural items or scenes – roses, the night sky, waterfalls, sunsets, and so on. Bullough illustrates his account of psychical distance by describing the experience of seeing a ship in a fog at sea. Art is mentioned almost as an afterthought, as if it is a straightforward matter to extend and apply the account to it. The primary focus is on nature, and on art only derivatively. But this must be unsatisfactory. It ignores the importance in art of the artist's agency, and of all that depends on this – representation, symbolism, expression, allusion, quotation, irony, and the rest. At the same time, it overlooks the relevance to the artist's achievement of the art-historical and socio-political backgrounds against which he works. Aesthetic theory often omits the human context from art's creation, and this makes it incapable of explaining the import of many of the properties on which the appreciation of art depends. For example, how can it account for the significance of a work such as Maya Lin's *Vietnam Veterans' Memorial* in Washington DC? If we are to put aside the work's social context and purpose, and also cannot consider whose names are listed and why, what remains of the work's meaning and identity? So, either aesthetic theory misdescribes the nature of aesthetic properties or there is much more to the proper appreciation of art than a concern with its aesthetic properties alone. On either count, positions like Stolnitz's do not adequately describe the concept of art.

Also problematic is the psychologistic approach to aesthetic experience. The appreciation of art does not require the adoption of a special frame of mind, or the use of a distinctive mode of attention, or an act of distancing the purpose of which is to keep practical concerns at bay. (In a famous critique of the notion, George Dickie points out that alleged examples of "interested" or "under-distanced" attention, as when a jealous husband in the audience is led by Shakespeare's play *Othello* to doubt his wife's faithfulness, or where the yokel leaps on stage to try to save the heroine, are better seen as cases of distraction or derangement.) What is needed for art's appreciation is attention to the work's artistic as well as its aesthetic properties. What makes this appreciation possible is an appropriate understanding of the piece's kind, of the social conventions in terms of which it is to be approached, of the practices of the artworld, of its medium and the constraints and challenges this poses, of how the artist amplifies or repudiates the work or art theories of his contemporaries and forebears, and so on. Theories like Stolnitz's do not explain, for instance, why we draw the boundaries around artworks as we do, so that we do not confuse the beauty of the painting with the beauty of its frame, or fault the play because an audience member's ugly hairstyle falls within our view of the stage. Moreover, there is no reason to suppose that a practical interest in an artwork inevitably excludes or opposes a simultaneous appreciation of it as art. A person who scrutinizes a painting in order to pass an art appreciation exam is motivated differently from the person who considers it for its own sake alone, but to succeed in the exam she probably must regard it in a similar way, and there is no reason to believe the difference in motivation must lead to a difference in the attention given or the experience that results.

Now, a dedicated aesthetic formalist might always dig in her heels. She accepts, of course, that the fact that a work is a *memorial*, say, is relevant to the history and sociology of art. She agrees, moreover, that we can interest ourselves in the techniques of production, the motivation for the work's creation, its significance to the artist, and so on. But she denies that these otherwise legitimate concerns amount to a proper focus on the artwork. Such matters are not part of its identity or content. Artworks are surrounded by a penumbra of emotional and political attachments, but it is not this mantle of social meaning that gives them their significance as art. To be considered as an artwork, and not as a piece of social history or as a civic monument, *Vietnam Veterans' Memorial* should be approached solely in terms of its formal and sensuous properties. In addition, the formalist can observe that, so powerful is the political and historical message that must be put aside in order to view this work aesthetically, an effort of will is likely to be needed if the viewer is to attain an appropriate detachment.

And so the argument is extended to all proposed counterexamples. The aesthetic formalist does not deny the human importance of art's associations and applications, but she rejects their relevance to art's proper appreciation as art. Appreciation should concern the objective properties apparent in the work when details of its origins, kind, and function are disregarded, she insists.

One way of meeting this response is by tackling the aesthetic formalist on her own territory. If recognizing the aesthetic significance of formal and other elements depends on acknowledging the external factors that the formalist dismisses as irrelevant, aesthetic formalism is undermined from within. Figure 3.2 is an example that may do the trick. The 1558 Brussels version of *Landscape with the Fall of Icarus*, by Pieter Brueghel depicts the moment when Icarus plunges headfirst into the sea. He fell from the sky because he flew too near the sun, which caused the wax holding together his improvised wings to melt. All that can be seen of Icarus are his legs, and these are insignificantly small parts of the depicted scene, which is dominated in the foreground by a man plowing and by a shepherd, both of whom are oblivious to Icarus's fate.

This work could be interpreted as a commentary on the world's indifference to individual martyrdom, but the aesthetic formalist would have us set aside such ideas, so let us focus on the painting's form. In purely formal terms, the composition is dominated by the plowman in the foreground. Only when we know what the picture represents does attention shift to the inconspicuous legs in the lower right. When it does, the legs become the work's compositional center. We experience the rest of the scene as organized around them. Even a strict aesthetic formalist must acknowledge that this picture's *composition* is deeply affected by the psychological weight placed on the lower right corner, which means that examination of the work's form cannot be detached from the story of what is represented; that is, from something that must be brought from outside. Not only must one know the title (and hence the story) to *understand* the picture, also the work's meaning is inextricably intertwined with the work's *formal* properties.

If the aesthetic formalist disregards the work's represented content and describes the legs merely as yellow-pink daubs, she could not explain their structural significance within the picture. But earlier I allowed to the aesthetic theorist that she can include what it represents as among the work's internal contents. In that case, the aesthetic formalist considers the elements of the work's composition as people, ships, and the like, not merely as colored patches. So, for her, the legs, the plowman, the sea, and the rest are part of the work's formal design. Nevertheless, what she can count as the work's represented content must be confined to what can be seen there, given only an understanding of the appearances of things and the conventions of pictorial representation. So, the formalist can allow that legs are depicted, but it is not apparent from the picture's appearance whose legs these are. If they were those of a swimmer who has just dived from the shore, they would not become the picture's gravitational center as they do when they are seen as Icarus's. The form of this work is revealed only to the spectator who understands that the legs shown are those of Icarus, who has fallen from the sky and who is to die. To acknowledge all that must be brought to bear on an appreciation of the form of this picture it is necessary to go beyond what is licensed by aesthetic formalism.

The impossibility of separating formal factors from aspects of content that are not straightforwardly visible is apparent from further consideration of the human body. The aesthetic formalist does not regard the body merely as an assemblage of cylinders, cubes, orbs, and the rest. But once it is seen as the root of human existence and agency, as infused with consciousness, as the mode through which we engage others and the world, how can we draw a line between the human *form* and *life* in its wider manifestations? The point is yet more vivid when we attend to important parts of the body, such as the face or the eyes.

Consider Caravaggio's *Deposition of Christ* (1604). The central compositional element of this picture is the downward thrust of the arc created by the heads and hands of the figures, a movement that ends in the lifeless hand of Jesus. But this central formal feature depends upon the psychological weight of heads and hands, a weight recognized by the European artworld since the early Renaissance in that contracts often stipulated that the master himself had to paint the heads and hands of the figures (other body parts, drapery, foliage, and architecture were often left to apprentices). If heads and hands did not have a special meaning for us, they would not in themselves — that is, in purely formal terms — jump out so prominently in pictures and so would not be able to do important compositional — that is, formal — work, like that found in Caravaggio's picture.

3.4 Artworks that Pose a Challenge to Aesthetic Theory

It was not artworks of the period just discussed that inspired the mid-twentieth-century critique of aesthetic theories of art. That role fell to works produced in the twentieth century. Two of the most philosophically influential were mentioned in the previous chapter: Duchamp's *Fountain* and Warhol's *Brillo Boxes*. What is striking about these artworks is that the relatively minor perceptual differences between them and the ordinary things they resemble play no part in explaining why the artworks have such different meanings and value. Perceptually equivalent objects share the same *aesthetic* properties, according to traditional aesthetic theory, but in that case it has no way of explaining why Duchamp's *Fountain* is an artwork while other urinals that came off the same production line are not. A related point emerges for the case in which it is different artworks that share the same perceptible features. Having created a work (of 1919–40) in the form of a postcard copy of Leonardo's *Mona Lisa* to which he added a beard, a moustache, and the sign "L.H.O.O.Q." – when pronounced, this sounds like the French phrase that translates as *She has a hot bum* – Duchamp went on to produce *L.H.O.O.Q. Shaved* (1965), which looks like *Mona Lisa* in miniature. And image appropriators often produce works that resemble those of the artists whose pieces they appropriate. For example, Sherrie Levine, an American artist, has displayed as her own artworks photographs she has taken of the art-photographs of others, such as Edward Weston and Walker Evans. Christopher Hobbs, a British composer, creates his works by drawing from a bag the pieces of a cut-up score of a classical music piece. By chance, one of Hobbs's works could have the exact note sequence of its source. The moral is similar: if two different artworks are perceptually the same, aesthetic theories like Stolnitz's cannot explain what distinguishes them since, by his account, they should display identical aesthetic properties. When artworks resemble non-artworks or other artworks, the differences must depend on their non-perceptible aspects or relations, not on aesthetic properties as traditionally described in aesthetic theory.

If the appreciation of art rests entirely with an experience of its aesthetic properties, then the observation that additional factors are involved among the artwork's *identifying* conditions might seem comparatively harmless. Aesthetic theorists then could not fully account for the identifying conditions of artworks but could still explain how they are to be understood and why we value them. But this response to the cases just described misses the full significance of the critique. Artworks that are outwardly similar to other artworks or to non-artworks can differ not only in their identities but also in their *contents*; that is, in features central to their artistic meaning.

Here are some examples. Duchamp's *Fountain* invokes the tradition of sculpting in white marble, which other porcelain urinals do not, and it offered a challenge to the presuppositions and prejudices of the artworld of its time which urinals located elsewhere in the art gallery do not. *L.H.O.O.Q. Shaved* makes a witty connection both to *L.H.O.O.Q.* and to *Mona Lisa*, whereas Leonardo's work contains no such reference. Sherrie Levine's photographs make an art-political point about the fact that women typically gain entry to the gallery via the works of male artists, whereas the works she appropriates have no such content. In another case, the Argentinian Jorge Luis Borges has written a story about a twentieth-century French author, Pierre Menard, who (without copying) creates a work that shares its text with part of Miguel de Cervantes' Spanish novel *Don Quixote* (written in 1605 and 1615). The narrator of Borges' tale records many artistically salient differences between these two works. Whereas Cervantes' piece is in the popular linguistic idiom of his time, Menard adopts the affectation of writing his story in archaic language; while Cervantes could write what came, Menard took on the more challenging task of reconstructing an earlier work; where Cervantes mouthed the opinions and platitudes of his age, Menard worked deliberately against the intellectual climate of a more complex and sophisticated later era. We might question the comparative evaluation made by the narrator, who says *Cervantes' text and Menard's are verbally identical, but the second is almost infinitely richer.* Nevertheless, it is plausible to argue that the two works differ in many of their content-relevant properties.

In fact, it is not uncommon for non-perceptible factors of the work to play an arguably important role in its identity and contents. Compare *Piss Christ* by the American Andre Serrano with an otherwise identical work that fills the bottle containing the crucifix with cream soda, not urine; or one of Rembrandt's self-portraits with a clone that is painted as an imaginative fiction by a South American Indian who has never heard of the seventeenth-century Dutch painter; or illustrations in a medical textbook that are indistinguishable from a homosexually erotic male nude by the artist Robert Mapplethorpe; or Charles Ray's *Cube*, which is a 7½-ton white cube of solid lead, with a doppelganger made of polystyrene foam.

A second lesson emerged from further consideration of the same kinds of example. Much twentieth-century art fails to live up to the aesthetic expectations we are criticizing. It downplays the sensuous aspects of its appearance in favor of cognitive properties such as wit and reference. The person who delights in the gleaming whiteness of Duchamp's *Fountain* has missed the point; Duchamp went out of his way to choose a piece that is aesthetically neutral. Some conceptual artworks, such as the self-explanatory *All that I once knew but cannot now remember* (to use a rapidly growing work of my own invention), present no aesthetic (or other) properties to perception. Also, some artworks are made to be anti-aesthetic, in that they set out to eschew beauty for expressive power, semantic complexity, or plain ugliness.

These cases cannot be dismissed as unusual or aberrant. The political, religious, or moral messages conveyed by much art of all periods is far more crucial to its significance than are the aesthetic qualities of its appearance, as was illustrated earlier in the discussion of figure 3.1 (supposing that this Balinese picture is art). Consider how little would be understood about the 50-ton sculpture *Gates of Sorrow* by Jim Gallucci, commemorating the tragedy of September 11, 2001, by a person who did not know (or who knew, but dismissed such matters from her mind in order to adopt a disinterested attitude) that it is shaped from steel beams taken from the remains of the World Trade Center and that it was made to commemorate those who died? Moreover, one central artform, literature, cannot easily be accommodated by aesthetic theories. While books, as material objects, present some aesthetic properties to the senses, the stories they contain need not be mentally imaged as they are read and followed. On the face of it, the traditional account of aesthetic properties does not include purely narrative artforms within its ambit.

Also relevant is the fact that, because artworks refer to and influence each other, the history of art cannot be merely the temporal succession of its works. As Arthur C. Danto has emphasized, what can become an artwork and the significance it has depends on when and where it is offered. Robert Rauschenberg made an artwork of his bed by applying paint to it in 1955, but Leonardo could not have done the same in the late fifteenth century, because neither he nor his contemporaries could have conceived of the result as art, given the tradition of painting to that time. And the production of art also implicates social institutions and practices, if it is also true that what becomes art depends on who offers it as such. A child can paint his bed so that it happens to look just the same as Rauschenberg's, but it would not follow that he produces an artwork. Rauschenberg was a recognized artist who, in painting his bed, was deliberately rejecting the range of media that seemed to have been prescribed by the tradition against which he was reacting. His work takes much of his significance from that, whereas the infant has no such standing or understanding.

To recapitulate the negative conclusions reached previously, the strands of post-Enlightenment aesthetics that became dominant in Anglo-American philosophy by the early twentieth century fail to account for our concept of art, because they wrongly suggest that an artwork's aesthetic properties confer on it its identity and appreciable content, and that awareness of the work's aesthetic properties provides for a full understanding of it. Also, the focus in aesthetic attitude theories on the psychological experiences of the individual is inadequate to explain all that is involved in the appreciation of art as such, for it overlooks how the appreciator's knowledge of appropriate social practices and conventions should direct and structure her response. At this stage we might try to save the theory by expanding the notion of an *aesthetic* property, so that now it includes, as well as perceptible properties internal to the object of appreciation, all the other kinds of properties that are significant to the identity and content of artworks. In taking this line, we would have moved far from the conception of the aesthetic as it was traditionally presented, however.

Whichever way we go – whether we say that there is more to art than the aesthetic or say that the aesthetic can be widened to include much more than aesthetic theories acknowledge – it is an error to maintain that our concept of art originated in and continues to reflect theories that have promoted the centrality of the aesthetic. If the current concept of art accommodates the twentieth-century artworks discussed above – and recall that many of them have never been controversial and the rest are usually now accepted as art – then either earlier aestheticians had a different concept of art or they failed fully to understand the concept of art they shared with us. Of these two ways of describing the situation, I prefer the second. Though the human understanding of many things has changed over the centuries, there is no basis for describing this always in terms of radical conceptual revision. Several centuries ago, some people believed that emotions were the result of perturbations in the movements of inner bodily fluids, and that gold could be made from base metals by alchemy. That these beliefs were mistaken does not mean that they did not share with us the same pre-theoretic, basic notions of emotions or of gold. And if a child comes to learn that milk comes from cows, not from a mountain spring as he was told at an impressionable age, it is not his concept of milk that is changed but, rather, some of his beliefs about milk. Similarly, there is no reason to argue that earlier aestheticians differed from later ones because they operated with and analyzed a different concept. Instead, they had the same pre-theoretic concept of art, but, as we can now see, their analysis was inadequate in parts. This is not something for which they should be blamed, of course. They did not have the advantage of seeing where artists would take the artworld or how the practice of art would unfold.

3.5   Art's Contextually Relative Properties

Many contemporary philosophers of art have come to think that the sociological, historical, and cultural context in which art is produced and consumed is relevant to its identity and content. If an artwork can be perceptually indistinguishable from a non-artwork, or another artwork, and possess not only a distinct identity but also quite different contents or properties, then something that is not directly perceptible plays a role in giving the work its identity and content. It follows that a piece's aesthetic properties cannot alone settle its identity and content, since such properties always are potentially perceptible, according to the traditional account of them. Factors beyond the work's boundaries affect its nature and meaning. The most important of these is likely to be the art-historical context that forms the backdrop to the work's creation. The work's identity and content depend in part on relational features; that is, on connections between the context of its production and the material and perceptible features of the piece. Just as one cannot identify people as aunts and uncles solely on the basis of their appearance, so one cannot recognize the relational properties responsible in part for an artwork's identity and content solely by examining its immediately perceptible characteristics.

What aspects of the art-historical context are relevant? One way of addressing this question is to imagine of a work that we are initially mistaken about some aspect of the context of its production, and then to ask if we should revise our understanding of it when our error comes to light. For example, consider a painting depicting a man dressed as Napoleon and a woman in early nineteenth-century dress. At first we believe the work is titled *Napoleon and Josephine* but later learn that the title is *The artist's neighbors posed prior to the fancy dress ball as Napoleon and Josephine*. In this case, we should revise our opinion concerning the work's content. It turns out that the painting represents quite different people from the ones we previously supposed. And notice that what settles this is not a straightforward matter of the resemblance between those who are in the painting and people in the actual world, because we might have known all along that the artist's neighbors posed for the work. It is quite standard for a painting to resemble the model who sat for it though it represents a historical or mythical character. So the title, as sincerely given to the work by its artist, is something we might need to know about, because it can affect what the work is about, as was apparent previously in the discussion of Brueghel's *Landscape with the Fall of Icarus*.

The case of representation suggests that an artist's intentions can be crucial to the nature or content of her work. If a painting depicts one of two identical twins, it will be the artist's intention that settles which one that is. (The artist might use Tweedledum as her model for a portrait of the absent Tweedledee precisely because she can rely on capturing the likeness of Tweedledee by using his identical twin.) Other art-significant features in which the artist's intentions could play a determining role are those of reference, allusion, allegory, quotation, parody, symbolism, irony, and metaphor.

Other facts about the author and her collection of works can also be relevant. Whether a work comes from the artist's juvenilia or from her mature phase will depend on her age and experience when it was done. If a certain work is the second in a trilogy, it needs to be taken in conjunction with its accompanying volumes. More generally, where a series of works share a common theme or related intent, they might reflect on each other. The artist's personal style and "fingerprint" can also be displayed across many of her works, and provide a significant connection or organizing principle within them.

Another consideration is the artwork's genre. Imagine a musical piece that was in fact a suite, though at first we mistook it for a symphony. As soon as it has been reclassified, different features become salient. Whereas formerly we might have wondered why there were six movements, many of which have a dance character, this now is predictable and of no special significance. And whereas before we might have criticized the piece for its avoidance of dramatic contrast and development, these no longer are seen as faults. Or to take a different case, imagine that we watch a film we at first take to be a comedy for children, only to realize later that it is a suspense thriller aimed at an adult audience. We are bound to revise our understanding of the earlier scenes, and of the kinds of skills the writer and director display in them. Depending on the case, we might find the movie either to be disunified or to cleverly create and exploit expectations for the sake of the dramatic impact that goes with defeating them later.

The medium of the piece and what is involved in working with it are also relevant. One does not have to be a violinist to recognize how difficult the concertos of Niccolò Paganini are to play, and appreciation of the

composer and performer presupposes this awareness of the music's virtu-
osic character. If an intricate miniature sculpture that one assumed
was done in diamond turned out to be carved from ice, one would be
inclined to reassess it as presenting the artist with different problems and
as requiring different techniques. Similarly, if a sculpture one took to
be of marble is revealed to be done in white soap, or that one took to be
of mahogany is of dark chocolate, it would need to be reconsidered.

This last example also can be used to show the relevance of the work's
wider social setting. To fully appreciate a woman's bust cast from chocolate or
soap (as in Janine Antoni's *Lick and Lather*), the audience needs to realize that
chocolate is a luscious, sensual food that invites the viewer to imagine licking
and biting the sculpture, and that soap is to be rubbed against the body.
Meanwhile, recognizing that a work is an allegory, critique, commentary, or
satire on actual political events, religious dogma, social movements, or class
manners can be vital to understanding what it is about. Unless one brings to
one's reading a sense of the outrage and scandal with which the patriarchs of
former periods viewed wives' adultery, one could not fully grasp Euripides'
Medea, Sophocles' *Women of Trachis*, Aeschylus' *Agamemnon*, the Arthurian
legends, canto V of Dante's *Inferno*, Nathaniel Hawthorne's *The Scarlet Letter*,
Leo Tolstoy's *Anna Karenina*, or Flaubert's *Madame Bovary*. Picasso's *Guernica* is
yet more powerful when seen as a protest against the bombing of the town by
fascist forces in the Spanish civil war.

Not surprisingly, the social and historical context most likely to be
relevant to the work's identity and content is that of the artworld and the
art tradition of the time in which it is made. Whether a work is original
depends on its relation to other works in the tradition. The same is true of
the influences it displays, of whether it is neglected or changes the course
of art history, of whether it marks a radical departure from the dominant
style or represents its apogee. Édouard Manet's provocative portrayal of a
known prostitute in *Olympia* makes reference to Titian's *Venus of Urbino* and
comments on the whole tradition of painting reclining nudes. Igor Stravinsky's *Pulcinella* borrows musical themes and gestures of the eighteenth-
century Italian Giovanni Pergolesi and makes little sense, either in the
context of Stravinsky's other works or of early twentieth-century music
generally, unless this is taken into account. If we believe a play to have been
written in the nineteenth century, only to learn that it belongs to the
middle of the twentieth, we might cease to be intrigued by its apparently
forward-looking treatment of character and temporal order and, instead,
see it as derivative and conservative, or as self-consciously adopting an
outdated style for the sake of commenting ironically on the earlier period

and its art. We might then be struck by oblique allusions to the plays of Bertolt Brecht that could not have been present in the earlier work. Meanwhile, the style and conventions will be more prominent in the experience, since these were not thoughtlessly adopted as the nearest theatrical idiom to come to hand but, instead, were carefully chosen to the exclusion of more contemporary and accessible approaches.

In this section, I have maintained that the relationship of the artwork to the context of its production plays a role in determining its identity and content. Among the contextual features that are likely to be relevant are the identity and intentions of the artist, the work's genre, style, and media, the artworld tradition that it assumes, draws on, or reacts against, and wider social elements and factors to which it makes reference or some other connection. Further implications of this position – call it *ontological contextualism* – are explored in chapter 4.

3.6   Art for Art's Sake, Again

According to traditional aesthetic theory, we should appreciate and value art *for its own sake*. Contemporary philosophy of art can try to preserve the spirit of this observation, while rejecting implications drawn from it by its rival. In aesthetic attitude theories, appreciating art for its own sake requires that it be approached in a manner that sets aside a concern with where it comes from, or functions it might perform, or anything else that is not perceptually apparent in the item to someone with taste but who is otherwise oblivious to what it is. The view defended above objects: in that case, the *it* in *for its own sake* is not the *artwork* as such. To identify an artwork, and to locate the properties that belong to it as an artwork, it must be seen in relation to those things outside its boundaries that contribute relationally to making it what and how it is. If a play is a seventeenth-century revenge tragedy, to appreciate *that* play for its own sake the audience must see it in terms of the art traditions, conventions, and so on, that make it what it is. And if art of the kind in question usually is functional – for example, having the purpose of glorifying God and communicating religious lore – then that too will have to be acknowledged in coming to a full understanding of the artwork, which is not to say that the appreciator has to endorse or share that religion. To appreciate something for its own sake is to grasp it as the individual it is. Where the object of appreciation is an artwork, it can be taken and understood as the individual it is only if we consider it in relation to the socio-cultural contexts, traditions, and functions that contribute to its identity and content. In an important sense, it is true that art typically is to be appreciated "for its own sake." But the sense in which this is true cannot be fully acknowledged if we adopt the approach sanctioned by aesthetic theories like Stolnitz's, which force us to leave out of consideration factors that make a vital contribution to a piece's identity and content as an artwork.

Applications and Connections — Copies and Misattributions, Viscera and Understanding

In this chapter we have encountered an argument with the form:

> An artwork, X, and some other thing, Y (which might be another artwork or not), are perceptually similar and, as a result, display no aesthetically significant perceptual differences. Nevertheless, X has features relevant to its recognition and appreciation as art that distinguish it from Y. Therefore, some of X's artistically significant features must depend on some of its non-perceptible properties.

This argument has been used to criticize aesthetic theories maintaining that only straightforwardly perceptible aesthetic features are relevant to the identification and comprehension of art. The same argument can be applied to other issues. One is that of forgery.

Suppose a painter copies another's painting so accurately that the two works cannot be perceptually distinguished. A common argument has it that they must therefore have identical aesthetic properties and equal value as artworks. If one is beautiful, so too is the other. But this is not the way they are treated. When one is discovered to be a copy of the other, critics are liable to revise their estimate of it, now finding faults or weaknesses they had not previously acknowledged. This shows that their judgment is clouded by political, moral, and other factors that should have no place in the estimation of art. The argument concludes, the judgment of art should confine itself to aesthetic considerations only, and in this respect the two works are identical.

As Alfred Lessing puts it:

The matter of genuineness versus forgery is but another nonaesthetic standard of judgment. The fact that a work of art is a forgery is an item of information about it on a level with such information as the age of the artist when he created it, the political situation in the time and place of its creation, the price it originally fetched, the kind of materials used in it, the stylistic influences discernible in it, the psychological state of the artist, his purpose in painting it, and so on. All such information belongs to areas of interest peripheral at best to the work of art as aesthetic object, areas such as biography, history of art, sociology, and psychology.

As argued earlier, most of the factors listed by Lessing, rather than being irrelevant to an appreciation of the piece as the artwork it is, are likely to be pertinent to establishing its identity or content. Learning new facts about the work's origin and influences can change how it should be assessed. That it is a copy of an earlier work, or is done in the style of some other artist, is relevant to an evaluation of what its creator has achieved. If we mistake the copy for an original, we place it wrongly within the art tradition and this can lead to the misidentification of its art-relevant features. When our factual error is corrected, it often is appropriate to revise our view of those features. What previously was original, unusual, and provocative, when mistaken for a seventeenth-century Dutch work, now is seen as conservative, derivative, and as affecting an archaic style when known to be a twentieth-century creation. In effect, this work does not belong to the genre it apes. Copies might be regarded as constituting a special genre of their own (one in which faithfulness to an earlier piece, perhaps for the sake of mastering the relevant skills, is a virtue), and genre membership is one among many relational properties that affect a work's content. Instead of exposing the art critics as frauds, Lessing betrays his own failure to realize there is more to an artwork's identity and content than its perceptually accessible aesthetic properties.

Now consider this outwardly similar argument: there have been occasions when works wrongly identified as by males are re-described by art critics and historians after they are discovered to have been done by women. The critics now detect a lack of skill or power, where formerly no "feminine weaknesses" were apparent. But the paintings did not change; they look the same as ever. So the change in opinion reveals a sexist bias against women artists, and the re-evaluation of the works cannot be justified on art-historical grounds.

Even if one agrees with the conclusion in this case, the argument must be inadequate as it stands, because it is has the same form as Lessing's and that was seen not to entail the conclusion he drew. How could the feminist's position be improved? One might argue that skill and power are perceptible aesthetic properties of the ordinary kind, not ones depending on relations to external matters, so that properties of that sort can change only if the work's appearance does. This strategy is unlikely to deal with all the symptoms of artistic inferiority that the critics now claim to detect, however. What is needed, then, is an argument to the conclusion that the artist's gender is not among the external factors that contribute to determining a work's identity or content. But is that a conclusion we wish to argue for? If it is plausible that women might have distinctive interests and experiences apart from men's, with the result that, by depicting scenes with, say, violent, domestic, or sexual themes, they might express thoughts and feelings that would not be present in outwardly similar paintings done from a male perspective, then we should not desire to argue for the conclusion just proposed.

As an example, consider the twentieth-century German painter Paula Modersohn-Becker, who did several self-portraits showing her naked and holding bowls of round fruit (usually oranges or apples) in close proximity to her breasts. The gender of the artist is key in understanding these works. Unlike a male (heterosexual) painter who continues a long tradition in which the female nude is a paradigmatic subject, as a woman painting herself it is inevitable that she separates herself from that tradition and comments on it. Her works make an ironic critique of the longstanding artistic practice of comparing women with fruit. Moreover, as *self-*portraits, they draw attention to the situation then faced by a female avant-garde painter striving to succeed in a world designed by and for male artists.

With this in mind, the feminist should not condemn all gender-based criticisms. She should allow that the artist's gender sometimes affects the work's properties and sometimes does not. This does not prevent her from challenging the sexist critic on a case-by-case basis. If the critic appeals to gender in an inappropriate way, or where it is not relevant, he or she can be criticized for doing so. And where the artist's gender is a relevant consideration, obviously it cannot be assumed always to operate to the detriment of women's art. Where it should be considered, it often draws attention to distinctive ways in which women's art is meaningful and valuable.

Here is another issue that can be raised in response to the debate discussed in this chapter. It might be held that the position maintaining that our understanding and appreciation of art requires knowledge of matters lying beyond the artwork's boundaries is unduly demanding and overly cognitive. It is demanding in the sense that it requires of the audience that they be primed with knowledge of art-historical traditions, of relevant genres, of the society in which the piece is created, of the characteristics of different media, of the artist's other works, and so on.

And it might be thought to be excessively cognitive in that it expects the audience to bring this knowledge actively to bear on their experience of the artwork. In challenging this view, someone might suggest that the basic and most genuine response to art is visceral, unmediated by thought. Everything necessary for the fullest response is made available through direct contact with the work.

This challenge should be rejected, though. If the response appropriate to art were visceral and thoughtless, birds and other animals with senses similar to ours would be as well qualified to appreciate art as we are, but they are not. Moreover, even aesthetic theorists regard aesthetic experience as cognitively founded, insofar as it requires the conscious adoption of an appropriate mental attitude. Others, with Kant as a leading example, think the aesthetic response involves a playful interaction between the imagination and understanding.

The appropriate experience of art is not a passive registering but a thought-filled interaction, then. There is a difference, however, between thinking about something and reflecting self-consciously on one's thinking as one does it. The appreciation of art need not involve the latter. Usually, it is not accompanied by an internal commentary in which one describes to oneself what one is thinking and why. Similarly, the acquisition of knowledge need not always involve deliberate focus or study. We learn constantly through experience and exposure, without always noting that we are doing so. Most residents learn to find their way around their neighborhood without consulting a map. And once knowledge is acquired, it can often be applied unconsciously, as when one drives a car without concentrating on doing so. With some kinds of practical knowledge or know-how, people cannot always articulate the knowledge that is apparent in skills they perform. As a consequence, they often grasp more than they realize and are frequently unaware of how much that understanding informs their actions and judgments. The knowledge the spectator brings to her appreciation of art might be learned from a book, but more likely it develops through exposure to art by a kind of osmosis, and she applies that knowledge without having to think about what she is doing. As is common elsewhere, the appreciation of art is likely to be partial at first, but it can be developed subsequently by a kind of bootstrapping, without resort to the formal study of theory or history. The experience of art is cognitive and infused with knowledge, then, but the appreciator's focus is on the artwork, not on her thinking about it. Her knowledge facilitates her direct experience of the artwork without getting in the way of that experience.

If the appreciation of art is not purely visceral and thoughtless, what does this imply about popular culture? As already noted in chapter 1, commentators sometimes conclude that the products of popular culture could not be art because they call for a primitive, gut response, not the cognitive one previously described. The popular music of the day – rock or jazz, say – is a typical target. Such music is said to affect the body directly through its volume or beat, stirring animal passions that are not mediated by cognition. The style of the argument is usually negative and conservative. It concludes that popular music is deeply inferior to art music. Occasionally, though, popular music is defended on the grounds that the very features disqualifying it from the status of art allow it to achieve a more direct and significant connection with its audience than art music does.

This last argument should be regarded with skepticism. Rock music, to take that example, could be employed as a mind-numbing drug, but the same is no less true of classical music, and in neither case would this use be the most common or appropriate. Rock music has many different genres, is no less subject to styles and conventions than any other kind, and is riddled with intertextual references, influences, parodies, repudiations, and quotations. If the older generation does not "get it," that is not because their hearing is defective or because their guts cannot resonate with the bass but because they lack the experience and understanding needed to know what they should be getting. They are liable to hear only the most basic of common features and not be able to detect subtle departures from the norm. In the same way, the novice to classical music will not be able to make the discriminations that would allow her to judge Mozart's music to be better than that of his less talented contemporary at the Viennese court, Antonio Salieri. Rock music, like any other kind, must be followed with understanding if it is to be appreciated.

The claim is not that all kinds of music are equally good when judged by the same set of standards. Some music is designed to reward concentrated listening and repeated hearings. It can be deeply moving and uplifting. Other music is intended to be immediately accessible, undemanding, and entertaining. It can become charged with powerful associations – for instance, because it played constantly during the summer spent at the beach when one was 13 – but does not set out to confront or refine the ingrained listening habits of its target audience. Nevertheless, I suspect that when it comes to the better examples within all kinds of music, none is simple or mechanical, though considerable skill might go into making a piece appear inevitable and artless. The same goes for story-telling, drawing, dancing, acting, and the like. If it were really as easy to write a successful hit song, potboiler novel, TV soap, or musical, as is sometimes dismissively claimed by cultural elitists, there would be many more millionaires than there are!

It could be that rock usually calls for a degree of unselfconscious cognitive engagement to be appreciated, much as Beethoven's symphonies do, and yet remain the case that the rock song is a craftwork with the utilitarian function of being entertaining while the Beethoven symphony is an artwork that is to be appreciated for its own sake. Or alternatively, art might come in many species with a variety of functions, so both the rock song and Beethoven's symphony might qualify as art of different kinds. So, the observations made above do not settle the debate between those who think only high Western art qualifies as such and those who regard art as universal, ubiquitous, and often humble. But they do reject one reason sometimes offered for thinking that both could not be art; namely, that one kind requires a cognitively informed response where the other never does.

Questions

3.1   The American artist J. S. G. Boggs has a distinctive artform. His hand-drawn works look just like US currency notes. He always presents these as artworks, not as money, but sometimes trades them in return for things he acquires. Meanwhile, some of Billy Apple's canvasses take the form of giant receipts or invoices for their own sale. Are there aspects of these works that aesthetic theories like Stolnitz's cannot explain?

3.2   In terms of what categories (scientific, mythological, cultural, historical) should nature be viewed in order to appreciate it aesthetically *as nature*?

3.3   You examine what at first you believe to be an enlarged photographic print. You learn that, in fact, it is a handmade painting. Would you then expect to experience a change in any of its artistically significant attributes?

3.4   Imagine eight, identical-looking, seemingly abstract paintings that feature red and yellow swirls. One was carefully crafted by the artist to be as it is. In painting the second, the artist followed the instructions of a computer program that randomly specified what shapes and colors should be used on each part of the canvas. The third was painted by a chimpanzee. The fourth was the accidental byproduct of the work of a fifteenth-century portrait painter who used the small canvas as his color palette. The fifth is intended as a send-up of the work of a famous abstract painter. The sixth was done by a very young child, who says it represents people and animals. The seventh was the consequence of an explosion in a paint factory. The eighth is offered as a realistic depiction of a plate of cooked eggs and tomatoes that have been mixed together. Are they all artworks? Do they all have the same aesthetic properties and merit? Do they all have the same artistic properties?

3.5   Is the artist's age ever relevant to the proper appreciation of her work? In reflecting on this question, consider the following cases. Suppose that you encounter a piece you had not previously seen but by an artist whose work you know fairly well. From its style and content, you initially assume it is a youthful work. As it happens, the piece is from the artist's old age. Or suppose you view a self-portrait depicting a young woman and assume it shows the artist as she was when it was painted, only to learn that she did it in old age.

3.6   The artist Glenn Brown duplicates Old Masters. He does not copy them exactly. Indeed, some of his repaintings of Rembrandt's portraits of Saskia, his wife — such as *Dark Star* and *Death Disco* — give her an unearthly, ghoulish quality not present in the originals. Do Brown's works differ from forgeries only by being less exact than forgeries usually are? Do Brown's works differ in their artistic features and character from the works of the Old Masters that were their models?

3.7   The seventeenth-century Italian painter Artemesia Gentileschi painted very strong, heroic female figures, sometimes doing violence to men. Do facts about her biography — that she was a woman painting at a time when there were very few women painting, and that she was raped at an early age — change the way we should think about and see these pictures?

3.8   Some instrumental symphonies by the Russian composer Dmitri Shostakovich are thought to be based on unvoiced ideas critical of the tyranny of Stalin's political regime, under which Shostakovich lived. His works were often criticized and, like others, he faced censorship and the threat of imprisonment or worse. Olivier Messiaen, a French composer, wrote his *Quartet for the End of Time* during the Second World War when interned in a Nazi prison camp. The music is sad and solemn, but no words are sung and no descriptive text accompanies the music. Is the political situation at the time a work is created ever relevant to its appreciation as art? If so, when and how?

Readings

The nature of aesthetic properties is famously discussed by Frank Sibley in "Aesthetic Concepts," *Philosophical Review* 68 (1959), 421–50, and in "Aesthetic and Non-Aesthetic," *Philosophical Review* 74 (1965), 135–59, and also by Monroe C. Beardsley in "What Is an Aesthetic Quality?," *Theoria* 39 (1973), 50–70. *The Nature of Aesthetic Qualities* (Lund, Sweden: Lund University Press, 1988), by Göran Hermerén, provides an overview, and a useful collection is *Aesthetic Quality and Aesthetic Experience*, edited by M. Mitias (Amsterdam: Rodopi, 1988). Modifications in the notion of the aesthetic that address the criticisms of traditional theories mentioned in this chapter are provided by: Alan H. Goldman, "Aesthetic Qualities and Aesthetic Value," *Journal of Philosophy* 87 (1990), 23–37; Gary Iseminger, *The Aesthetic Function of Art* (Ithaca: Cornell University Press, 2004); and, less sympathetically, by Noël Carroll, "Aesthetic Experience Regained," *BJA* 42 (2002), 145–68.

The aesthetic theories of the early twentieth century mentioned in the text are Edward Bullough's " 'Psychical Distance' as a Factor in Art and an Aesthetic Principle," *British Journal of Psychology* 5 (1912), 87–118, and Jerome Stolnitz's *Aesthetics and the Philosophy of Art Criticism* (Boston: Houghton Mifflin, 1960), an extract from which is printed with the title "The Aesthetic Attitude," in *Introductory Readings in Aesthetics*, edited by J. Hospers (New York: The Free Press, 1969), 17–27. Other aestheticians of the period with similar views include David Prall, Curt J. Ducasse, and DeWitt Parker. Aesthetic attitude theory is combined with aesthetic formalism by the art critic Clive Bell, in *Art*, first published 1914 (3rd edn., Oxford: Oxford University Press, 1987).

Challenges to aesthetic attitude theories include George Dickie's "The Myth of the Aesthetic Attitude," *American Philosophical Quarterly* 1 (1964), 56–65; Marshall Cohen's "Aesthetic Essence," in *Philosophy in America*, edited by M. Black (London: George Allen & Unwin, 1965), 115–33; and Noël Carroll's "Art and Interaction," *JAAC* 45 (1986), 57–68, and "Beauty and the Genealogy of Art Theory," *Philosophical Forum* 22 (1991), 307–34. Arguments for the relevance of the work's art-historical context and genre are famously presented by Arthur C. Danto in "The Artworld," *Journal of Philosophy* 61 (1964), 571–84, "Artworks and Real Things," *Theoria* 39 (1973), 1–17, and *The Transfiguration of the Commonplace* (Cambridge, MA: Harvard University Press, 1981); and also by Kendall L. Walton in "Categories of Art," *Philosophical Review* 79 (1970), 334–67.

A useful collection on forgery is *The Forger's Art*, edited by D. Dutton (Berkeley: University of California Press, 1983). Among others, it includes Alfred Lessing's "What Is Wrong with a Forgery?," which first appeared in *JAAC* 23 (1965), 461–71. Another chapter in Dutton's collection is Mark Sagoff's "The Aesthetic Status of Forgeries," which first appeared in *JAAC* 35 (1976), 169–80. Sagoff argues that forgeries comprise a special genre of their own. Crispin Sartwell emphasizes the continuity between copying and creating in "Aesthetics of the Spurious," *BJA* 28 (1988), 360–7.

For debate about the experience appropriate to the appreciation of rock music, see: Bruce Baugh's "Prolegomena To Any Aesthetics of Rock Music," *JAAC* 51 (1993), 23–9, and "Music for the Young at Heart," *JAAC* 53 (1995), 81–3; James O. Young's "Between Rock and a Harp Place," *JAAC* 53 (1995), 78–81; and Stephen Davies's "Rock versus Classical Music," *JAAC* 57 (1999), 193–204. Theodore Gracyk's *Rhythm and Noise: An Aesthetics of Rock Music* (Durham: Duke University Press, 1996) and *I Wanna Be Me: Rock Music and the Politics of Identity* (Philadelphia: Temple University Press, 2001) cover many philosophical issues raised by the nature of rock and its reception.

Chapter Four

Varieties of Art

Ontology is concerned with the matter, mode, or manner in which things exist. If you ask, *Is it animal, vegetable, or mineral?* when trying to guess what item another person has in mind, your question is about the ontological character of that item.

This chapter is about the ontology of art. It considers the variety of forms in which art exists. Some artforms aim at spontaneous improvisation rather than the creation of works that persist and can be experienced on different occasions. Much jazz is of this kind. Nevertheless, the focus in this chapter will fall on the ontologies of *works* of art, since the vast majority of the arts package their output in works.

On its face, ontology is a dry and theoretical topic. The importance of ontological questions becomes apparent, however, when we rightly appreciate that they are crucial to locating and characterizing works of art. We have to be able successfully to pick out particular artworks and their contents before we can go on to analyze, describe, perform, appreciate, or evaluate them. These initial identifications inevitably involve assumptions about the manner in which the works in question exist and are constituted. Therefore, what we do and say about art presupposes ontological theories and commitments, whether we are aware of them or not. The explicit consideration of ontological issues draws these decisive assumptions to the surface where they can be scrutinized and analyzed. A deeper understanding of art's nature is not the only outcome. In the process we are faced by intriguing questions, such as *Do artworks exist eternally or are they created and, sometimes, destroyed? Does the identity of an artwork alter in response to its ongoing interpretation and reception?*

The position defended in this chapter builds on a key idea presented in chapter 3, namely that an artwork's identity and contents are generated in part by relations it holds to aspects of the socio-historical setting in which it was created. I call this view *ontological contextualism*.

4.1   Artworks as Public Items

Many people would hold that artworks must be, or be present in, public objects or events, with the result that they can be experienced directly via the senses and can be the topics of interpersonally objective judgments. We must be able to point to artworks, thereby identifying them and at least some of their properties in a public fashion. Indeed, it is widely maintained that first-hand perceptual acquaintance with artworks is essential for their fullest appreciation. A person who experiences a work only indirectly – for example, who knows a painting only through others' descriptions or through photographic reproductions – is not well situated to grasp all that is important about it as the artwork it is.

Despite these widely held intuitions, some philosophers – one example being R. G. Collingwood, an English philosopher who wrote in the 1930s – have maintained that artworks exist only in the private realm of the artist's mind. What the artist publicly produces is not the artwork but a prop or trace that assists members of the audience to duplicate the work in their own minds. This form of *ontological idealism* seems apt for the case in which a poet composes a poem in his head and never writes it down. Nevertheless, the position faces major difficulties and should be rejected. Like all forms of ontological idealism, this view cannot easily explain how we successfully make interpersonal references to artworks and identifications of their contents, and it runs counter to the conviction that we can have direct perceptual access to the artist's work.

Similar difficulties accompany an alternative theory according to which the artwork is to be identified with the artist's actions, not with the product that results from these. (Versions of this position have been developed by the contemporary philosophers Gregory Currie and David Davies.) Though actions differ in principle from mental experiences by being directly observable by third parties, in practice this theory makes the work nearly as inaccessible as the previous one does. The artist's actions are very rarely observed by his audience. And while it is true that we appreciate what the artist has done and achieved, we also value the product that is made and the qualities it displays.

Rather than debating these views, I will assume that artworks are public objects (such as oil paintings) or are instanced in public objects or events (such as cast sculptures or musical performances), or are specified via public instructions or encodings (such as playscripts or digital files of art-photographs) from which presentations of the work can be generated. The work does not exist until an appropriate public object or event has been suitably authorized: the novel is written down, the score is notated, or the dance is presented as an exemplar or model. The work need not be offered to an audience – a finished painting would be an artwork even if it were destroyed by fire before anyone other than the artist viewed it, and many a symphony has remained unperformed – but it must be incarnated in a manner that is potentially perceptible. To return to the earlier example of the poet, his work is not given its definitive form until it is publicly recorded or spoken and signed off. While it remains in his head, he can always change it. (Even if he told himself it was finished, he could always revoke this decision at a later time.) In presenting the work publicly, he might simply "copy" what is already in his head, but equally, he might decide to modify that earlier inspiration. In any event, the completion of the work involves some act of potentially public authorization.

As was hinted above, the manner in which a work is to be publicly presented or specified depends on what kind it is. Works for performance are usually indicated via sets of work-determinative instructions issued to the work's potential performers. The symphony is finished when its score is. Usually, works for performance can be performed many times, so long as the appropriate directives are followed. Other works can be specified in an encoded form. The silkscreen used for printing, the negative of a photograph, or the electronic pattern on a CD are examples of encodings. Computer files, stored as machine code, can encode artwork photographs or novels, for example. I would also regard the print of a movie as an encoding. While the frames look like (small, frozen) bits of the movie, many of the movie's crucial properties, such as seemingly continuous movement, are not revealed by viewing the reel of film. The reel needs to be screened before the work is presented.

When an encoding is decoded by an appropriate process – the inked or painted silkscreen is applied to paper in the required fashion – or by a device meeting the relevant conditions for accuracy and transmission – an industry-standard photo developer, CD player, computer CPU and screen, or movie projector – the work is presented. And if that process is repeatable, the work in question can have many instances.

Some other kinds of works are first delivered via exemplars, copies or clones of which instance the same work. Indeed, this can be common for works for performance – dances, songs – created in oral traditions. Yet other works, such as handmade paintings and carvings, are created through direct manipulation of the forms and features of physical objects. These artworks are singular.

Two ideas implicit in what I have just written are debated within the philosophy of art. I have assumed that the dependence of artworks on physical objects or events shows that they are created when the appropriate objects are made or events take place. Yet some philosophers maintain that artworks are eternal abstract patterns that are discovered (but not created) by artists. On this view, the physical objects or events artists create affect our access to the artwork, not its existence. The second assumption I have made is that some artworks are singular while others, at least potentially, can have many incarnations. Some philosophers would maintain, by contrast, that all artworks are potentially multiple. In the following two sections I defend both assumptions against those who would question them.

4.2   Are Artworks Created or Discovered?

It is plausible to conceive of works with multiple instances in terms of what their instances have in common, which can be regarded as a formal pattern. We might think of musical works as ordered combinations and sequences of notes. (Or, if the work does not always specify individual notes, for instance because it leaves it to the performer to vary or decorate the melody, we can consider it to be an ordered sequence of musical elements, including trills and stylistically appropriate flourishes.) And we might think of a novel as an ordered word-sequence in a particular language. (Or, if the story is not so specific as this, for instance because it survives translation into another language, we can view it as a structured sequence of narrative elements.) Again, for handmade, singular artworks, such as Michelangelo's *David* or Leonardo's *Mona Lisa*, the pattern or form of the matter that constitutes the work is crucial to its identity. *David* would be lost if the statue were reduced to shapeless rubble, though none of its constituent matter would have been destroyed. Not surprisingly then, artworks have sometimes been regarded as purely formal patterns, that are distinct from the physical items or events in which they are embodied or exemplified.

Formal patterns are abstract objects. Following the ancient Greek philosopher Plato, they are generally regarded as eternal and indestructible. The formal pattern that we call a square did not suddenly come into existence at some datable moment and cannot be sent out of existence, though particular, actual items exhibiting this form may be made at a given moment and destroyed at a later one. Formal patterns are not created by humans, but they can be discovered by them. That the DNA molecule inevitably takes the form of a double helix was a scientific discovery of the 1950s.

Now, if artworks are formal patterns, as was just suggested, they too are eternal and indestructible. Such a view — I call it *ontological Platonism* — is defended by the American philosopher Peter Kivy in discussing musical works. Beethoven drew attention to a certain note-sequence when he composed his Fifth Symphony, but the pattern pre-existed his efforts and, since the artwork is the pattern, so did it. Beethoven discovered the artwork, he did not create it. And if all copies of his score were destroyed, along with everything else from which we could derive an accurate copy of the score, what is lost is our access to the work, though the existence of the work remains unaffected. Extending this view, it could be suggested that Michelangelo's chiseling exposed the artwork that is the form exemplified in his statue of David, thereby making that pre-existing work available to the rest of us, and also that, if the statue is destroyed, what is lost is our contact with the work, though the pattern that is the work remains untouched.

A defender of this view might continue: discovery can be no less context-dependent than creation. Perhaps only a particular person, acting under particular influences at a particular time, could make the discovery in question. It took the invention of the camera, of light-sensitive papers, and the rest, before anyone was in a position to discover photographic artworks. And it took someone with John Donne's sexual psychology, interest in the science of his period, and religious commitments to write the sonnets he discovered at the beginning of the seventeenth century.

Plainly, this theory runs against the widely held intuitions that artists are creators and that artworks can be destroyed. We think of artists as creative, as free in their choices, and as makers, all in ways that discoverers are not. And if someone smashes the original molds and all the bronze statues cast from them, we would judge her for having annihilated the work, not for hiding it from us. What she does seems very different from the private collector who denies everyone access to an artwork by keeping it always locked in a vault.

Apart from relying on the strength of these intuitions, how can this theory about the ontology of artworks be challenged? Here is a first argument. The theory attempts to explain our alarm at the destruction of the statue or painting on which the artist worked by suggesting that we react not because the pattern that is the work is damaged but, instead, because we lose access to it. This argument fails, however, because it is not true that, when an oil painting such as Leonardo's *Mona Lisa* is destroyed, contact with the formal pattern it exemplifies is lost. Countless copies, drawings, and photographs of the original preserve the pattern of its form. Access to the formal pattern, which this theory equates with the work, is not inhibited by the painting's obliteration, so there should be no cause for alarm should this occur.

4.3 Are all Artworks Potentially Multiple?

At this point, a defender of the theory might question the second of the assumptions listed above. She might accept that nothing is lost in this case, but go on to argue that this is because *no* artwork is singular, since formal patterns always can be multiply instantiated. We are wrong to be alarmed at the destruction of Leonardo's painting because the work he discovered has numerous other embodiments. Many duplicates are faulty or inaccurate, but copies that cannot be perceptually distinguished from the original are equally legitimate as instances of the artwork. And if these survive the destruction of the particular painting on which he labored, the artwork is not lost after all.

One response to this new proposal might complain that it is no less contrary to our intuitions than was the theory's initial version. We do accord a special status to the oil paintings and carved sculptures that come from the artist's hand, and this is not merely because accurate duplicates are hard to make or because we attach a purely historical significance to the first of the items issuing from a production line. Imagine that science comes up with a matter replicator. It copies any material object down to the atomic level. If a stone is placed in one of its boxes and the switch is flipped, a duplicate appears in the other (and the original stone is otherwise unaffected). Now suppose the replicator is used to clone persons. It is doubtful that this would lead us to decide that persons are multiple after all. We are concerned with how they came to be and their histories, both up to the time when the cloning occurs and subsequently. We would regard the creation and history of the original person as distinguishing them from all the clones. Moreover, each clone would go on to have a distinctive history following the cloning process, and we are likely to be as interested in those differences as in the similarity that holds at the moment of cloning. The same is probably true for art, I suggest. If we could duplicate *Mona Lisa*, we are likely to be concerned to track the original and keep it separate from its clones, even if we judge that a clone is not inferior to the original when the goal is art appreciation. Though we accept the clones as substituting for the original, this does not mean that we also agree that the identity of the artwork must have been transmitted to the clones. (If your child was duplicated in the replicator, would you be indifferent about which one you took home afterwards?) Our conceiving of such works as singular stems partly from a commitment to the idea that the history of production contributes to the identity of the item that is manufactured.

In any case, suppose we *do* feel a need to revise our concepts when faced with duplicates and doppelgangers. What then takes place is a *change* in the concept, not a discovery that somehow the concept was that of a multiple work all along. In the absence of this technology, there is no reason to abandon our present ontological commitment to the singularity of hand-crafted paintings and hewn statues.

One aspect of this concern with the process of creation focuses on the medium used and the possibilities and challenges this presents to the maker, given the means of production. The idea that artworks are abstract patterns seems largely indifferent to the medium involved. The same formal pattern might be equally realizable in sponge cake, molten lava, and dead animals. Even if the abstract pattern displays features restricting the media that would realize it — for instance, it has notes with trumpet-like qualities, or has the appearance of marble-like stuff — there is a world of difference between achieving this by dealing directly with the medium and by synthesizing something that presents only the outward appearance of the medium. It matters that the result is achieved by playing the trumpet or chipping away at marble, as against pushing a button on a pre-programmed sound synthesizer or matter replicator, even if the outcomes are sensorily equivalent. Moreover, qualities of the medium are likely to become part of the artwork's content and message. A striking illustration is provided by works that self-destruct because of the nature of the media that constitute them, thereby making their ephemerality part of their point. Gustav Metzger, a German artist, produced self-destructive art in the 1960s, including plastic screens splashed with acid. He thought it was the artform most suited to the industrial age. More recently an English artist, Damien Hirst, has created works that contain dying butterflies and rotting meat. Sandy Skoglund, an American, has used 80 pounds of raw hamburger meat as the medium for *Spirituality in the Flesh*, a portrait of a seated woman. Her installation was made and photographed in one day and destroyed by her the next. It is surely wrong to regard the artwork in these cases as an abstract pattern that presents merely the *look* of corroded plastic, flapping butterflies, or uncooked meat. Hirst's work must be understood as including still-living insects, not disembodied appearances, while Skoglund goes to considerable lengths to disguise the meaty substrate of the portrait she creates.

Arguments of the sort that have just been offered should remind the reader of views developed in chapter 3, where it was argued that an artwork's identifying properties and its content typically depend on relations tying it to aspects of the context in which it originated, including its title, genre, medium, and the like. That more general argument, which applies both to works that can have multiple instances (such as novels, symphonies, cast statues, and prints) and to singular pieces (such as oil paintings and carved statues), is directly relevant to the debate in hand. It suggests that two items that are perceptually indistinguishable to a person who is unaware of their causal provenance can differ in their identity and content. One might be an artwork, the other not. Or both might be artworks, but where one is a humorous, postmodern pastiche, the other is not. To recall an earlier example, despite sharing the same text, Cervantes' and Menard's *Quixotes* display quite different artistic properties and meanings. The former is unselfconscious in its use of the contemporary idiom where the latter is a studied attempt at a historically dated style, and the latter contains allusions to nineteenth-century ideas that are absent from the former.

If these earlier arguments are convincing, they prove fatal to the theory that artworks are abstract patterns. Cervantes' and Menard's *Quixotes* share the same linguistic *pattern* and, on this view, should both be instances of the same single work. But this cannot be right, since they possess contrasting, context-dependent properties crucial to their art-relevant identity and content. If ontological contextualism succeeds, ontological Platonism can be rejected.

When we accept that artworks depend for their identity and content on relations enmeshing them within the art-historical and wider context in which they are produced, they can no longer be viewed merely as abstract, formal patterns existing in a pure realm of atemporal relations. By virtue of the contextual ties that contribute to their identity, artworks are embedded in the concrete reality of the space-time world of objects and events. As such, they can be created and destroyed. This is not to deny that the formal patterns they present contribute significantly to their identity and content. But it is to insist that factors in addition to their abstract, formal ones are no less necessary to their being the artworks they are. Artworks are perhaps better thought of as *designs* than patterns. Designs are the products of intentional activity and decision.

How are designs, as opposed to mere patterns, subject to creation and potential destruction? Some philosophers have argued that a design is created along with its first instance, without pre-existing eternally, because it is shaped by human decisions. This seems plausible when we consider human artifacts, such as the half-hour situation comedy TV show, the board game Checkers, or the 1972 Chevrolet Corvette Stingray. Others maintain that, as well as making decisions regarding the design of their works, the process by which artists create works includes indicating, projecting, or making normative what they do. In other words, the artist decides not only to select and draw attention to a design, but gives it a special salience and status by saying, in effect, *This, and this alone, is a well-formed instance of my artwork!* or *Perform or copy this, if you wish to make a well-formed instance of my artwork!* In creating the work, the artist makes it the case that the appropriate design is deliberately selected and presented as her work.

The media and modes of its practical realization, not solely its design, are factors relevant to an artwork's identity. A late nineteenth-century violin sonata, for example, is not solely a selected and shaped pattern of notes, because the means of sounding them (the violin), the genre (sonata), and the musico-historical setting (late nineteenth century) also contribute to its having properties relevant to its identity as the work it is. In fact, all the factors mentioned in chapter 3 as pertinent to a work's identity and content should be factored in. (These included the work's genre, style, and medium, its creator's intentions, and the work's relation to the artist's body of works, to other works to which it refers or by which it is influenced, to the art-historical setting in which it originated, and to the wider social and political environment.) The creation or destruction of an artwork depends on the treatment of its identifying elements, and these are as likely to include properties that depend on relations connecting the piece to the context of its production as to include its pattern or form.

4.4   Multiply Instanced Artworks

I have suggested that some artworks, such as handmade paintings or sculptures, are singular. They are particulars. However much two oil paintings resemble each other, they must be different in their identities (though they might be related as members of a set, or in other ways). Other artworks are multiple in their occurrence or presentation. Each of us might possess our own copy of Samuel Taylor Coleridge's poem *Kubla Khan*. Two paperbacks, movie screenings, cast statues, or performances might be similar precisely because they are instances or presentations of a single artwork.

How is the relation between a multiple work and its occurrences or presentations to be characterized? Some philosophers, Richard Wollheim being an example, describe the relation as that between a *type* and its *tokens*. (If you answer *Six* to the question *How many letters are there in the word "poorer"?* you are counting letter tokens. If you answer *Four*, you are counting letter types.) Other philosophers use different terminologies, writing of *kinds* and their *instances* or *classes* and their *members*. I will not debate the differences between these various approaches. In what follows, I refer to *works* and their *instances*, but that usage is intended to leave open the question of whether multiple works are types, kinds, or classes, and of what might hang on these distinctions. In terms of the earlier discussion, works are humanly created types, kinds, or classes of tradition-specific, media-specific, and genre-specific designs.

For some works with potentially many instances, the instances have to be very similar to each other if they are to qualify as faithful or undamaged. It is likely to be crucial to the accuracy of copies of a modern novel that they share the same word order, since the identity of this kind of work usually depends on the narrative it contains and the narrative, in turn, usually is specified at the level of a particular sequence of words or sentences. Similarly, two accurate copies of a movie should be (nearly) visually and aurally identical when screened under equivalent conditions.

In other cases, though, fully faithful instances of a work can differ markedly in their content or qualities. With works for performance, such disparities are often attributable to differences in *interpretation*. Two performances of Shakespeare's *King Lear* or of Beethoven's Fifth Symphony might offer contrasting interpretations. But divergence between accurate instances can be found also in some arts that do not involve performance. Two prints might come from the same woodblock or lithograph and yet be in different colors.

Where fully faithful instances of a work can vary markedly in their content or qualities, this is because the work underdetermines aspects or details displayed in its instances. This is not to say that such works are incomplete. (The classical Viennese composer Franz Schubert's "Unfinished" Symphony is incomplete because he stopped before all the movements were written, but his "Great" C major symphony was finished, even if it is designed to allow for differing interpretations.) Rather, we should say that the identities of such works encompass certain parameters of indefiniteness. It is their nature to be vague in parts. Because their concrete realizations cannot be vague in the relevant respects – even if the authorized prints from a woodblock might be in any color, each print of it must be in some particular color or colors – the person who produces an instance of the work has the job of resolving its indefiniteness. Since there is more than one way of doing this legitimately, equally and ideally faithful instances of the work need not display all the same features or properties.

A further distinction in the ways multiple works of art exist should be noted. Some multiply instanced artworks, such as novels and poems, must have *at least one* instance. For these, the first instance serves as a template or exemplar the copying of which results in further instances. Other multiple artworks can exist with *no* instances. This is the case with an uncast bronze, an unprinted silkscreen, an unscreened movie, or an unperformed symphony or play. For some of these, the work is finalized when the mechanism for creating it – the mold, movie print, or silkscreen – is made. And for others that are for performance, the work comes into existence when an appropriate set of instructions addressed to performers – an authorized score or script – is produced.

It was just implied that modern movies are not works for performance. That might seem strange, given that movie actors do more or less the same kinds of things that stage performers do in live theater. Here is the explanation: movies are for screening, not performance. The movie is completed when the masterprint is finalized. That print and its subsequent clones encode the work. The work is presented when the celluloid print or digitized disk is screened in the usual fashion and in a theater of the appropriate kind. The movie's delivery is via a mechanical process, and the person who activates this process, the projectionist, is not normally regarded as performing or interpreting the movie. (By contrast, silent movies that were to be given a live musical accompaniment should be regarded as multi-media works that are for performance in part.) Purely electronic musical compositions that are issued on disk are like modern movies. The disk contains an encoding of the work. The work is played when the disk is decoded on an industry-standard CD player and amplifier-speaker system. Such a work is for playback. The person who sets the machine going by pushing the *play* button is not a performer or interpreter of the work that is sounded.

Movies and electronic musical works might be made without the assistance of actors or musicians. The cartoonist who draws and animates the movie, or the composer who works directly on her computer to generate the sound files that make up her work, are creators, not performers, of the works they produce. In other cases, though, actors or musicians are involved. Their contributions, which are filmed or taped, add to the process in which the work is created. Before the work is completed, those films and tapes are edited, intercut, mixed, and so on. The movie star might be no less an actor than the thespian who plays Hamlet in the theater, and the two might prepare and present their roles in ways that are similar, but their contributions to the outcomes differ. Unlike the theater actor, the movie actor provides material from which the work is made. He does not interpret a work that is already finished. The same comparison holds between the musician who performs Beethoven's "Moonlight" sonata live and her counterpart in the studio who plays material under the composer's direction that is taped for inclusion in the composer's purely electronic composition. The former performs a finished work, while the latter contributes to a piece that, when completed, will be for playback, not performance.

4.5   New Works Based on Old Ones

These examples remind us that the material from which artworks can be made includes, as well as pigment, stone, notes, gestures, words, and the like, human artifacts with their own identities. For example, in 1912 Picasso and Georges Braque began experimenting with collage – that is, they took parts of newspapers and other items and stuck them to the surfaces of their paintings, incorporating them into the works' overall content and design.

On some occasions, the artifacts appropriated or used by the artist are already works of art in their own right. For example, a movie can be based on a novel. Even if the movie faithfully follows all the dialog in the novel and remains true to all that it describes, what results is not another instance of the novel but a new work. Because of the intimacy of their relation, this new work reflects on its source, and can be called an adaptation of it.

I would characterize movie remakes as similar. The movie *The 39 Steps* (based on a novel by John Buchan), was first directed by Alfred Hitchcock in 1935 and subsequently redone by Ralph Thomas in 1959 and by Don Sharp in 1978. *The Ladykillers*, directed by Ethan and Joel Coen and released in 2004, is based on a comedy made by Ealing Studios in 1955. The remakes share the originals' stories and much else besides. Moreover, this is no accident, since the one movie is based on the other. Yet we are inclined to view the remakes as separate, though related, works, because they involve distinct groups of creators and production processes. The original and remake, both based on the same story, can be compared to the case in which two artists paint the same model in more or less the same fashion. The two works will be intimately related, given their common source and creative circumstances, but they have distinct identities. (By contrast, when a movie is re-edited, as when the "director's cut" is released, or where the DVD includes deleted scenes and an alternative ending, we might prefer to talk of different *versions* of a *single* work.)

These are examples of a general practice: that of generating a new work from another by subjecting it to a change of medium. In the case of music, the result is called a *transcription* or *arrangement*. When J. S. Bach's music is electronically synthesized, a new but derivative work results. And if its instrumentation is essential to a symphony's identity, as was true by the mid-nineteenth century, an arrangement of the piece for piano produces a new but similar piece. Again, what is important is the change of medium, from an ensemble of different instruments played by a large number of performers to a piano played by one person.

Of course, piano transcriptions of this kind were common in earlier times as a way of disseminating music to those who could not afford to attend concert halls and opera houses. Accordingly, the transcriber usually aimed to preserve the nature of the source work as accurately as the new medium permitted. But the approach of those who derive new artworks from older ones can be much freer than this, as when the goal is to create an entirely original piece. Hiphop artists provide an interesting example. Earlier I observed that the person who operates her CD player is not a performer in her own right, but that is not also true of the hiphop DJ who scratches and samples others' recordings in producing his own songs. He is a performer–composer who appropriates the works of others in making his own. In doing so, he also transforms what in other contexts is merely a mechanical decoding device – namely, the record player – into a musical instrument that is performed on. This is not unlike the case of Duchamp's *L.H.O.O.Q.*, mentioned earlier. Duchamp creates one work by appropriating the image of another and in the process transforms the postcard into an artistic medium where previously it was merely a way of recording or representing an artistic medium, that of oil painting. Works of these kinds, because of their self-conscious intertextuality – that is, their deliberate reference to the source work via allusion, pastiche, quotation, caricature, homage, or whatever – potentially possess a rich and complex artistic significance.

4.6   The Ontological Variety of Works of Art

Another point to have emerged from the earlier discussion deserves to be highlighted. Works within a single artistic type can display considerable variety in their ontologies. Take music again. There can be improvised musical performance that is not the performance of any work, as is the case with much jazz. There can be oral traditions in which works are conveyed by an exemplar that subsequently is copied. Folk music traditions are often like this, as is much rock. There are works for performance that are specified not by a model instance that serves as a paradigm but by a notated score that has the function of prescribing to potential performers what they must do and achieve in order to instance the work. Classical works of Western music are notated and taught via notations. Meanwhile, in some traditions of liturgical chant which call for strict adherence to the model and reject ideas of interpretative freedom, faithful instances of the work resemble each other nearly as closely as copies of novels do. In other cases, a great deal of freedom for interpretation is allowed to the work's performer, and faithful performances can vary widely. (Those who re-record rock songs can adopt this free approach, as was apparent when Jimi Hendrix "covered" Bob Dylan's music. Nevertheless, many cover bands attempt to ape their models, eschewing originality for emulation.) In addition, there are computer-generated, electronic musical works that are for playback, not performance.

As well, there is a useful distinction to be drawn between works intended for *live* performance and ones for *studio* performance. These latter, which include most popular music, call for performances involving the kinds of electronic interventions, effects, and editing that depend on the electronic resources of the studio or recording suite, and the perform-ance is issued on disk. Subsequent recordings of the same rock song result in disks that encode new performances of the same work. The differences in what is normative in works for live and studio performances explains why a pop star might mime to her record, or rely on backup singers to do harmonies that on the disk were multi-tracked, while an opera singer cheats if she does not do all the singing the part requires of her.

Musical works, then, are not homogenously of a single ontological type. Some performances are not of works. Some works are not for perform-ance. Some works for performance are for live playing and others are not. Some works are "thin" in that they underdetermine many of the details of their faithful rendition, while others are "thick" with constitutive detail. An appreciation of what the composer has done and how, and what instead is due to the performer, if there is one, presupposes an understanding of what ontological variety of music is in question.

Another useful illustration of the ontological variety among works in a single artform is provided by ballet. Some ballets seem to take their identity from the music composed for them. An example is Stravinsky's *Rite of Spring*, which has received many different choreographic treatments. The work's identity cannot derive solely from the music, however. (After all, it is at least a necessary condition for something's being a ballet that dancers take part if the performance is to be complete.) The importance of its choreography to the ballet's identity is apparent in other cases. One is that in which the music already has an established identity before it is appropriated for use in the ballet. An example is George Balanchine's *Concerto Barocco*, which is based on J. S. Bach's concerto for two violins in D minor, composed 200 years earlier. Another case is that in which the dancers' movements trigger the music as their bodies break electronic beams or their feet land on pressure plates. An example is *Variations V* by Merce Cunningham and John Cage. And a final illustration of the importance the choreography can have for the work's identity is that in which no music goes with the dance. *Moves*, by the American choreographer Jerome Robbins, is such a ballet. There is a continuum, from ballets in which the music is fixed and notated while the choreography is open-ended, to ones in which it is the choreography that is fixed and notated while the range of possible musical accompaniments, including the silent one, is open-ended.

Ballet is a hybrid artform. It unites dance, mime, drama, living sculpture, costuming, décor, and music. Other hybrids include opera and musicals, which combine music, song, and drama. Also, most songs meld narrative and music, and many involve poetry as well. Within hybrids, there is considerable scope for ontological variation, depending on which elements dominate and in what fashion.

Even if we carefully work out the range of ontological types different artforms employ, puzzling and difficult cases are bound to remain. Some artforms are ontologically ambiguous. This is true of poetry, where there may be nothing to choose between reading the poem silently and speaking it as if one were its narrator or subject. Taken one way, poems are a special form of literary narrative. Taken the other, they are dramatic works that are for performance. We should accept poetry's ambivalence, without trying to force it unnaturally to fit only one ontological category.

4.7 Is the Identity of an Artwork Fixed or Evolving?

In chapter 3 we saw that perceptually indistinguishable artworks can have different contents as a result of being created in different art-historical contexts. However, a question arises from the fact that artworks persist through time, which means their ongoing cultural setting alters with history's ebb and flow. Is there reason to think that the work's context continues to affect its identity *after* its creation, with the result that it remains self-identical yet crucially altered? The idea has been defended by the American philosopher Joseph Margolis, for example. Living things retain their identity though they change over time. An oak tree can be one and the same as a past acorn with which it shares few properties. A given person can, at different times, be young and blond and old and bald. So, does an artwork have an evolving identity, much as a living person does?

Some may do so. Gardens, supposing some qualify as artworks, are intended to change with the growth of the flora and the yearly cycle. These works change while retaining their basic identity only because their media and constitutive elements are living. It is less plausible to suggest the same for other artworks, I suggest.

Like anything else that persists, artworks acquire new properties with the passage of time. They become older, more influential, interpreted in new ways, thought about by different people, banned, neglected, water-stained, digitized, sent into space, and whatever. Consider, for example, Michelangelo's ceiling and Judgment Wall in the Sistine Chapel. Following the works' completion in 1512, clothing was painted over the loins of many of the naked figures. Moreover, centuries of candle smoke and pollution darkened the ceiling more than anyone realized. When the works were cleaned at the close of the twentieth century, the colors were so bright that critics questioned the long-accepted judgment that it was Titian who was the master of color while Michelangelo was the master of form. As well, changes to a work's social and art-historical context can be no less significant than its physical deterioration in making it difficult or impossible for the present audience to see it as the artist's contemporaries did. In viewing Leonardo's *Mona Lisa*, we are not likely to forget that it is the most reproduced art image in history, worth a president's ransom, once shot at, and so on. But there are ways of accounting for the acquisition of such properties without adopting the view that factors crucial to the work's identity alter after its initial creation, as I now explain.

If the president of China sneezes, everything in the world permanently acquires a new property – that of having existed when the president of China sneezed – yet we would not see this as affecting each thing's identity. Some of a thing's properties are crucial to its identity but many are not; changes in properties of this latter kind leave its identity unmodified. What matters, then, is whether changes in an artwork that are a consequence of events after its creation affect those of its characteristics that are central to its identity. The following argument denies that this is so.

Of course we can discount as irrelevant to a work's identity constant change in the number of sneezes through which it has existed. We can also discount other developments that come much nearer to home, as it were. The course of history may be one in which a particular work is influential, initially overrated, the culmination of a stylistic tradition, and the last of its kind. More generally, the *significance* of a work can be affected by its later treatment and reception. It can become an icon for some later period, be ignored, be revived, and fetch millions at auction. But none of these are alterations to the kinds of properties that seem most relevant to its identity: namely, its creator, genre, time of creation, and content.

This is not to deny that features relevant to a work's identity and present at its creation might not become appreciable until later. Laurence Sterne's novel *Tristram Shandy* uses techniques that anticipate postmodern developments in twentieth-century literature. His audience of 1759 did not know the future and, anyway, might not have noticed aspects of the book that later seemed prescient, but the use of those techniques was present at the work's creation. Such properties are revealed by history, which is different from their having been acquired at an historical remove from the work's creation.

Suppose, though, that a work turns out to be the first of a trilogy. Doesn't the creation of the later two works affect the identity of the first? Not simply by following after it. Also needed is an intention on the part of the artist. But now suppose the intention to write a trilogy was not formed until some time after the completion of the first work. In that case, we might agree that its identity is changed, but this is possible only because certain actions artists perform can create uncertainty about when labor on the piece has come to its conclusion. The nineteenth-century Austrian composer Anton Bruckner regularly revised and rewrote his symphonies after their first performance and publication. Perhaps he was changing their identity. Where there is an ambiguity among versions or uncertainty between various possible completion dates, there will be a corresponding lack of clarity about the work's identity. To allow this, though, is far from accepting as a general claim that events taking place long after the artist's death can change her work's identifying properties.

A final case to consider is that in which the work receives a critical interpretation that would have been impossible at the time of its creation. For example, the interpretation hinges on giving a word a meaning that it did not acquire until after the creation of the work in which the word is used. William Blake's phrase *dark satanic mills*, from his Preface to *Milton* of 1804, is interpreted in this way if it is read as referring to the textile mills of the British industrial revolution that came later in the nineteenth century. Something similar appears to be true when Freudian psychoanalysis is applied to works that pre-date it, as when it is held that Hamlet hesitates because he is paralyzed by Oedipal guilt, or when Marxist or feminist interpretations are proposed for pre-nineteenth-century works. Such interpretations concern the works' content and imply that this has changed since the works' creation, because the theories the interpretations rely on were invented at a later time.

Different strategies of reply are appropriate to different examples. In some cases, we can say the work is misidentified and thereby misinterpreted. In others, we can point out that the interpreter is not in fact making claims about the work's content but, instead, is playing with the text; for example by considering what it *might* mean. And Freudian and Marxist interpretations may not be anachronistic if all that is implied is that earlier artists, who could be astute observers of human nature and social relations, recognized the outward signs of the syndromes and power structures that Sigmund Freud and Karl Marx later analyzed. After all, Sophocles authored the Greek tragedy *Oedipus Rex* millennia before Freud came up with the theory of the Oedipus complex partly on the basis of contemplating Sophocles' play.

According to a long-established philosophical maxim, we should not adopt a more profligate or exotic ontology than is necessary to account for the mode in which something exists. If we can explain the direction of an electrical current without positing the existence of green but invisible gremlins that direct all electronic traffic, then we should refrain from including gremlins of that sort in our ontology. For art, we can account for the manner of its existence without resorting to the special kind of ontology that is used to explain the persistence through change of the identity of living creatures. So, if we accept the principle of keeping our ontologies as simple as possible, we should reject the position according to which changes in a work's socio-historical setting subsequent to its creation affect its identity-relevant features.

Applications and Connections — Musical Recordings, the Movie of the Movie, the Matter Replicator

Jazz is an art of improvisation. But suppose one of Charlie Parker's saxophone solos is later notated. Does that result in the creation of a work of which he is the composer? Perhaps not. Not all musical notations have the purpose of specifying works. Some have a *descriptive*, not a *prescriptive*, function; their goal is to record what a musician did. For example, ethnomusicologists and folklorists write down musical perform-ances to document them for the purposes of analysis and description. When Parker's solo is written down, what is notated is not a work but an improvisation. This is not to deny that, in making up the music, Parker displays many of the skills of the composer. Nor is it to object if the suggestion is that his improvisations are "works of art." What is denied is that he composes a musical work, as we normally understand such things: namely, as compositions intended and created for repeated performances.

Parker could have intended to compose musical works and written them in an improvisatory way, while relying on the help of assistants who were skilled in the use of musical notation. Apparently, this is how John Lennon and Paul McCartney sometimes worked in creating their songs. What is claimed is not that Parker *could* not compose, but that he *did* not. He did not intend to prescribe via his act of improvisation that others perform what he did.

In that case, what should we say about recordings of jazz? If the musicians intend their music to be evanescent, can it survive being canned? There is reason to think it will be damaged, if not killed. The difference between hearing the live performance and listening to the recording is like that between watching an exciting sporting event as it takes place and viewing a replay of the game when one knows the outcome. In the live situation, the avid fan recognizes when a risky strategy has been put in place and the threats to which it is intended to respond, yet, like the coaches and players, cannot yet know if it is to prove a tactical masterpiece or a dismal failure, whereas the viewer of the replay probably cannot prevent herself interpreting earlier events in the game in light of what transpires later. This can be an appropriate way of listening to a symphony, say, since symphonies are intended to be heard on more than one occasion, but it is likely to corrupt the experience most apt in appreciating jazz.

Mention of recordings brings up a new issue, this time to do with works intended for live performance. When Johannes Brahms's Second Symphony is recorded in the studio, the musicians can make multiple takes that are later edited together, they need not begin at the beginning and end at the end, they can always redo a section that contains a mistake, and filters and other devices modify the sound, yet the work is intended for live performance, which requires continuous playing from the beginning to end without electronic manipulation of the output. Why do we count the recording as a performance of Brahms's work? The quick answer is because we expect norms to be followed that make it reasonable to hear the recording as a *simulation* of the live performance that would sound as it does. The correct number of musicians per part should be observed, large chunks (minutes rather than seconds) of the piece should be recorded in a single take, all the notes that make it onto the recording should have been played as written on the specified instruments, and the musicians should be capable of playing the piece to a professional standard in a live performance. Meanwhile, the editors and engineers should aim at verisimilitude to the sound made by such an orchestra under the acoustic conditions of a concert hall.

By contrast, pop recordings typically present *virtual* performances rather than simulations of live ones, because they can be heard to make extensive use of multi- and back-tracking, mixing, filtering, and the rest. When musical works intended for live performance are subject to this kind of treatment in a recording – for instance, when Bach's pieces are electronically synthesized – the result is what was earlier called a *transcription*; that is, a work that is new by virtue of how its medium differs from that of its source, but also a work that retains a close connection to, and reflects on, its model.

The standard recording of a musical work created for live performance can be compared to a film of a play that deliberately confines itself to presenting the action as it would appear on stage and avoids close-ups and the like. A movie of that sort might count not as a new piece but as a (simulated) performance of the play. As cinema, the film would be odd, though. It is liable to strike its viewer as boring, even as distractingly artificial. A more cinematic approach would introduce close-ups, slow motion, flashbacks, pan and dolly shots, varied angles and perspectives, rapid editing with cross-dissolves, montage, and like effects. Also, the stage would be abandoned for appropriate locations or studio sets. The film of a play, then, would be like the film of a novel, that is, a separate but derived work.

If there is a continuum between the movie that presents a simulated performance of the play and the movie that presents a new but imitative work, can there be a clear boundary between the two? Perhaps not. If the boundary is vague, cases that fall in the gray area will be ambiguous as to their genre, and perhaps also as to their ontology (and there is no harm in that!). But like other distinctions drawn within continua, the majority of cases can be clear – like red versus orange, say – even if borderline ones are not.

Here is another issue that also raises questions about the ontological status of movies. Some people object to the colorization of movies made originally in black and white and others, including the Canadian philosopher, James O. Young, defend the practice. One argument used by Young is that the colorization of the movie amounts to what was called above a *transcription* of the original. The movie of the movie is analogous to the movie of the play or the movie of the novel. In other words, the colorized movie is a new and separate work.

The process of colorization is not destructive of the black-and-white original. In this it differs from some other examples of the generation of new works from old ones. Francis Picabia painted over one of his most controversial works and called the new painting *The Fig-Leaf*. Robert Rauschenberg created *Erased de Kooning* by erasing a line-drawing by the older and then more famous artist. And the contemporary Australian artist Jet Armstrong spray-painted "crop circles" on two landscape paintings, retitled them, and displayed them as his own work. In this case, the original artist, John Bannon, threatened to take legal action. Where its creation entails the destruction of another piece, we might not welcome the new work, especially if it is of lower merit. That concern is not relevant to the debate about colorizing movies, however, because the process leaves all black-and-white prints of the movie unharmed.

So the defense of colorization continues as follows: the colorized movie is a new and different work from the original. Just as Duchamp took the image of *Mona Lisa* and created from it *L.H.O.O.Q.*, so the colorizer takes the images of the old movie and makes a new one. The original work is not damaged, as was also true of *Mona Lisa* after Duchamp's creative act. So how can there be a basis for objection? Indeed, should we not accept colorized movies as welcome additions to the temple of cinema?

The rhetorical questions just posed might be answered in various ways. We could allow that the colorized movie is a separate and related work and still identify resulting harms about which we might be concerned. In practice, given the policies of TV stations and video stores, the availability of the black-and-white movie is likely to be reduced. And there might be disrespect being shown to the artists responsible for the original. We might forgive Duchamp his cheek, given the wittiness of his work and how far removed from us Leonardo is, but we might not feel so well inclined toward colorizers, since their contribution is not artistically clever and is driven by the industry's desire for profits.

A stronger line, though, would say the colorized print is a (defaced) version of the original, not a new and separate piece. The case for colorization is bound to be weakened if the process amounts to messing around with the work, not creating a new one. Sometimes the prints of movies are damaged by wear and handling; they are scratched, frames may be missing, and so on. What one sees when a damaged print is screened is a defective version of the original movie. A critic of colorization might maintain that the same is true of the colorized version. The movie is altered for the worse, but not so much or in such a way that it undermines its identity as an instance of the original work.

Here is a situation where we must decide, if we can, whether the changes involved in colorizing a movie produce a new work or merely a version of the old one. We should ask, is the absence of color essential to the preservation of the movie's identity? If it is, the colorized movie is a different piece. If it is not, the colorized movie is merely a print of the original. On the second view, the colorized version is defective, just as a scratched print is, but it instances the same movie as the black-and-white print, not a new and different one.

There are films in which the absence of color is part of what makes it the movie it is. When they made *Raging Bull* and *Manhattan*, Martin Scorsese and Woody Allen deliberately rejected the option of color. It is reasonable to regard their decisions as affecting the works' identities. This conclusion might not be warranted where all film stock is in black and white, however. Under those circumstances, black and white is a standard, not a variable, property of the medium. As a result, its use cannot properly be interpreted as being intended to add content to the work. (Similarly, before the genres admitted other possibilities, no significance can be read into the two-dimensionality of paintings, or the sepia tone of old photographs.) This is not to deny that filmmakers are not guided in what they do by attributes of the medium. Usually they are sensitive to these and exploit them. Not only do they film *in* black and white, they film *for* it. (Similarly, a painter can exploit the flatness of the canvas in depicting some of the surfaces shown in the work. And a photographer can take account in organizing her photograph of how the sepia tone of the print affects the clarity of its formal arrangement, say.) But this does not mean that the film's medium becomes part of its content, as opposed to being what facilitates the realization of that content. And where the medium does not affect the content, it does not affect the work's identity. Black-and-whiteness is a defining property for one or more genres of film, but as such it does not contribute to the identities of the individual films that fall within those genres.

Against this it might be observed that changes in color can affect a film's mood and that a film's mood is among its contents. The color-tinted print might be less stark and somber in its emotional feel than the black-and-white original. This is true, but the inference that a change of mood completely undermines the print's status as an instance of the original movie is not established. A scratchy or distorted soundtrack might affect the film's mood without destroying the identity of the print as an instance, albeit a less than ideal one, of the film. An alteration to the original's mood might count as a flaw in a colorized print, but not as one that disqualifies it from instancing the source movie. And if we allow that a film can come in more than one version (black and white plus many possible colorized variants), it is plausible to consider the versions as analogous to performance interpretations, which certainly can differ in their expressive moods while instancing the same work.

Overall, it seems sensible to reject the defense of movie colorization that argues that the process results in a new work. Rather, the outcome is a *version* of the original film. That does not end the debate, which can continue by considering whether the change disfigures the original, or whether that matters. It might also be relevant to distinguish between movies that make a claim to be artworks and those that do not, to think about the impact of colorization on the availability of the original and perhaps also on the audience's appreciation of the history of cinema, to consider the motives both of movie-makers and colorizers, and to reflect on the degree of toleration we show to adaptations of movies for screening on commercial television. The concern here is not with the longer discussion, though, but with the maneuvers concerning film ontology with which it begins.

Let us return to the matter replicator that was discussed earlier. Previously I considered and rejected the idea that we mistakenly regard some artworks as singular only because we do not have the technology to produce such a machine. Here I want to raise another question. If a clone could substitute adequately for the original as the object of aesthetic appreciation, despite its very different origin, does this undermine the claim that artworks take their identity and content in part from the natal setting in which they are first produced? I would answer *No*; the possibility of the replicator does not challenge the ontological contextualism discussed earlier, which privileges the art-historical setting in which the work was created over others that obtain later.

We already have equivalents of the replicator for some artworks. When considering the relational properties of an art photo, movie, or purely electronic musical composition, our focus is on when the negative or master was first made, not on when the particular print or disk we are viewing or hearing came into existence. It may be that new prints of Orson Welles's movie of 1941, *Citizen Kane*, were cloned from a master only last year, but that does not make the work a postmodern one. Where the replicating process is mechanical or automatic, we regard the copy as if it inherits the original's properties or provides for knowledge of them. Faced with a clone of *Mona Lisa* and knowing it as such, still we "see" brush strokes, the artist's way of treating light and shade, and so on, though we are aware that no brush or artist was involved in making the simulacra we are viewing. In other words, we treat the duplicate as a window allowing us direct access to the original. (Many people are content to view only the copy of Michelangelo's *David* that stands in Florence's Piazza della Signoria and would say they have seen Michelangelo's famous work, though they did not visit the nearby Accademia delle Belle Arti where the original is housed. What they assume is that the copy gives them access to the original's features because it is a faithful copy.) The story of the matter replicator does not undermine the argument for ontological contextualism, but it does remind us that we might be prepared to treat copies as substituting for the original and its circumstances if the cloning process is faithful (and especially so if the cloning process is automatic).

Questions

4.1   Suppose you read an English translation of *War and Peace*. Have you read Tolstoy's novel, which was written in Russian, or a related but different work? Is *translation* equivalent to musical *transcription*, or does it produce a *version* of the original work and not a different one? If the equivalent question is asked about translations of poetry or works in verse, not novels, are you inclined to answer the same way?

4.2   If a singular work, such as a carved marble sculpture, deteriorates over time, should we restore it to its original condition if we can? Suppose the process of restoration involves re-creating lost parts, or replacing damaged ones. Should the changes be integrated into the original, or should they be marked or indicated somehow? Suppose that, as a result of many restorations over the years, all of the material of the original has been replaced. Does that mean the artwork has been destroyed?

4.3   A piece by Damien Hirst — a sheep cut in half and suspended in formaldehyde — was vandalized by having Indian ink thrown into its tank. The gallery spent a great deal of money to restore the work to its former appearance. It would have been simpler and cheaper to start again, with the carcass of another, similar sheep. Had they done so, could they represent the work as Hirst's? Would it make a difference to how the previous question should be answered if the gallery obtained Hirst's approval before making the replica?

4.4   Imagine an artist who, inspired by the Swiss sculptor Jean Tinguely's *Homage to New York* of 1960, creates a sculpture that self-destructs. It runs down a hill and tumbles off a high cliff above a deep lake, shedding parts and burning as it does so. This event is filmed under the artist's direction. Here are three possibilities. The artwork is the *event of the sculpture's self-destruction* and the film is merely a record of this event. In this case, the artwork was singular and is now lost, but a record of it survives on film. Second, the artwork is the *film of the event* and the sculpture's self-destruction was merely a medium for the work's construction. The artwork — that is, what is encoded on the film of what happened — can be screened on potentially many occasions and was not destroyed. Third, the artwork is a *complex event involving both the statue's self-destruction and the filming of it*. Unless the filming of the statue was itself filmed in a way that showed both, no record of the work survives. How might we decide between these possibilities, or what would indicate that the work is ambiguous between them?

4.5   In the past, it was common for composers to "recycle" some of their ideas. Passages that first appeared in a religious oratorio might be used later with different words in an opera. A comparable practice occurs still. The punk band the Ramones reused material from its early songs in its later ones. Do these cases show that the musicians involved did not have the concept of a musical work?

4.6 If you see *Swan Lake On Ice*, have you seen the famous ballet? If so, how do you account for the fact that none of the performers wear ballet shoes? If not, how do you explain why the words "Swan Lake" figure in the title of the show and that it has the same story?

4.7 Is the movie of a novel an interpretation of it (as well as being a new but derivative work)? If so, how does it differ from a critic's description and analysis of the novel? How is the adaptation of a novel for the movies both similar to and different from the interpretation of a musical work through its performance?

4.8 If Ansel Adams's photographs of Yosemite were colorized, would they become different works? If the movies of Ingmar Bergman, the Swedish film director, were colorized, what properties would they be likely to lose and what new ones would they take on?

Readings

For the view that artworks exist in the mind of the artist, see R. G. Collingwood's *The Principles of Art* (London: Oxford University Press, 1938). Gregory Currie, in *An Ontology of Art* (London: Macmillan, 1988), and David Davies, in *Art as Performance* (Oxford: Blackwell, 2003), both argue that it is the artist's actions, not the product he makes, that is the artwork.

The thesis that musical works are pure sound structures that are discovered by composers is defended in Peter Kivy's "Platonism in Music," *Grazer Philosophische Studien* 19 (1983), 109–29. Jerrold Levinson presents a contrary view in "What a Musical Work Is," in *Music, Art, and Metaphysics* (Ithaca: Cornell University Press, 1990), 63–88, and John Andrew Fisher challenges the idea that they are discovered, not created, in "Discovery, Creation, and Musical Works," *JAAC* 49 (1991), 129–36. The ontological variety of music is emphasized in Stephen Davies's "Ontologies of Musical Works," in *Themes in the Philosophy of Music* (Oxford: Oxford University Press), 30–46.

Works of art are characterized as types in Richard Wollheim's *Art and its Objects* (2nd edn., Cambridge: Cambridge University Press, 1980), and in Joseph Margolis's "Works of Art as Physically Embodied and Culturally Emergent Entities," *BJA* 14 (1974), 187–96. They are described as norm kinds in Nicholas Wolterstorff's "Towards an Ontology of Artworks," *Noûs* 9 (1975), 115–42. The suggestion that types can be created, rather than existing as eternal abstractions, is defended by Robert Howell in "Types, Indicated and Initiated," *BJA* 42 (2002), 105–27.

Discussion of the ontologies specific to some particular varieties of art, apart from those already listed for music, are: Robert Howell's "Ontology and the Nature of the Literary Work," *JAAC* 60 (2002), 67–79; Noël Carroll's "The Ontology of Mass Art," *JAAC* 55 (1997), 187–99, and his "Toward an Ontology of the Moving Image," in *Philosophy and Film*, edited by C. A. Freeland and T. Wartenberg (New York: Routledge, 1995), 68–85; Dominic McIver Lopes's "The Ontology of Interactive Art," *JAE* 35:4 (2001), 65–81; Joel Snyder's "Photography and Ontology," *Grazer Philosophische Studien* 19 (1983), 21–34; and Francis Sparshott's *A Measured Pace: Toward a Philosophical Understanding of the Arts of Dance* (Toronto: University of Toronto Press, 1995), ch. 19. A rare discussion of hybrid art genres, such as collage, kinetic sculpture, mime, and opera, is found in Jerrold Levinson's "Hybrid Artforms," in *Music, Art, and Metaphysics*, 26–36.

The special ontological status of recordings is considered in Theodore Gracyk's *Rhythm and Noise: An Aesthetics of Rock Music* (Durham: Duke University Press, 1996), 1–37 and 228–32, where he argues that, in rock, the work is purely electronic. Also on this topic is John Andrew Fisher's "Rock 'n' Recording: The Ontological Complexity of Rock Music," in *Musical Worlds: New Directions in the Philosophy of Music*, edited by P. Alperson (University Park: Pennsylvania State University Press, 1998), 109–23. Lee B. Brown argues, in "Phonography, Repetition and Spontaneity," *PL* 24 (2000), 111–25, that an appropriate experience of jazz's improvised freedom is lost to the person who listens to a recording.

For sympathetic presentation of the idea that the artwork changes its identifying properties after its creation as a result of its subsequent interpretation see Graham McFee's "The Historicity of Art," *JAAC* 38 (1980), 307–24, and Joseph Margolis's "The 'Nature' of Interpretable Things," *Midwest Studies in Philosophy* 16 (1991), 226–48. And for a critical review of the thesis, see Jerrold Levinson's "Artworks and the Future," in *Music, Art, and Metaphysics*, 179–214.

James O. Young argues that a new work is created when a black-and-white movie is colorized in "In Defense of Colorization," *BJA* 28 (1988), 368–72. For a good general discussion of issues raised by colorization, see Yuriko Saito's "Contemporary Aesthetic Issue: The Colorization Controversy," *JAE* 23:2 (1989), 21–31.

Chapter Five

Interpretation

When the significance of something is not apparent on its face, interpretation is involved in seeking to explain and understand it. Because there is a great deal we wish to comprehend, interpretation is a perennial human occupation. We try to predict the weather by interpreting cloud and wind patterns, for example. More generally, both scientific theories and practical wisdom are based on interpretations of relevant data.

The behaviors, emotions, and thoughts of humans provide rich materials for interpretation, as do the outcomes and products of their actions. Many human artifacts and creations are ripe for interpretation, but among them artworks stand out. Most artworks are made *for* interpretation. There are several senses in which this is true.

For dramatic and musical pieces, the work's performance is inextricably linked with its interpretation. If we think that the performance interpretation of a work is the overall expressive and structural vision of it planned and intentionally projected by the performer, most performances will embody an interpretation of the work they are of. Meanwhile, narrational artworks usually call for interpretation to the extent that the worlds they present are under-described, so that the audience's imaginative input is needed to flesh out the story. Moreover, such works are often made to be ambiguous, enigmatic, multi-layered, or otherwise challenging in ways that demand of the audience that it adopts an interpretative approach to appreciating the story. The power of such works to elicit interpretations sustains and gives point to the practice of story-telling.

Someone might object that, if art encompasses not only recent, high Western art but also more quotidian kinds (as was discussed in chapter 1), artworks are not always demanding in the way just described. Mass art and popular art often have an unsubtle, formulaic content that leaves the audience's imagination with little to do. In replying to this objection, we can accept that the role of interpretation in appreciating the content of such works sometimes is minimal, but then go on to highlight another mode of interpretation that is crucial in following both low and high art with understanding. Narrative and representational art can (and should) be scrutinized for the way the use of the medium structures, or otherwise affects, the content that is narrated or represented. Because it is always appropriate with art to consider the treatment of the medium and how this interacts with and permutes the message that gets to be expressed, even artworks whose content is bland are usually subject to interpretative consideration. The resulting judgment of such works is not always negative, because it takes more skill than is sometimes acknowledged to create mass and popular artworks that are accessible and appealing to a broad (but not thereby unintelligent or unsophisticated) audience.

In this chapter we concentrate on theories about the interpretations offered of artworks by commentators who set out to describe and understand them. (Other kinds of interpretations, such as those made by musicians and actors through their performances, and critical reviews of such performances, are not discussed further in what follows.) While all kinds of art are subject to critical interpretation, and though there are specific issues associated with the critical interpretation of paintings, sculptures, and movies, the spotlight here falls on the interpretation of literary works. What is involved in interpreting a novel or poem? What purposes are acceptable in interpretation and what limits if any should be placed on how one derives an interpretation from an artwork?

5.1 When Is Interpretation Necessary?

Interpretation is called for when a thing's meaning or import is not obvious. When your friendly neighbor wishes you *Good morning* as usual, no interpretation is required. When you face your sworn enemy in mortal combat, her *Good morning* will be a candidate for interpretation. Here are some other cases in which interpretation is likely to be appropriate: where what is said is literally false (and the speaker should realize this), or does not cohere with the rest of the discourse, or is incongruous in the situation, or is vague or ambiguous. In many cases, the suspicion that the speaker does not believe what she appears to avow – *I never realized that clothes could be hung in a closet!* – can suggest that interpretation is in order. But in others, where the utterance is normally rhetorical or conventional, it might need interpretation if it is spoken too deliberately and sincerely, as when one's neighbor's *Good morning* is too hearty, probing, and solicitous. And to mention one of the most important cases, interpretation is likely to be needed in understanding complex, multi-layered, extended discourses offering the possibility of more than one reading.

Interpretation is concerned with grasping the full meaning of an utterance. This requires going beyond the obvious to uncover meanings that are not plainly stated. Why would we be interested in doing this? For many reasons, perhaps. One, often primary, motive is that the speaker meant more than she said literally or plainly, and we are interested in all that she meant. We want to understand her meaning, and that requires some interpretation of what was said if, as is common even in ordinary contexts, not everything that she intended to communicate was baldly stated.

5.2 What Is Interpreted?

The object of interpretation was just referred to variously as a thing, an utterance, and a discourse. The types of items subject to critical interpretation usually are speech or writing, actions, events, and human artifacts. These objects of interpretation are not blank nothings, as it were, but items identified, perhaps only implicitly, as falling under a certain description. If your mortal enemy speaks Vgyth and if what sounds like *Good morning* is Vgyth for *Now you will die!*, what is needed is not interpretation but translation, or the discovery of what is literally meant. When it was suggested that *Good morning* is a candidate for interpretation if uttered by one's mortal enemy, it was assumed that the words were English and spoken by someone competent in the language's use. What needs to be interpreted is not mere sounds – at that level there is nothing to discriminate between English and Vgyth – but a greeting made in English and used on an incongruous occasion.

This point is important. The identification of the object of interpretation precedes the kind of interpretation that looks to uncover meanings beyond those that are plainly presented. Picking out the object of interpretation and identifying it is a prerequisite for its interpretation. Since its content, including basic semantic content, can be among its identifying features, some content must be established and acknowledged before the interpretative project of seeking out (further) meanings begins. If the object of interpretation is the greeting in English, *Good morning*, the primary dictionary meaning of the terms and phrase are part of what identify it as the utterance it is. In that case, its subsequent interpretation does not concern these directly, but looks for additional meanings the phrase might have in the context of its use on this occasion. If the object of interpretation is the

English sentence *He was hoisted by his own petard* and the auditor does not know the meaning of the word *petard*, the interpretation can start only after uncovering what *petard* means, and the discovery of that meaning is not part of the interpretation as such. Not all acts of understanding are acts of interpretation and not all meanings are made apparent through acts of interpretation.

In earlier chapters I argued that artworks depend for their identity and content not only on the raw, material properties found within their boundaries but also on relations between these and features of the work's creation. For example, it was suggested that a work's title and genre contribute to its identity and content. Now, if one's goal is to interpret a particular *artwork* as such, one must first locate the artwork and that means it must be regarded in relation to the art-historical setting in which it was produced. This places constraints on how it can be interpreted. For example, if words used in the poem subsequently changed in meaning, and there is a potentially interesting reading that relies on these new meanings, that reading must be rejected. If an eighteenth-century poem contains the line *The stars were terrific on the night when Oscar came*, the poem cannot be interpreted as alluding to Hollywood awards, *star* can refer only to celestial bodies, and *terrific* must mean *liable to cause terror*. The poem contains no references or allusions to the world of cinema, and interpretations assuming that it does so have misidentified the poem.

Even if an interpretation correctly identifies a work it can be silly, eccentric, unsuccessful, or just plain wrong. But what makes it an interpretation of the work, even if it is a poor one, is not solely that the interpreter has nominated it as such. The interpreter must also be able to identify the work and its most basic contents and the interpretation must be answerable to them. The interpretation made by a person who does not understand or who ignores the meaning of a poem's words fails to hit its target. It is a non-interpretation, not a poor interpretation of the work in question. There is nothing to prevent an interpreter basing some interpretation on a (deliberate) misreading of the poem, but the result is an interpretation *after* the poem, or *inspired by* the poem, not *of* the poem.

If not the poem, what is the object of interpretation in this case? To help answer this question, consider the difference between a *poem* and a *text*. As was noted in chapter 4, the poem is more than its word sequence. The identity and content of the poem depend on a particular use of the words it contains to make a poetic utterance (against the background of a particular art-historical moment). This use results in a poem that excludes many of the possible meanings that an equivalent text – a slab of language regarded ahistorically and apart from any occasion of use – could be given. To return to the earlier example, though the poem cannot be about movie awards, a text with an identical word sequence can be interpreted that way. The business of interpreting the poem's word sequence as a text, and not as a particular poem, is far less constrained than is the poem's interpretation. The interpretation of the text surveys the many potential uses it could be given in making meaningful utterances. One possibility, then, is that the commentator disregards the poem in order to focus instead on an equivalent text that yields a greater variety of possible interpretations.

The interpreter could go yet further. She might consider the object of interpretation not as a *text* but as a *string of characters* that could be in code. This string can have as many meanings as there are sentences that can be generated from it via any rule or principle of coding we can come up with. Or to be yet more profligate, she could regard the object of interpretation merely as an *inscription* or as a set of marks of unspecified origin, not even presupposing any language. It would then be a source of an infinite number of potential interpretations. Any imaginable principle mapping the inscription to a content or meaning generates the possibility for a new interpretation. Here the interpreter is limited only by the fecundity of her imagination, not by constraints set by the meaning and content of the object of interpretation.

Several lessons can be drawn from this discussion. It can be very confusing to talk of interpretations without making clear under what description the object of interpretation is to be regarded. To return to works mentioned in chapter 3, is the interpretation of Cervantes' *Don Quixote* or Menard's? Both use the same text but to different purposes and in different art-historical settings, so the resulting works differ also in their identities and meanings (as I suggested in chapter 4). Or is it of neither artwork but of the slab of text they share in common? The second lesson is that there is virtually no limit to the number of interpretations that can be on offer, and no law to prevent a person availing herself of any of them, depending on how abstractly the object of interpretation is characterized. In the case of works of art correctly identified as such, usually the range of plausible interpretations is not unlimited, however. There are lots of interpretative games that can be played with the *text* of William Words-worth's *The World Is Too Much with Us*, but if an interpretation is to be of that *particular poem*, it must not only nominate the poem so titled as its subject but also acknowledge and respect the poem's identity-conferring contents, even if it then goes on to put an implausible spin on those.

The artist's intention can be crucial in establishing the identity of her work, including its identity-relevant contents, because those intentions can determine the work's title and perhaps also its genre. As well, they are central to what it represents and to the unpacking of its metaphors, allusions, allegory, irony, quotations, satire, and so on. To accept all this is not yet to allow that the work's proper interpretation should concern itself exclusively (or even primarily) with what the artist intended it to mean. Intentions that are relevant to fixing the work's identity are one thing, while intentions about what meanings belong to the work, beyond the plain ones it wears, are another. We take account of intentions of the first kind in locating the work of art as the object of interpretation. Whether we must be directed or restricted by intentions of the second kind remains to be considered.

5.3　Actual Intentionalism

When we converse, our interest is in what the other means by what she says. We attend to what is said because that provides excellent evidence for what is meant. If the two come apart, however, we converge on what was meant rather than what was said. There are several ways in which these two can diverge. A person can misspeak, either by making a slip of the tongue or because she is not fully competent in the language used. She says *ostrich* when she means *eagle*. Sometimes errors of this kind can be detected, along with what should have been said instead. On other occasions the error escapes notice, and to that extent the communication is less than perfect. Or the hearer is not sure whether there was an error or not, and might then ask for clarification. What is clear is that in the conversational or communicative context, decisions about what is meant are to be settled by reference to the speaker's intentions, even if what was said in error could make sense in the context. A common case is that in which an utterance is ambiguous: *When the sewer became blocked, the building superintendent stepped in*. If only one of the possible meanings is intended, the other should be put aside. In ordinary communications, speakers' intentions control how what they say should be interpreted, supposing interpretation is needed.

Some philosophers claim that literary artworks are to be interpreted as their authors' communications, so they conclude that the intentions of authors are no less determinative of how their works should be interpreted than are those of other communicators. The view that accords them this significance is known as *actual intentionalism*. It holds that the work's meaning, both explicit and implicit, is what its author intended. As it stands, this position appears to be too strong (though something like this strong version has been defended by the American literary critic E. D. Hirsch), because it does not leave space for the possibility that the author fails to achieve what she intended. If she gets things so badly wrong that what is produced could not plausibly support the meaning she intends, her intention is unrealized and the work does not mean what was intended. A qualified version of the theory, call it *moderate* actual intentionalism, addresses this problem (Noël Carroll and Gary Iseminger are among the contemporary proponents of this version of intentionalism). Moderate actual intentionalism allows that the author's intention determines the work's meaning only if that intention is carried through successfully. (There is disagreement among moderate actual intentionalists about the criterion of success, though. Some insist only that the intended meaning is one that it is *possible* to understand the work as having. Others require that the intended meaning is the one *most likely* to receive uptake from the intended audience.) Moderate actual intentionalism can acknowledge the prospect that the work has meanings *beyond* those determined by the author's intentions, provided these are not at odds with what is intended and would not be disavowed by the author were they drawn to her attention. The work's meaning encompasses all that is successfully intended by its author, but perhaps not only that.

One objection often raised to actual intentionalism maintains that the intentions of others are inaccessible to us in principle. Two observations might be offered to support this idea. The first insists that we can be sure about what goes on in others' heads only if we have the same access to their mental lives as they have, which we don't. The second holds that our only route to others' intentions is through things (words or actions) that *themselves* have to be interpreted in terms of yet further intentions. A regress ensues and it seems that we cannot ever get to that nugget of an inner state that could stop it. The conclusion in both cases is that questions of meaning cannot be settled by reference to speakers' intentions.

Skepticism about the existence of other minds, or about the possibility of knowledge of other minds, has attracted more philosophical discussion than can be reviewed here. The fact is, we often take what people say or do as revealing their mental lives. Direct experience of mental states is not the only method by which knowledge of them can be obtained. But now the second argument kicks in, suggesting that, as we peel back the layers, what is revealed is a stream of behaviors or states that in their turn have to be interpreted by reference to underlying intentions, and this process is endless, so that, in the end, we never get our hands on the intentions we were seeking. If this argument can be blocked, there cannot be an infinite regress; that is, we must come to evidence that cannot be denied about what the relevant intentions or mental states are. In other words, whatever room for doubt or interpretation the reflective philosopher claims to find, we must all believe there is none, and subsequent events must bear out the appropriateness of those beliefs. Earlier I stated that interpretation is required only when the significance of something is not apparent on its face. Sometimes intentions are plain in this way, notwithstanding the possibilities for hidden meanings detected by the philosophical skeptic.

It might help here to remind ourselves of biological facts of the kind evoked in chapter 1. To survive, we need to interpret our situation accurately. We must identify its possible dangers and opportunities. We often do so by conscious reasoning. At other times, though, we react unthinkingly, relying on non-conscious modes of processing and judging that we inherited from earlier species that survived successfully without cognition, thereby becoming the distant ancestors of our own species. The commitments of belief are not always considered or revisable. We cannot help but give them. And this applies to our acknowledgment of the reality of an external world, of our sharing that world with other, mentally alive humans, and of our recognizing, engaging, and empathizing with their cognitive and emotional states. We have evolved to be mind-readers who are sensitive to what others think and feel. And that is how the regress is blocked. It runs into the brute nature of our unconsidered certainty on particular occasions that we know what others think, believe, intend, and feel because they betray or express these states in what they say or do. Of course it is true that sometimes we may be unsure of someone's intentions and have no way of resolving our doubts, but this is not universal or inevitable.

Recall that we have not always been cognitively sophisticated adults able to articulate ideas in a public language. As children, we had to learn our mother tongue from adults who spoke it. We could do so only by trusting that they expressed themselves and their intentions successfully. (A young child who doubts such things would reject as unfounded the intuition that leads other children to find consistency and pattern in the use of the sounds these large creatures make. As a result she could learn nothing.) That trust is given without calculation. It precedes the weighing of evidence and philosophical argument. Accordingly, the fact that the skeptic can enunciate her concerns in well-formed English, a language she acquired as a

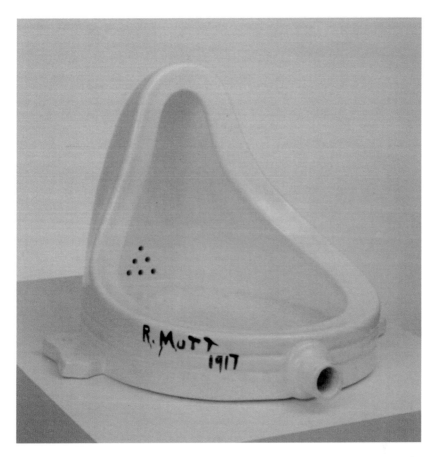

Figure 2.1 Marcel Duchamp, *Fountain*, 1917/1964, glazed ceramic with black paint; 38.1 cm x 48.9 cm x 62.55 cm

San Francisco Museum of Modern Art. Purchased through a gift of Phyllis Wattis.

Photography: Ben Blackwell. © by Artists Rights Society (ARS), New York/ADAGP, Paris/Estate of Marcel Duchamp.

Figure 2.2 Andy Warhol, *Brillo Box*, 1964, synthetic polymer and silkscreen on wood, 17" x 17" x 14"

© 2005 by The Andy Warhol Foundation for the Visual Arts, Inc. / ARS, NY and DACS, London. Digital image © 2005 by The Museum of Modern Art, New York / Scala, Florence.

Figure 3.1 I Made Berata, *Balinese picture*, ca. 1990.

Figure 3.2 Pieter Brueghel, *Landscape with the Fall of Icarus*, ca. 1555, oil on canvas

Musées Royaux des Beaux-Arts de Belgique, Brussels/Giraudon/www.bridgeman.co.uk.

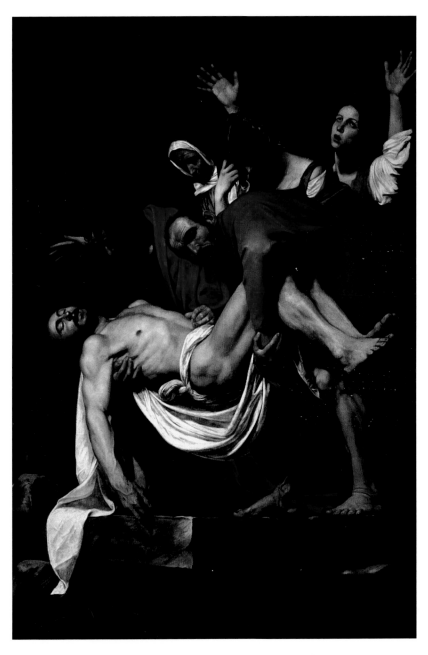

Figure 3.3 Caravaggio, *Deposition*, 1602–4, oil on canvas
Vatican Museums and Galleries, Vatican City, Italy/www.bridgeman.co.uk.

Figure 6.1 *É la vita*, designed by Bijan of Florence

US agents: Florentine Masks, POB 822, Malibu, CA 90265, www.maskart.com. Photograph by Peter John Steen-Olsen.

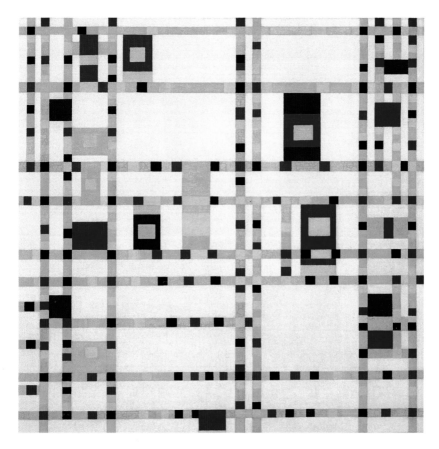

Figure 7.2 Piet Mondrian (1872–1944), *Broadway Boogie Woogie*, 1942–3, oil on canvas, 50" x 50"

Figure 7.3 Vincent Van Gogh, *The Night Café in Arles*, 1888

child, already provides grounds sufficient for questioning the doubts she expresses.

I assume, then, that we are not barred in principle from discovering what others, including literary authors, intend. In most cases, the best evidence of an author's intentions is found in the work she produces. Unless there is special reason to think otherwise, we can usually take for granted that these works mean what they say.

Does this make the appeal to authors' intentions circular and irrefutable? No. We can often tell when a person has misspoken (and even what she intended to say instead). The same can be true of authors, despite the fact that they sometimes cannot reliably declare their intentions for a work prior to the process of creation in which those intentions are clarified and crystallized, that sometimes they cannot say what they intended even on the work's completion, and that sometimes they are content to sign off a work that falls short of what they wanted though it contains no obvious blunder. In some works, it is obvious that something has gone badly wrong and that what resulted could not have been intended as such. We detect or suspect that the author has miscalculated, which shows that we do not assume automatically that the work always accurately reflects what was intended. In addition, there may be corroborative or relevant evidence in sources other than the work from which we can determine that the author's intentions were not all successfully realized in her work.

Intentionalists do not assume naively that everything that preoccupied the author in the period of creation carries over to her work. If her letters and diaries are full of her private feelings, it does not follow automatically that these were transmitted to her works (as is discussed further in chapter 6). Also, intentionalists will be careful not to accept everything at face value. Authors can be insincere, untruthful, or forgetful about their purposes, or can become distanced from them over time. Intentionalists do not have to be unsophisticated about such matters. But on the other hand, if the author explains in her letters and diaries what she was trying to do and how she was trying to do it, and there is no basis for doubting her sincerity or reliability, intentionalists maintain that what is written there can be crucial to the work's interpretation. The moderate actual intentionalist not only regards the author's intentions as a determinant of a work's meaning, she also argues that external sources can provide valuable evidence about such intentions.

This last point leads to a much-discussed objection that sees appeal to external evidence of literary authors' intentions as fallacious. In claiming to identify this fallacy in the mid-twentieth century, William Wimsatt Jr. and Monroe C. Beardsley maintain that, either the intention succeeded, in which case one does not need to look outside the work for its meaning, or the intention failed, which means external evidence of the author's intentions does not point to a meaning that can be found in the work. There are several things to notice here. First, the point is a worthwhile one if its purpose it to warn against extreme forms of biographical interpretation, in which critics largely ignore the text of the work in favor of projecting into it stories about the author's love-life, neuroses, and so on. (Clearly, it is biographical styles of criticism prevalent at the time they wrote that are the primary target for Wimsatt and Beardsley.) Also observe that the objection is not to intentionalism as such, but instead to inappropriate reliance on external sources of evidence about an author's intentions. Wimsatt and Beardsley do not argue that it is fallacious to consult far-flung evidence of an author's intentions in arriving at interpretations of a work, provided that what is uncovered is tested against what is manifestly in the work. We can easily overlook interpretationally relevant features of the work and re- course to data about its author's intentions could be helpful in guarding against this danger. In other words, Wimsatt and Beardsley hold that an author's intentions never *alone* determine the contents of a work, but this does not also entail that reference to those intentions cannot be germane to detecting meanings that have been conveyed successfully to the work.

There is, however, a difficulty with the argument that there is an intentional fallacy. It assumes that the work's import is sealed hermetically within it. External indications of its meaning can shed light on its internal meaning, but the internal meaning is supposed to exist independently and as something against which these outside claims can be tested. The problem with this idea was foreshadowed in chapter 3, where it was argued that the content of artworks often depends on relations between the work's internal features and contextual factors that lie beyond its boundaries. We need to consider the work's relation to the art-historical context of its creation in order to detect its content. In other words, *internal* meanings depend in part on *external* factors. In consequence, it cannot be true that external evidence can serve only to confirm what is indicated independently by internal evidence of the work's meaning. To take a crude example, what a poem means "internally" depends on the meanings of the words it contains, and their meanings depend on their uses in the wider linguistic environment. Not surprisingly, Wimsatt and Beards- ley are forced to compromise their argument by conceding that there can be *intermediate* evidence – evidence that is neither wholly internal nor entirely external – relevant to interpreting a literary work's meaning.

This objection would be harmless to the argument for the intentional fallacy if it turned out that authors' intentions are never among the external factors that cooperate with internal features to determine their works' content. Once we allow that some aspects of the work's contextual setting – such as its genre and art-historical location – play this role, however, it is implausible to think that its author's intentions never are involved. As well, irony, allusion, metaphor, and quotation, to name a few literary devices likely to be mentioned in interpretations, all appear to require the backing of an intention to qualify as such. So the case against intentionalism is not yet proved.

Another challenge offered to moderate actual intentionalism rejects the idea that artworks have only one meaning, this being the one intended by the author. In art, we expect great works to invite multiple, even contradictory, interpretations. In reply, the moderate actual intentionalist can allow (as explained above) that the work has meanings additional to those that are intended. And a more important point is that artists deliberately make their works to be complex, richly layered, and tantalizingly ambiguous or vague precisely because they intend to produce art allowing for a variety of plausible interpretations. The multiple interpretability of artworks is consistent with the tenets of moderate actual intentionalism, so the proposed objection misses its mark.

5.4   Hypothetical Intentionalism

A rival to actual intentionalism is hypothetical intentionalism, contemporary advocates of which include Alexander Nehamas, Jerrold Levinson, and Jenefer Robinson. According to the hypothetical intentionalist, the work's meaning is determined by the intentions the audience is best justified in attributing to the author (whether or not these are the ones she actually had). In effect, the audience works out what intentions a *postulated* author would have had and interprets the work on this basis. (Proponents of the view differ over how the appropriate audience is to be described – possibilities include the intended audience, an ideal one, and an experienced one from the time of the work's creation – and over the extent to which public facts about the actual author – for instance, about her personality, values, and attitudes, or about her other works – should be used to fill out details of the postulated author.) Hypothetical intentionalists, even if they require that the author who is postulated must be much like the actual one, tend to reject appeals to information about the actual author that is private or restricted, presumably on the grounds that such details could not be expected to be known by the appropriate audience. If a work contains a coded message intended only for one other, who was given the key by the author, that message might contribute to an interpretation offered by an actual intentionalist but be ruled inadmissible by a hypothetical intentionalist.

For the case in which it is allowed that the postulated author matches what is known about the actual author and there is no reason to think idiosyncratic or very private codes lurk in the background, actual and hypothetical intentionalism can appear to be very similar. Interpreters of both stripes use hypothetical reasoning, relying not only on what is apparent in the work but on facts about its actual creator, to arrive at what was most likely intended. And in the majority of instances, the process of hypothetical reasoning leads to the same answer as regards the work's proper interpretations. (Where different intentions are equally attributable, as will often be the case, more than one interpretation will be possible.)

There is one kind of possibility, however, over which the two theories diverge. It can be described abstractly as follows: the given work allows for contrasting interpretations, one of which is clearly superior to the other. Nevertheless, the actual author asserts unequivocally that only the inferior one was intended. Here the actual intentionalist is obliged to abandon the superior reading for the intended, inferior one, whereas the hypothetical intentionalists sticks with the superior reading on the grounds that it is the more plausible and thereby the one we are most justified in hypothesizing to have been intended. Both theorists chalk up a demerit point against the artist, but whereas the actual intentionalist now judges the work to be poor, the hypothetical intentionalists continues to hold that it should be interpreted in the fashion that makes it superior.

Cases of this kind are not easy to come by. Two are often cited in the literature. One is by the British poet A. E. Housman. His "1887," part of *A Shropshire Lad*, was written on the occasion of the fiftieth anniversary of Queen Victoria's ascent to the throne of England.

1887

From Clee to heaven the beacon burns,
The shires have seen it plain,
From north and south the sign returns

And beacons burn again.
Look left, look right, the hills are bright,
    The dales are light between,
Because 'tis fifty years to-night
    That God has saved the Queen.
Now, when the flame they watch not towers
    About the soil they trod,
Lads, we'll remember friends of ours
    Who shared the work with God.
To skies that knit their heartstrings right,
    To fields that bred them brave,
The saviours come not home to-night
    Themselves they could not save.
It dawns in Asia, tombstones show
    And Shropshire names are read;
And the Nile spills his overflow
    Beside the Severn's dead.
We pledge in peace by farm and town
    The Queen they served in war,
And fire the beacons up and down
    The land they perished for.
"God save the Queen" we living sing,
    From height to height 'tis heard;
And with the rest your voices ring,
    Lads of the Fifty-third.
Oh, God will save her, fear you not:
    Be you the men you've been,
Get you the sons your fathers got,
    And God will save the Queen.

Approached one way, the poem is shallow and jingoistic, with its comfortable assumption that God will want to preserve the British sovereign and what she stands for. But one can also consider it as an ironic rejection of unquestioning claims for the absolute rule and moral integrity of Britain's monarch. This second, subversive interpretation is more subtle and interesting and presents the poem as artistically superior. Yet it was rejected by Housman, who protested: *I never intended to poke fun . . . at patriotism, and I can find nothing in the sentiment to make mockery of: I meant it sincerely.*

Another example is by the American novelist Henry James. His *The Turn of the Screw* might be read as a simple ghost story, in which ghosts threaten the children the governess is charged with looking after. Alternatively, the ghosts are figments of the governess's imagination and the book is not a moral fable about the protection of innocence from evil but is instead a tale about psychological disintegration. The second account, which is no less compatible with the story's text than the first, is superior, because it deals with a more complex and provocative theme. Nevertheless, James claimed he intended no more than a ghost story.

Though the sincerity of the artist's declaration is likely to be contestable sometimes, let us suppose it is beyond question for a relevant, particular case. Then the actual intentionalist must reject the artistically superior reading, though it is perfectly compatible with the work's text, because it is disowned by the artist, whose intended meaning was successfully carried through to the work. By contrast, the hypothetical intentionalist can adopt the unintended but preferable account of the work. If we assume (as we usually should) that the postulated author is highly skilled, we are better justified in going for the interpretation that shows the work in the more favorable light, just because it is reasonable to hypothesize that this interpretation is the one intended, given the author's competence.

What this shows is that hypothetical intentionalism discriminates between competing interpretations by reference to the light they shed on the work's possible merit. The interpretation that makes more of the work's value is the one to be preferred. If two otherwise equally supported interpretations differ in the worth they assign to the work, we should favor the superior reading since it is reasonable to hypothesize that the artist would have intended her work to be better rather than worse. It would be a mistake to assume from the theory's title that it is more concerned with intentions than with artistic value. What is hypothesized is unaffected by facts about the author's *actual* intentions, and *hypothetical* intentions are not *intentions* any more than *false* friends are *friends*.

5.5   Value Maximization

For the reasons just given, hypothetical intentionalism might not be far from a third approach, which sees the point of interpretation as concerned with *maximizing* the work's artistic value rather than with understanding it as a communication. Once created, literary works of art are autonomous and separate from their authors. We are interested in the interpretations they will bear, not solely ones that were, or might have been, intended. We are bound to be interested in what authors say about their works, because they are usually well placed to have insights about what interpretations will be rich and rewarding. And even when we have information about what was actually intended, we are likely to speculate about what alternative intentions would have been possible. But any interpretation, whether based on reference to actual or hypothetical intentions, is legitimate provided it is compatible with the work and its contents. There may be many. Among them, the ones to be privileged are those that present the work in the most artistically rewarding light. Contrasting interpretations can be equally but differently valuable, so this approach allows for multiple interpretations. We adopt this maximizing approach, it is held, because we interpret works of art primarily for the sake of the appreciative satisfactions they can yield. This non-intentionalist, maximizing theory is sometimes known as *conventional-ism*, because it regards the meanings targeted by interpretations of artworks as mainly generated by relevant artistic and non-artistic conventions.

The maximizing theory is usually criticized for being too liberal. Any artwork, interpreted in the right way, could be a masterpiece. An incom-petent and formulaic piece can be interpreted as a brilliant postmodern satire about incompetent and formulaic works of art. Such an interpret-ation will be preferred by the theory, because it maximizes the work's artistic value. Yet that interpretation surely should be rejected, because it falsely represents the work by treating mistakes as if they are sophisticated, deliberate transgressions. The interpretation needs to be *true to the work*, not merely *consistent* with it.

The reply can take this form: to be truly represented as being of the given work, the interpretation is constrained to respect the work's iden-tity-conferring features and contents. Among these are its title, what it represents, and its genre. The maximizing interpretation cannot depart from these and continue to be of the work in question. To take a work not as belonging to its given category but to a different one is to fail to interpret the work in question, not to interpret it poorly. Just as forgeries or copies should be regarded as belonging to a category distinct from that of the works or styles they mimic, so should satires, lampoons, caricatures, and ironic utterances. Accordingly, we cease to interpret the mediocre work when we imagine it to be a brilliant send-up, and that strategy is therefore not advocated as part of the maximizing theory. In other words, the maximizing theory, like others that take the artist's creation as the interpretation's target, accepts the relevance of the artist's intentions where these are crucial in fixing the identity of the work that is to be interpreted.

A second objection to the maximizing theory goes this way: certain features of the work must be analyzed intentionally. These include the work's title, what it depicts, as well as allusion, quotation, satire, allegory, symbolism, metaphor, and irony. If the maximizing strategy allows no place for the artist's intentions, it also allows no place in interpretations for reference to such features, yet they are the kinds of things that should be discussed within any adequate interpretation. Alternatively, if the maximizing strategy does admit the relevance of such features in interpretations, it must be smuggling in indirect reference to the author's intentions while denying that it does so. So, the maximizing theory is either inadequate or internally inconsistent.

Again, there is a response: we cannot maximize the value of the work in hand by attributing to it an allusion or quotation it could not possess as the work it is. This rules out the legitimacy of anachronistic interpretations, for example. A given work cannot be enriched by an interpretation imputing to it an indirect allusion to computer chips if it was written in the nineteenth century and therefore contains no such allusion. As for what remains among the work's (non-identifying) contents, the maximizing theory can interest itself in the *appearance* of intentionality whether or not the relevant features were intended in fact. In this, it falls into line with hypothetical intentionalism. If it is reasonable to hypothesize that an allusion (symbol, metaphor, or whatever) could have been intended in the work (correctly identified as such), then we can approach it as having an allusive character and consider the interpretations this permits even if its author did not intend to make an allusion. The maximizing interpretation does not implicitly assume the presence of intentions that did not exist. Rather, it appeals only to what *could have been* (but was not in fact) intended for the work in question.

A third objection to the maximizing theory observes that we are more interested in understanding artworks, including recognizing their faults and inadequacies, than in maximizing their merit. The maximizer can answer that, whether good or not, to be judged fairly the work must be seen in the best light that is consistent with preserving its identity. And she can agree with the objector that the satisfaction we seek from art should go with critical awareness and understanding, not mindless thrill-seeking or purely sensuous titillation. In other words, the value-maximizing theory does not endorse strategies of the kind objected to here, which are inappropriate by being unsuited to achieving appreciation of the work as such, so the dart misses its target.

Here is a summary of the relations and tensions between the three theories considered so far. Moderate actual intentionalism differs from the other two in automatically disallowing candidate interpretations that are at odds with what was successfully intended, along with ones that are disavowed by the artist. Interpretations aim primarily at making sense of the work of art as a communication. Even if moderate actual intentionalism is correct, however, it may prove inadequate. This would be the case if works of art typically have meanings stretching far beyond (though not inconsistent with) what is intended, because then much of what we would want to consider in an interpretation would not be controlled by the artist's intentions. By contrast, the maximizing theory regards the primary purpose of interpretation as the favorable presentation of the work, since this is the approach most liable to produce a satisfying experience of it. Interpretations must respect the work's identity, however, if they are presented as being interpretations of that work. Hypothetical intentionalism falls nearer the maximizing theory than its name suggests, because it also adjudicates sometimes between competing interpretations by preferring the interpretation that reveals the work in the best light. The more the interpreter assumes that the postulated author is like the actual author, however, the nearer hypothetical intentionalism comes to actual intentionalism. But these two theories cannot meet so long as hypothetical intentionalism insists that successfully realized actual intentions do not always trump hypothesized ones. All three theories allow that an artwork can be multiply interpretable, though moderate actual intentionalism is likely to countenance the legitimacy of fewer interpretations than the other two approaches.

5.6 Uses for Interpretation

The three views considered so far agree that the proper object of critical interpretation is the artist's work viewed as such, and not, say, merely its text. They differ, though, over the primary purpose of interpretation; over whether it is to discover what the artist was trying to communicate, to learn what someone like the artist might have meant by it, or to maximize the artistic rewards derivable from it. Are these accounts of interpretation consistent with critical practice? What is the primary purpose of an interpretation, or are there many, equal goals?

If we look at the behaviors regarded as acceptable within professional criticism, there are many. Interpretation is not always confined to the artist's work. Sometimes it jumps off from the bare text, considering what possible meanings that could bear without regard to the artist's creative use of a token of that text in producing her work. And even when the work is the focus of critical attention, its interpretation can have many motivations and purposes. Sometimes we are interested in what the artist meant, or in what could have been meant, or in maximizing the work's value, or in considering simply how it could be construed, irrespective of how this reflects on the work's merit, or in analyzing how it is put together, or in drawing lessons for life from it, or in situating the work with respect to theories, such as those of Freud or Marx, to events and social movements with which its creation coincided, to archetypes and myths, or to the interpretative tradition it has received.

If all these methods of interpretation are acceptable, we might be inclined to dismiss the question about which is primary. That could be too hasty, though. One or more approaches to art might be foundational, not by being more frequent or by being historically prior to others, but by being presupposed somehow in the activity of art-making. The idea is that there would have been no point to making art were it not fit for certain kinds of interpretation, or interpretation with certain purposes, though once art does exist, lots of other reasons for interpretation and styles of interpretation can come into play.

5.7 Theory-Driven Interpretations

Before pursuing this last point, let us extend chapter 4's discussion concerning Marxist, psychoanalytic, and feminist approaches to art's interpretation. As interpretative strategies, these seem to be very different from those considered so far, in that their use often appears to be anachronistic.

Some works of art explicitly invite interpretation in terms of Marxist, psychoanalytic, feminist, or critical race theories. Doris Lessing's African novels appeal to Marxist ideas, and no doubt many Soviet works had the purpose of illustrating the virtues of economic socialism. Philip Roth's novel *Portnoy's Complaint* is presented as a monologue related by the protagonist from the psychoanalyst's couch. Marge Peircy's and Margaret Atwood's novels address feminist themes. The poetry of bell hooks deals with issues of race, gender, and identity.

Moreover, because such theories have become part of our regular cultural heritage, they can be considered as background to works that postdate their appearance but do not apply them self-consciously. Social realist British plays and novels of the 1950s – such as John Osborne's *Look Back in Anger* and John Braine's *Room at the Top* – make much of issues of class and can be considered in terms of Marxist theory, for instance. James Joyce's *Ulysses* and J. D. Salinger's *Catcher in the Rye* are novels ripe for psychoanalytic interpretation. The writings of Virginia Woolf and Sylvia Plath can be fruitfully approached from the direction of feminism. The relation between Huckleberry Finn and the escaped slave Jim in Mark Twain's novel of 1883 clearly draws attention to the racist assumptions underpinning such associations. Plainly it is legitimate to invoke such theories in interpreting works of these kinds, and these interpretations fit the models discussed earlier; that is, they might be concerned with what the author meant, or what might have been meant, or about understanding the work in a favorable way. Even where the works in question pre-date the public presentation and acknowledgment of Marxist, psychoanalytic, feminist, and critical race theories, the ideas in these theories can be pressed into the service of interpretation in several ways.

Classism, neuroses, sexism, and racism existed long before the systems developed to analyze them. As was suggested in chapter 4, these phenomena might have been recognized as such by artists who also anticipated some of the insights of the theories that came later and applied these in their works. (If we regard these theories of behavior to be fundamentally mistaken about human nature, it will be confusions, not insights, that artists prefigured.)

At other times this style of criticism is polemical. This is apparent, for example, when feminist critics "read against the grain" in order to bring out a work's sexist assumptions and biases, both in the presentation of its material and in the values and interests it takes for granted in its intended audience. In a related approach, psychoanalysts consider works for the light they shed on the psychology of the artist. In doing so, they treat the work as a resource for analysis on a par with the artist's dreams and fantasies; that is, as a symbolic representation of the artist's unconscious desires and processes. Freud's essay on Leonardo is a case in point. And Marxists also write sometimes of art in terms of its use as an emblem of class and power, while race theorists look for the hidden racist premises in works of art. In such cases, the goal is that of validating and illustrating the theory, not of understanding the artwork on its own terms, which is why such analyses often do not aim to present an encompassing, coherent view of the work as a whole.

On yet further occasions, the intent is more playful. The theory provides one way among many others to clothe the piece. And if in the process the artist's work slips from view, because there is no description under which it imports or contains the theoretical apparatus that is applied to it, then so be it.

Both the polemical and playful approaches to interpretation are acceptable, as I noted before. Interpretation need not confine itself to providing consistent, integrated accounts of artists' works viewed as such, as opposed to the texts associated with those works, which may be taken up by the interpreter and used for her own purposes.

5.8 Does Interpretation Change the Work's Meaning?

I have accepted that, as well as being directed to the artist's work viewed in relation to the art-historical context in which it arose, interpretation can legitimately interest itself in other matters, as was just indicated with respect to the varied purposes of Marxist, psychoanalytic, feminist, and critical race theories of art. One possibility to consider, albeit one that sounds surprising, is that interpretation is at its most relevant and fruitful when it moves beyond the artist's historically bound work. If, as is sometimes said, authors are dead and readers can create meaning via their acts of interpretation, the potential value of interpretations would be reduced if those interpretations were to be confined to the artist's work as it was originally created. According to proponents of this view, such as Joseph Margolis and Michael Krausz, the artwork is altered through the accretion of new meanings and associations. If the critic is to interpret the work for the present, she must address not its former incarnation but its contemporary one, which has been shaped over time through its critical reception and its interaction with other social changes.

In chapter 4, I denied that actors and musicians complete the works they perform. The same can be said of critics; their interpretations do not complete the works they write about. The work is changed by the interpretation, but only in the trivial sense that it acquires the property of having been interpreted in the way specified. Interpretation may be creative – dramatic and musical performances assuredly are – but what is created is a new interpretation, not a new work. Also, I argued that artworks do not change their identity over time. Their significance can alter markedly, but this does not change the meanings and other features that are responsible for their identity. The current proposal differs somewhat from the ones rejected previously. It maintains not that the work's *identity* is changed by interpretations, but that its *meaning* is. Call this view *meaning constructivism*. In what follows, I argue against the plausibility of meaning constructivism.

We should distinguish a work's *significance* from its *meaning*. The work's significance is a matter of how we think about it and relate it to values and ideas that lie beyond it, whereas its meaning is something it possesses in virtue of its semantic, symbolic, or other properties. Its significance is what we make of its meaning when we consider the relation between its meaning and matters of interest or value to us. I readily allow that interpretations can change a work's significance, but do they also change its meaning?

As noted previously, the fact that a work is interpreted changes it by making true something that was not so before: namely, that it has been (again) thought about in a certain way. Apart from trivial changes of that sort, the object of interpretation is unaffected by being interpreted, in that what was true and false of it before remains so afterwards. For example, an interpretation might draw attention to some previously overlooked feature of the work, or might bring certain of its elements into prominence by giving them emphasis, but the result is a change in how we regard the work and what we find in it, not in the work as such. The properties uncovered or stressed by the interpretation are not affected in their existence or character by the interpretative process. Either they were there all along or they were absent, and the claims of the interpretation, insofar as these are about the existence and nature of those properties, are true or false (or plausible or implausible) accordingly. In general, the only modification we achieve in things by pointing at them or by describing them is to make it true that they have been pointed at or described thus-and-so. We point at or describe things not to alter them but to change if and how they are seen and appreciated by other people. Interpretations are no different.

Moreover, if meaning constructivism is proposed in order to justify the observation that artworks are multiply interpretable, it is unconvincing. According to meaning constructivism, each interpretation changes the meaning of its object. The work receives multiple interpretations, but the meaning of the work is altered by the interpretations it receives, so no two interpretations target the same work-content. Effectively, the multiplication of interpretations entails the multiplication of interpreted meanings. This is not a happy conclusion, because what is usually thought to be interesting about the variability of contrasting, even conflicting, interpretations is that these can be equally plausible or convincing when they target a particular work as having the same, unchanging meaning. If the work's meaning constantly changes, there is nothing surprising or challenging about the fact that interpretations of it will also differ. So, meaning constructivism can explain the multiple interpretability of works of art only by describing art's susceptibility to a variety of interpretations as different from and less interesting than we originally supposed.

5.9   What is Interpretation's Primary Purpose?

We can now return to the questions posed earlier. What is the primary purpose of the interpretation of art? As was noted before, many purposes are accepted as legitimate. It remains possible that none of these is more central than the others. That is unlikely, though. Interpretative approaches may focus more on the work's text than on the work itself, or can be interested in the work only to the extent that it throws light elsewhere, perhaps by illustrating a theory or by backing up some didactic observation. Though all such approaches are acceptable, it is reasonable to suppose that ones attending more closely to the work and viewing it in its entirety and as art are more likely to be conceptually pivotal in explaining why we make and appreciate art as we do.

Given this, is the primary mode of interpretation more intimately linked to the work as it was when it was created or to the work in relation to its current setting? If meaning constructivism provides a convincing analysis of art's interpretation, the art interpreter's focus should be fixed on the present, even if the art historian looks to the past. But the tenets of meaning constructivism were challenged and rejected. To focus only on what survives to the present through the extended process of interpretation is to risk undue concentration on the social significance that artworks attain rather than on their meaning as such. There is much of importance to be understood about art's changing significance, but all too often that significance depends on accidents, fashions, and distortions that have little to do with the business of making and appreciating art. So, the kind of interpretation that is primary is likely to be that which aims at understanding and appreciating the nature and content of the artwork, both as it is in itself and as it is in relation to the art tradition that it reflects on. In chapter 4 I argued that artworks depend for their identity and content not only on their material properties but also on how these relate to elements of the art-historical context in which they are created. Given this, the kind of interpretation that will be primary in the sense indicated above should start from the historically located work that is the creation of its artist.

The idea is simple enough. The appreciation of good art can be extremely rewarding. For that matter, the entertainment provided by forms of art that do not aspire to greatness and seriousness is of considerable worth. But artworks, both great and modest, are not easy to create. Usually, they require considerable skill, talent, and thought. Many artists are motivated to produce art of substance only if they think it has a fair chance overall of being received at its true value. In other words, the production of art tends to presuppose the possibility of an audience with the knowledge, interest, and application to appreciate what is created. And the art that is produced is historically indexed, because its identity and content depend on relations tying it to its natal setting. So, the mode of interpretation that aims at the comprehension of the historically situated work, viewed as the creation of its artist, is primary. If that had not been a common form of interpretation, now and in the past, it is difficult to understand why art would have been made at all. Once art is made, interpretation can be directed to a myriad purposes, including ones that are interested only incidentally and partially in the artwork and its acknowledgment as art. But insofar as these presuppose the existence of art, they are secondary to the mode of interpretation that might encourage the artist to create; that is, to the mode of interpretation that aims at appreciating the historically situated work that is the artist's product.

I began by discussing three theories of interpretation: the purpose of interpretation is to uncover what the artist meant (provided that intention was successfully realized in the work), or to arrive by imaginative hypothesizing at what might have been intended and meant by a postulated author, or to maximize the rewards of appreciation, consistent with respecting the identity and content of the work. As they were presented, these theories share a commitment to the contextualist ontology for art that was discussed in chapter 4. In that respect, they are all potential examples of the mode of interpretation that is here identified as primary. Hypothetical intentionalists and value maximizers are perhaps less likely than moderate actual intentionalists to tie the work's identity directly to the identity of its artist, but all three theories specify that some features of the context in which the work is produced contribute to its individuality and content, which together establish the limits of interpretations that can be truly described as being of the artist's work as such.

Questions

5.1 How is the interpretation of ordinary communications, such as letters, both like and unlike the critical interpretation of a poem or novel?

5.2 How is the interpretation of state constitutions, bills of rights, and treaties of sovereignty both like and unlike the critical interpretation of a poem or novel?

5.3 How is translation both like and unlike interpretation?

5.4 How is the kind of interpretation that is involved in performance both similar to and different from the kind of critical interpretation that has been the focus of this chapter?

5.5 Samuel Beckett's enigmatic play *Waiting for Godot* is difficult to understand but is widely taken to be a serious allegory about the meaning (or meaninglessness) of life. When asked, Beckett maintained he intended to write only a comedy. If you were a moderate actual intentionalist, would you be inclined to stick with the "serious" interpretation and therefore to assume that Beckett was being disingenuous? What grounds could you have for doing so and what kind of evidence could show that you were wrong?

5.6 It is widely held that Hamlet fails to act decisively in avenging his father's death at the hands of his uncle. Yet some critics have argued against this interpretation, pointing to the fact that Hamlet shows his determination and haste in killing Polonius and in having Rosencrantz and Guildenstern murdered. Does this show that Shakespeare's tragedy is self-contradictory? If not, is it possible for both interpretations to be equally and highly plausible?

5.7 Does the contemporary significance of Leonardo's *Mona Lisa*, as the world's most famous and reproduced artwork, mean that it can no longer be appreciated as the artwork it is? If so, does this show that its meaning has changed?

5.8 How does the interpretation of musical scores and playscripts – that is, of the notations by which such works are communicated to their potential performers – differ both from performance interpretation and critical interpretation?

5.9 How does the critical analysis and interpretation of works differ from the critical review of performances?

Readings

Two useful modern collections on art's interpretation are *Interpretation, Intention, and Truth*, edited by G. Iseminger (Philadelphia: Temple University Press, 1992) and *Is There a Single Right Interpretation?*, edited by M. Krausz (University Park: Pennsylvania State University Press, 2002). Robert Stecker argues that the meaning of an artwork is what its artist successfully intended, and also that interpreters can interest themselves legitimately in matters other than what it means, in *Interpretation and Construction: Art, Speech, and the Law* (Oxford: Blackwell, 2003).

The idea that it is fallacious to regard authors' externally expressed intentions as determining the meanings of their works is proposed in a classic article, "The Intentional Fallacy" of 1946, by William K. Wimsatt Jr. and Monroe C. Beardsley. This paper is found in *Problems in Aesthetics*, edited by M. Weitz (2nd edn., New York: Macmillan, 1970), 347–60, and in many other collections on aesthetics.

A famous statement of actual intentionalism is by E. D. Hirsch Jr., *The Aims of Interpretation* (Chicago: Chicago University Press, 1976). Among the first to propose the theory that interpretation considers what a hypothetical author might have intended is the literary critic Wayne C. Booth in *The Rhetoric of Fiction*, published in 1961 (Chicago: Chicago University Press, 1983). Philosophers holding the view include Alexander Nehamas, in "The Postulated Author: Critical Monism as a Regulative Ideal," *Critical Inquiry* 8 (1981), 133–49, and Jenefer Robinson in "Style and Personality in the Literary Work," *Philosophical Review* 94 (1985), 227–47. For reviews of the dispute between moderate actual intentionalism and hypothetical intentionalism, see Noël Carroll's "Interpretation and Intention: The Debate between Hypothetical and Actual Intentionalists," *Metaphilosophy* 31 (2000), 75–95, and Gary Iseminger's "Actual Intentionalism vs. Hypothetical Intentionalism," *JAAC* 54 (1996), 319–26, both of which favor the former theory, and Jerrold Levinson's "Hypothetical Intentionalism: Statement, Objections, and Replies," in *Is There a Single Right Interpretation?*, 309–18, which prefers the latter theory. The view that interpretation typically is directed to finding the most rewarding reading the work can support is defended in Stephen Davies's *Definitions of Art* (Ithaca: Cornell University Press, 1991), ch. 8. For critical discussion, see Carroll's "Art, Intention, and Conversation," in *Interpretation, Intention, and Truth*, 97–131, and Stecker's "The Role of Intention and Convention in Interpreting Artworks," *Southern Journal of Philosophy* 31 (1994), 471–89.

Sigmund Freud's psychoanalysis of Leonardo, based on his painting *Madonna and Child with St. Anne*, is in *Leonardo da Vinci: A Memory of his Childhood* (London: Ark Paperbacks, 1987). For critical discussion of theory-driven interpretation, see Arthur C. Danto's "Deep Interpretation," in *The Philosophical Disenfranchisement of Art* (Columbia: Columbia University Press, 1986), 47–67, and Peg and Myles Brand's "Surface and Deep Interpretation," in *Arthur Danto and his Critics*, edited by M. Rollins (Oxford: Blackwell, 1993), 55–69.

Joseph Margolis defends the view that interpretations of works of art alter their meanings in "Reinterpreting Interpretation," *JAAC* 47 (1989), 237–51. Similar conclusions are presented in Michael Krausz's *Rightness and Reasons: Interpretation in Cultural Practices* (Ithaca: Cornell University Press, 1993), see especially 66–92. Criticism of the position can be found in Davies's "Interpreting Contextualities," *PL* 20 (1996), 20–38, and in Stecker's *Interpretation and Construction*, ch. 6.

Chapter Six

Expression and Emotional Responses

According to psychologists, the evolutionary function of emotions is to make salient parts of the environment that can be relevant to our survival and flourishing. Nothing focuses a person's mind more sharply, I expect, than the sight of a charging elephant bearing down upon her. The emotions concentrate our attention on what is important within the buzzing confusion of data that constantly bombards our senses.

The emotions of other people have a double significance for us. As a social species, it is vital that we concern ourselves with how others see and experience the world. When they are lit up by emotions, we can learn about what they feel and value and about how they think about their situation. As well as seeing that someone is happy, we also observe that she esteems the friendship that is the source of her contentment. In addition, the emotions displayed by others can alert us to things they have noticed about the environment that we have so far overlooked but that are no less relevant for ourselves.

Once our emotional capacities are in place, they tend to be triggered by the imaginative worlds created by human narrators, not solely by the actual world of immediate experience, though in this case there may be no immediate or direct pay-off in terms of survival or benefit. Some narratives, such as those told by historians, aim to describe the way the world is or was or will be. Others, including many works of literature, generate fictional worlds. Some of these fictional worlds contain characters or events "borrowed" from the actual world, of course, but many do not. We respond affectively to what happens in fictional worlds irrespective of whether we believe these to reflect real-world occurrences. When we do so, our emotions play their usual role of directing our focus to what is of interest within the world, but in this case the world in question is that of the story.

For much of the time, we experience emotions and they guide our thoughts and actions without our reflecting self-consciously on how or why this is so. Something about our environment calls forth a response and we give it, without introspecting on the mental and other processes involved. It is sometimes the same when we respond to the worlds created by narratives, or to the abstract sound-worlds of musical pieces. Plato, writing more than two millennia ago about the ideal Greek state, suggests that music induces emotions according to the tuning system employed, and he recommends that the kind of music that makes people feel warlike should be banned. He is echoed, of course, by twentieth-century conservatives who have argued for the suppression of jazz and rock 'n' roll because they detect there an undercurrent of raw sexuality that they fear could corrupt the feelings and behavior of the young people who listen to such music.

The triggering of emotional responses need not always be so blind, however. Sometimes we become aware that a narrative is manipulating our feelings in a manner we want to resist. For example, it tries to elicit a stronger reaction than is warranted by its content, or it tries to get us to sympathize with values and attitudes we do not share. Instead of reacting as the author intended, we reject the first work as mawkishly sentimental and the second as misguided in its judgments or morality. In these cases, we shift our attention from the content of the narrative's world to the methods used in creating and developing that world. We become aware of the medium, not simply the message; of the telling, not merely the tale.

Some narratives – and now we come to those with a claim to be artworks – invite us to be simultaneously aware of the response we should have and of the techniques by which the author tries to control this, and we are meant not simply to observe the connection but, as well, to reflect on how it is achieved. According to the contemporary British philosopher Peter Lamarque, literary artworks require of us that we adopt both *internal* and *external* perspectives on their fictional worlds. The internal approach involves direct imaginative involvement in the world of the work, including recognition of emotions it expresses and reactions to these and other features of the story. The external approach focuses on the fictionality of the worlds depicted, on narrative structure and the means of literary representation, on the work's theme and genre, and on possible interpretations. These two perspectives interact in the experience of the work's reader. For example, the response to a character is guided by awareness of the structures of representation. We react to a character not solely in terms of her situation – poverty, say – but also in terms of how this is represented in the story – for instance, as contrasting with the wealth of others who are shown to be morally corrupt, so that monetary transactions are seen to function as a metaphorical thermometer for the moral condition of the story's world and its inhabitants.

The expression of emotion in art is a major source of its value, and this value comes in various forms. First, we rightly admire the skill required to portray, express, or describe emotions in ways that are psychologically plausible and relevant to the work's overall construction. As well, we esteem the power of art to call forth a response and thereby to secure our focused involvement in the world it presents. This imaginative and emotional engagement can be a means to further rewards. One work might educate us about the real world through the manner in which it directs our sentiments and attitudes. In another, our absorption in the work provides a welcome release from real-world cares and concerns. The various sources of art's value are discussed at some length in chapter 8; here the point is that both the expression of emotion in art and the arousal of affective responses in its audience are crucial at every point to what invests art with human significance and worth.

Despite this, it is philosophically puzzling that some art expresses emotion or that we respond emotionally to art as we do, or even at all. We are often moved by the plight of characters we know to be fictional, whereas, in the standard case, we need to believe something exists before it can become the target of our emotional reaction. On realizing that I mistook a stuffed toy for a lion, my belief that I am in danger disappears and along with it goes my response of fear. Why, then, am I moved by the death of Romeo and Juliet, when I know they have never existed and, therefore, never loved and died? Is the response to a fictional character irrational, or not genuinely emotional, or something else? And again, usually we avoid unpleasant feelings if we are able, yet we seek out works that, because of their tragic or horrific contents, evoke negative emotions. Is this because not all negative emotions are unpleasant to experience, or because we are masochists, or, again, because we are irrational, or for some other reason? And in the case of "pure" instrumental music, which apparently tells no story, how can it express emotion, and why are we moved by the feelings it expresses given that these seem to be abstracted from the realm of human experience?

As a prelude to addressing these issues, we need a general account of the elements of emotions.

6.1 The Nature of Emotions

Emotions usually are described as having physiological, perceptual, cognitive, and behavioral aspects. These can be illustrated using fear as an example. Typical physiological accompaniments of fear are sweating, increased pulse, dryness in the mouth, erection of the hair on the neck, and a feeling of inner tension. Perception is directed at the source of fear: for instance, the shadow of an intruder. We can distinguish the *intentional object of perception* (what the person believes they see) from the *material object of perception* (what is actually seen). Usually these two coincide, but they are distinct when perceptual errors are made, as when a person mistakes the shadow of a tailor's dummy for that of an intruder. In some cases, the relevant perception will be introspective, rather than directed outwards, as when a soldier fears that he might act in a cowardly fashion. The *intentional object of one's fear* is what one is frightened of or about: in the earlier example, an intruder. The cognitive elements of emotion typically include characteristic *beliefs* and *desires*. Fear for oneself usually involves the belief that one is threatened by harm and the desire to flee, freeze, or fight. In order to envy you, I must believe you have something I do not have and that I value and want. To feel pride in myself, I must believe I have achieved something or am in some other way worthy of admiration. The behaviors that may express or betray an emotion include the behaviors to which the relevant desires lead, as well as bodily attitudes, facial expressions, and the like. Fear leads to flight, freeze, or fight behaviors, and can also be apparent in a bodily attitude of tense alertness, a grimacing face, and so on. Deeply sad people may give way to weeping and display a downcast demeanor. Embarrassed people are inclined to blush.

Some philosophers insist that all emotions presuppose belief (or, alternatively, make-belief, some would allow) and are characterized by the kinds of beliefs (or make-beliefs) they involve. On this view, for example, fear for oneself always involves the belief (or make-belief) that one is in danger. Other philosophers, along with many psychologists, are more inclined to regard as essential only the element of affective sensation. I cannot canvas the detail of this wider debate here, but I prefer an alternative, which is that *none* of the elements listed above is *necessary* to all emotions.

Patriotic feelings might have no physiological accompaniments and might be expressed behaviorally in a huge variety of ways. Moods are not always directed at or about any thing or event. Some "gut" emotional responses seem to be triggered automatically, bypassing cognition in the process. (A person might flinch from a striking snake, even knowing she is separated from it by an unbreakable window.) In other cases, the emotional response occurs in the face of beliefs that should prevent it, as when one's fear is irrational, phobic, or reflexive. (A person might have an uncontrollable fear of birds though she has been taught and genuinely accepts that they are harmless.) Some emotions seem to have universal behavioral and facial expressions. Psychologists who have studied these, Paul Ekman being a famous example, identify happiness, sadness, fear, anger, and disgust as belonging to this category. Nevertheless, many emotions – such as regret, jealousy, pride, hope, guilt, and shame – do not appear to have universal behavioral and facial expressions.

Some affective responses, such as disgust, seem primitive, reactive, unsubtle, and not cognitively based. Others, such as feelings of patriotism, are much more obviously cognitive than physiological. Some, such as sadness and happiness, can fall in either camp, depending on the circumstances. The happiness occasioned by a good meal after an exhausting day's labor is of the kind that goes with the satiation of basic appetites, whereas the happiness that comes from solving a mathematical puzzle is much more cognitively based, and the happiness of winning a sporting competition mixes a spread of elements.

We could attempt to tidy up this variability by distinguishing emotions from moods, phobias, and feelings, or by rejecting the general term in favor of more precise categories. Or, instead, we might accept the complexity of our affective lives as reflecting the fact that we are an evolved species with brains containing centers both for complex, conscious reasoning and for "quick and dirty" unconscious reactions. On the one hand, if we share at least some emotions with other species, as seems hard to deny, the emotions in question are unlikely to require self-awareness and complex conscious calculation. But on the other hand, given that we are capable of self-awareness and complex conscious calculation, and given also the crucial role played by emotion in directing our attention to aspects of the environment that may be important to us, it is not surprising that higher thought is no less deeply infused by emotion than are more basic and reflexive responses. We can consider the many possibilities that lie before us, and we do so not in a cold fashion but in terms of the ways in which our commitments and investments can be projected into the future. As a result, we feel hope, yearning, anticipation, and apprehension to a degree that less cognitively developed creatures cannot. Diversity in the kinds of emotions humans experience is consistent with the complexity and variety of human natural and cultural history. Provided we are sensitive to the mixed and miscellaneous character of emotions, it may not be necessary to revise or reject what the term purports to cover. In any case, the general, "folk" notion of the emotions will serve for our purposes in this chapter.

6.2 Identifying Others' Emotions

How do we identify the emotions others experience? We could have indirect access to physiological changes taking place in their bodies: for instance, if they are hooked up to a brain scanner and to monitors of pulse, skin conductance, and the like. This is not usual and may not be very helpful anyway, since it is unlikely that we could individuate many different emotions solely by reference to the body's internal states. The best source of information, then, is through observation of their behavior. For a start, we might follow their gaze and discover the intentional object of their emotion. If their perception is not mistaken and their response is not phobic or irrational, knowledge of its object might suffice to identify the emotion. If the object of a person's emotional reaction is a charging lion, chances are that they are experiencing fear for their safety. Further information about their attitudes, beliefs, or desires will often be neces-sary, however, before we can read off their emotional state from its object. For example, we can know that a person is interested in what might be in the mail, but not be sure of her emotion because we do not know if she is dreading a court summons or expecting a tax refund. Or we can know that a person has just registered that his parents are coming unexpectedly to visit him, but not be sure how this makes him feel until we learn about his attitude to unexpected visits, his parents, and the rest. We can learn about others' beliefs, attitudes, desires, and values because they describe them or from observing consistent patterns in their behavior over time.

Can we tell what emotion a person is experiencing solely from her behavior, without knowing its intentional object or her cognitive states? If psychologists' studies are correct in showing there are universally recog-nizable facial expressions for certain emotions, we can do so. The sadness in the briefly glimpsed face of a stranger might be unmistakable. In most cases, though, we need to be able to place expressive behavior in a wider context. Whether a person is running for exercise, for pure joy, to flee something behind her, or toward something, may not be apparent solely in the manner and direction of her running. If some identifications of emotion are more or less instinctive, others clearly depend on experience and learning. We smile and laugh at babies rather than frowning at them because we expect them to instinctively respond to smiles, but we have to learn the cultural significance of a raised forefinger.

One other way we frequently learn what others feel is often overlooked: they tell us. Though people can be confused about their feelings, or can have reasons not to respond honestly, mostly they are reliable truth-tellers when it comes to reporting their inner life. So, we can ask a person what she is feeling, or she may volunteer the information without being asked. Alternatively, a person's descriptions of the world can indirectly indicate how she feels. Where one person characterizes the situation as involving a glass that is half full and with interesting challenges ahead, another sees a half-empty glass and the threat of failure. From what she says, one person may unintentionally convey that she feels superior to those of other races, while another cannot help revealing that he pines for a lost love.

In general, a number of features of the situation – knowledge of a person's character and values, of the object of her response, of the actions she chooses or bodily attitudes she displays unconsciously – go into our estimation of what another feels. According to some philosophers, the process by which we arrive at such judgments involves simulating what we would feel if we were like the other and in their situation, while other philosophers maintain we have a theory of cognitive psychology that we apply to the case in hand. It is only rarely that differences between these accounts lead them to contrasting descriptions of the expression of emotion in art, however, so I will pass by the debate between these camps.

6.3   Identifying the Emotions in Art

We identify the emotions of the characters in novels, paintings, plays, sculptures, songs, poems, operas, and movies in the same way that we recognize the emotions of others in ordinary life. In È la vita – see figure 6.1 – the facial expressions of joy, anger, and sadness are unmistakable, though the intentional objects of these responses are not represented.In Shakespeare's Othello, the Moor's jealousy is revealed in his actions, culminating in Desdemona's murder, and in what his words declare, both directly and indirectly. Until near the end, every action of Butterfly, in Giacomo Puccini's opera, declares her naive faith in and love of Pinkerton, as well as her confidence that he will return to be her husband and the father of her child. By the manner in which he describes his former wife while viewing her portrait, the Duke in Robert Browning's poem *My Last Duchess* betrays the irritation and petty jealousy he felt because she did not reserve all her smiles and pleasantries for him, and he unwittingly indicates that he had her put to death rather than stoop to discussing his dissatisfaction with her. Robinson Crusoe variously exhibits fear, anger, courage, determination, and delight, as well as the universal yearning for human companionship, in Daniel Defoe's novel.

As well as the usual ones just described, art provides special resources for revealing its characters' emotions. One is the title. We do not have to labor to realize what emotions are likely to feature in a novel called *Pride and Prejudice*. In many works, an omniscient narrator tells us what the character experiences and feels. Via arias and soliloquies, we can observe, as we cannot in real life, what a character thinks or says when she is alone and reflecting on her inner state and situation. And in movies and dramatic works, the lighting and music can clue us to the character's mood. The gloomy lighting of *film noir* establishes an appropriate emotional tone for the depressive dramas associated with the genre. Tense chords, brittle harmonics, or a pulsing bass in the movie's orchestral accompaniment can alert us to coming dangers and threats, even as what is shown is yet calm and placid, while a soaring melody might testify to the hero's love where his impassive face does not.

It is not difficult, then, to explain how we identify the emotions experienced by the inhabitants of artworks. But these are not the only emotions we encounter. The work itself may convey an emotional attitude to the actions or feelings it describes or represents. For example, the protagonist might be shown to feel fierce patriotism and courage while the work in which he features expresses quiet rage about the way the blindness of such passions leads men to brutal war and useless sacrifice. Where one work might express admiration for its characters' self-abasing religiosity, another dealing with the same story or theme might be disapproving in its tone. The mode of expression in these cases can be direct — *Here is a tale of betrayal most foul* — but often is not. Usually it is conveyed by the manner in which the events of the story are represented or described. Percy Bysshe Shelley's poem *Ozymandias* is about a ruler who celebrates his achievements with a portrait in stone and the inscription *Look on my works, ye mighty, and despair!* The poem indicates the futility of this gesture by describing how only the wreck of the statue survives in the featureless desert. The work *refers* to or indicates one emotion but *expresses* another.

How can works of art, and not only characters in them, express emotions? A plausible suggestion is that the emotions in question belong to someone who gives expression to them through the work's creation or presentation. An obvious candidate is the artist. And often enough this will be true. The fear and loathing of totalitarianism that emerge so powerfully from the novels *Nineteen Eighty-Four* (written in Britain in 1949) and *Animal Farm* belong to George Orwell, as we know from his own account. In general, though, it is unwise to assume fictions must be autobiographical. Attitudes and emotions expressed in the work toward its other contents should be attributed to the work's author only where there is independent confirmation that this is justified, though we expect the author to take responsibility for the work's overall point of view.

To whom can they be attributed in other cases? The stories of some works are explicitly presented by a narrator. The attitudes expressed to the tale might be those of its teller. Again, this account will pass for many works, but for others it will not. Just as the narrator might express feelings toward characters and events in the tale she relates, so the work might express feelings toward the narrator's attitudes, as well as to those of other characters. The narrator might be presented by the work as biased or as self-deceived, for instance. An example is Vladimir Nabokov's novel *Pale Fire*.

Another possibility is that we should posit a narrator or fictional author who stands *outside* the story and is not a character in it; attitudes and feelings attributable to the work are ones she expresses. The idea is that every story is presented from a narrational point of view, which is the point of view of an authorial persona who is external to the work. This authorial persona usually should not be equated with the work's historical author.

As before, there are some cases in which this seems implausible. In a movie, the shot might first be from above, then at shoe level, and so on. Why is the fictional narrator leaping about like that? And some of the shots are from the perspective of the characters, not of any narrator, as when we see the hero staring deep into his love's eyes and cut to a close view of her eyes as seen by him.

Whenever we consider a person – the author, an internal narrator, or a hypothetical external narrator – as the owner of the emotion or attitude expressed, a residue of expressiveness seems to remain unaccounted for. An alternative approach might focus on the suggestion that descriptions and representations can be expressive in their own right, even when dissociated from describers and depicters, whether real or fictional. But instead of pursuing that idea directly, I turn to another problem that brings up some similar issues.

6.4 The Expression of Emotion in Music and Abstract Art

Earlier it was suggested that, in a movie, the accompanying music can establish a mood or emotion that is not yet apparent in the story or action. I presumed that the reader would agree and think of examples from his or her own experience. Though the case is a familiar one, on reflection it should also seem philosophically puzzling. We think that music can express emotions without the help of words or pictures. In the most striking case, we say that purely instrumental music in an abstract tradition, such as the classical symphonic one, can be happy or sad. Sometimes a consistent expressive mood pervades a whole movement, as is the case with the exuberant sunniness of the last movement of Beethoven's Seventh Symphony. At other times, the mood shifts back and forth, as in the third movement of Mozart's Fortieth Symphony, where the tense, restless, nervous, drive of the minuet is replaced in the central "trio" section by calm serenity.

So striking is its expressive power that music is sometimes regarded as the most expressive of the arts. Yet music cannot feel emotion, does not clearly point to or characterize objects apt to elicit emotions, and does not depict or involve behaviors, such as weeping, frowning, skipping, and yelling, that are naturally expressive of emotions. In song, it is appropriate to think of the music and words as joined to give expression to the feelings of the character represented by the singer, though it would remain to explain what the music's contribution is. In the case of purely instrumental music, though, it is not clear that *anyone's* emotion is expressed, yet we experience the music as emotionally expressive. Instrumental musical works can be sad or joyful, calm or angry, though their being abstract entails that they are not representational, either of persons who experience the emotions expressed or of contexts that invite emotional reactions. (The same can be true of abstract works of painting and sculpture, but I will concentrate on the musical case in what follows.)

It might be held that musical expressiveness is subjective in the sense that different people can quite properly attribute different expressive properties to a musical piece without disagreeing. According to this view, it can be true for me that the music is sad and true for you that it is happy, and there is no other kind of truth for this matter. If this position is correct, music's expressiveness is not an objective property of it, and a philosophical account of the nature and basis of that expressiveness will have to focus as much or more on what is distinctive to the individual listener as on what is distinctive to the music. We should begin, then, by considering whether musical expressiveness is subjective or objective.

The evidence usually brought forward for the subjective nature of attributions of expressiveness to music draws attention to the lack of coincidence in different people's judgments about the expressiveness of individual pieces. Is this evidence conclusive?

For a start, we should discount as uninformed the judgments of people who are unfamiliar with the style of the music in question, or who are otherwise not well placed to appreciate the music. As was explained in chapter 4, a person who does not know a work's genre and the conventions, practices, and traditions it presupposes cannot easily locate the work or correctly identify its contents. If a listener is not situated to recognize and appreciate the work in what she hears, her reactions are not a reliable indicator of its qualities. When the responses of listeners who are not appropriately experienced with music of the kind in question have been put aside, how much variety in judgment remains? On the surface, there may be a great deal, but it is arguable that this appearance is misleading.

If music is very fine-grained in its expressiveness, slight contrasts in the emotional qualities attributed to the music will be indicative of disagreement. Those who think the expressiveness of purely instrumental music is fine-grained argue that this accounts for its ineffability; that is, for the difficulty we sometimes experience in trying to say precisely in words what it expresses. The composer Felix Mendelssohn made the point by stating that what music expresses is not too *in*definite to put into words but, on the contrary, too definite. The opposing position maintains that music expresses only broad categories of emotion, in which case there is no substantive difference indicated by judging variously that the music is sad, morose, grief-laden, gloomy, downcast, or miserable. It continues: what makes for the expressive uniqueness of individual works is not the specificity of the emotion expressed but the particularity of the musical means used to achieve its expression. There are many ways of expressing a given, general emotion in music. Therefore, differences between works by no means entail that those works express diverse, very specific emotions. It is not difficult to name the emotions expressed by music, though it can seem to be so if we mistakenly attempt to identify finer, more precise emotions than are there.

If we adopt the first view and regard music's expressiveness as fine-grained, we have to admit that listeners disagree among themselves about what it expresses. But if we take the second, the level of agreement is much higher, which may be a reason for favoring it.

As just observed, when the emotions expressed by music are identified at a rather general level, there is a great deal of intersubjective agreement about the expressiveness of musical works (as well as about emotions they could *not* be expressing). This agreement could be coincidental or could be the result of widespread indoctrination, perhaps, but a more likely suggestion is that it rests on the recognition of objective properties or powers of the music. That observers with good eyesight agree in daylight that healthy grass is green suggests that their experience of its color depends no less on objective properties or powers of the grass than on the (shared) nature of human perceptual capacities. I suggest that something similar holds for music's expressiveness. If one person thinks the music is sad and another hears grief in it, they do not really disagree. But if one person thinks the music is sad and another hears happiness in it, they do genuinely disagree and, unless a quite complicated story can be told – perhaps they are listening to very different performances of the same piece – at least one of them is wrong.

So, we are seeking an account of how music's expressiveness can be an objective property of it. Many – conflicting – theories have been proposed.

One view attempts to explain music's expressiveness as *associative*. Through being regularly associated with emotionally charged words or events, particular musical ideas become connected with emotions or moods. These are recalled later when the relevant passages, rhythms, or harmonies are employed in musically abstract pieces. Some of these associations can be individual, as when a song becomes linked for me to an emotionally significant but personal event. Other associations are more widely shared. Trumpets and drums, or snare drums and fifes, are associated with the excitement and danger of war, certain hymns go with funerals, protest songs evoke the 1960s, and so on. When they use appropriate tunes or instruments, composers can rely on such shared associations to impart a predictable, widely recognized expressiveness to their music.

There is no doubt that music can often invoke former contexts in which it was heard and the emotions with which they were infused. It seems very unlikely, though, that music's expressiveness is always associative in this way. One problem is the lack of sufficient specificity in the associations deemed relevant. As well as with war, trumpets and drums can be associated with many other things, such as smoky jazz cafes. Anyway, thoughts of war surely do not always recall a specific set of emotions:

for some they occasion nostalgia, for others sadness. The associations invoked are likely to tie the music to an era or movement, rather than to an emotion as such. Songs connected with wartime, such as *We'll meet again* (composed in Britain by Albert Parker and Hugh Charles in 1941), might instantly transport the hearer to the past, but that does not mean they are correlated with any particular emotion.

A more obvious point is that the most powerful connections between music and other contexts seem to rely on an expressiveness that the music contributes in its own right. Instead of music's being emotionally neutral but inheriting a tinge of expressiveness from its social setting, more often it adds its own affective character and thereby strengthens or complements the context's emotional profile. But in that case, the expressiveness it contributes is something it already possesses, not something it acquires by association. Music taken from Gustav Mahler's Fifth Symphony deepens the sadness of Luchino Visconti's film of Thomas Mann's story *Death in Venice*, while part of one of Mozart's C major piano concertos sets the tone (pastoral calm tinged with sad yearning) for Bo Widerberg's Swedish film *Elvira Madigan*. Surely the music was selected not because the directors thought it was charged with appropriate associations – after all, a majority of the audience's members would not have known these classical works – but rather because its expressive character chimed with the emotional effects the directors were trying to create in their films. In fact, where an association is produced, it can be to the music's detriment. When classical music is appropriated for its cheerfulness and joined to words advertising toothpaste, or when Beethoven's Ninth Symphony is used in Stanley Kubrick's movie of Anthony Burgess's novel *A Clockwork Orange*, it is the music and its expressiveness that suffer from the connection.

At this stage, the familiar move of identifying this or that person as the one whose emotions are given expression in the music can be tried. One view, known as the *expression theory*, holds that, if music is sad, this is because it stands to its composer's sadness as an expression of it. (This is a more specific theory than the general thesis, mentioned in chapter 8, that the creation of art involves some form of self-expression.)

Objections to this position are easy to come by. Compositions can take months or years to complete, and their composers no doubt ran the full gamut of emotions over the period. Composers have not been inhibited in writing sad requiems by their glee at receiving the commission for the work. Also, the act of expressing sadness by writing a symphony is a very sophisticated one, and while it is easy to see how an audience might read off the composer's feelings from the tears to which she gives way under the force of those feelings, the assumption that they do something similar when they hear sadness in the symphony requires more discussion. In other words, the act of musical composition is not expressive in a basic and transparent way, as tears are and so the manner in which the act of composition becomes expressive by resembling natural and easily under-stood forms of expressiveness is not obvious or clear.

Rejecting the expression theory does not entail denying that composers sometimes express their emotions in the music they write. They can deliberately set out to create a work that expresses their feelings by matching them. The act of expression, then, is closer to that of expressing one's feeling of sadness by carving a sad-looking facemask than by bursting into tears. The adjective *sad* is applied to the mask, not the carver, and it would remain appropriate even if the carver were happy, but where the mask has been made to mirror what the carver feels, it thereby expresses her emotion. (It remains, though, to explain how music can be sad-sounding, or the facemask sad-looking.) What is rejected is the expression theorist's proposed analysis of musical expressiveness, according to which what makes it true that the music is expressive is that it presents an emotion the composer felt.

A third view, called *emotivism* or the *arousal theory*, argues that what makes it true that the music is sad, say, is that it moves the hearer to sadness. (Or in a variant proposed by Derek Matravers, a British philoso-pher, it could be argued that the listener is moved to pity, which is an especially apt response to sadness.) To deal with cases in which conditions are not conducive or the listener is not able to follow the music, the theory could be revised to say that the music is sad if it *should* arouse such feelings in a suitable listener under appropriate conditions.

Again, objections come easily. Even when the auditor and conditions are ideal, the response is not inevitable. The listener might hope to cheer her mood by listening to happy music and fail, though she attends appropri-ately to the music. In another work, the listener might recognize and appreciate the music's sadness yet remain unmoved, or might instead feel admiration for the composer's skill in creating the expressive effects. Meanwhile, the arousal theory seems to get things back to front. We would normally think it is because the music is sad that it moves the listener, not that the listener's being moved is our basis for calling it sad. The response is not merely caused *by* the music, it is a response *to* the music and, specifically, to an expressive character we recognize in it.

Peter Kivy denies that sad music makes people feel sad, or that happy music makes them feel happy. Holding to this position entails claiming that many listeners are deeply confused about their responses to music, because they are inclined readily enough to describe their reaction as echoing the music's expressiveness. We need not go so far before rejecting the arousal theory, however. It can be accepted that audiences can be moved to feel what the music expresses. (It remains, though, to explain how music can be sad.) What is rejected is the arousal theorist's proposed analysis of musical expressiveness, according to which what makes it true that the music is expressive of an emotion is that it moves the listener to that emotion (or to another, which is an especially apt response to that emotion).

Here is a fourth tack. According to Jerrold Levinson and Jenefer Robinson, we hear expressiveness in music by experiencing the course of the music as a "story" about events or experiences undergone by a *hypothetical persona*. That is, we make believe of the unfolding of the music that it is an episode in the life of an imaginary person and on this basis judge what emotions that person must undergo. To aid us, the waxing and waning of tensions in the fabric of the music establish the *pattern* of the events that we imaginatively fill out.

One objection to this theory observes that many competent listeners who are sensitive to music's expressiveness are not conscious of playing this imaginative charade as they listen. Another is that the patterning of the music is insufficiently complex or precise to constrain the listener's imaginative engagement with the music. Of course, what is required is not that all listeners make believe the same story, but that they agree in their judgments about the music's expressiveness as a result of imagining whatever they do. But even then, there is reason to doubt that this coincidence in judgments should occur. One listener might hear anger expressed where another detects happiness and a third hears sexual ecstasy, because losing one's temper might be dynamically very like bursting with joy or sexual release. And again, one listener perceives changes in the moods of a single persona and tries to integrate them, where another hears irreconcilable differences between the emotions of a series of distinct personas, and a third imagines the case of a mother who thinks about the divergent personalities of her children.

It can be accepted that listeners sometimes adopt such modes of hypothetical listening in coming to grips with music's expressiveness. As a heuristic device, a listener might imagine of the music that it is about a person's reluctance to follow the path society has set down for her, and consider what then would be expressed. What I reject is the proposal that what makes it true that the music is expressive of an emotion is that the listener hears that emotion in it as a result of making believe that the music's progress tracks episodes in the life of an imagined persona.

The theories just considered seek an owner who feels the emotion to which the music gives expression – the composer, the listener, or a hypothetical persona. Perhaps we should focus more on the idea that the expressiveness resides in the music, without depending on anyone's feelings. In that case, we might regard talk of music's expressiveness as *metaphorical*, since music is not literally capable of feeling sadness and the like. But this is not a promising path to take. Even if we were convinced by analyses of *linguistic* metaphor, it is not clear how they could be applied to the idea that *music* is sad in a metaphorical way. And whereas metaphorical descriptions of music – for instance, as stormy, cold, or hard-edged – usually can be eliminated in favor of different ways of saying the same kind of thing, there are no adequate substitutes for expressive predicates. Technical analyses might explain how expressiveness is realized, but they do not mean the same. How, except with *sad* and its cognates, can we capture the feeling-tone of the slow movement of Mahler's Fifth Symphony? Finally, it is a characteristic of live metaphors that they are not recorded in dictionaries, but under *expression* one will find among the meanings listed "the depiction of feeling, movement, etc., in art; conveying of feeling in the performance of a piece of music." If the metaphor once was live, it died long ago, so talk of the musical expression of emotion is no less literal than talk of a home key, of notes being high and low, of melodic movement and pace, or of rivers having mouths and bottles necks.

The primary use of terms such as *happy* and *sad* is in relation to the experiences of people. Secondary uses of the same terms are common. These secondary uses may derive historically from the primary one but have become established so that they are no less literal. Where there is no question of sentience, such terms are used to attribute an expressive character to the appearance that something presents. In this vein, we describe willows as sad, some rock formations as exuberant, house and car fronts as presenting faces that are happy or sad, and facemasks as happy or sad. For that matter, we also talk of the expressive character of the appearance of creatures that are sentient and capable of experiencing emotion, but in the use under discussion we do so without regard to what they actually feel. We note that the basset hound has a sad-looking face and make this attribution as a description of the face's appearance, implying nothing about what the dog might be feeling (particularly so, given that dogs do not reveal sadness, when they feel it, through their facial expressions). We can also concern ourselves in a similar way with the expressive appearance of human faces, bodies, and comportments. A person's face can be sad-looking without her feeling the way her face looks, and we can be interested in describing her face's expressive character without inferring from that anything about what she feels. There is no contradiction expressed by saying *He always looks miserable but take no notice; usually he is in a happy mood.* So the claim here is that, when we describe music using terms that designate emotions, we are attributing *an expressive character to the sound it presents, without regard to what anyone feels.* If the attribution is justified, it is literally true in this secondary use of terms like *happy* and *sad* that the music's sound has a happy or sad character, just as it is literally true that the mask of comedy presents a happy appearance.

On what basis is this secondary use derived from the primary one in which emotional terms refer to experienced emotions? As was explained earlier, sometimes we can identify others' emotions in their behavior, bodily attitudes, and facial expressions, because these can be symptomatic of the inner, affective states they betray. The flavor of expressiveness lingers, however, when relevantly similar behaviors and bodily bearings occur in the absence of the appropriate feeling or emotion. In that case, the expressiveness attaches to the character of the behavior's appearance, though no felt emotion is expressed or betrayed. In this way, the previously described secondary use of emotion terms, in which they identify emotion characteristics in appearances, trades on their primary use, in which they refer to experienced emotions and feelings. What grounds the secondary use is a resemblance to behavior or to bodily poses that, were an emotion being expressed, would easily be recognized as giving expression to it. The face of a basset hound looks the way a person's face would look if that person were sad and showing it.

In the case of music, what resemblances might be relevant? One possibility is that the form of music maps the dynamic structure of the physiological patterning of emotions. Another is that music is experienced as resembling expressive human utterance or vocalizations. A third, I think more plausible, suggestion is that the movement of music is experienced in the same way that bodily bearings or comportments indicative of a person's emotional states are. In other words, music is experienced as dynamic, as are human action and behavior. And when music is experienced as like behaviors presenting characteristic appearances of emotion, it is experienced as similar to the behaviors not only in its dynamic profile but also in its expressive profile. Just as happy people move in a fashion that is energetic, fast, and sprightly, so does happy music, and just as sad people move slowly, as if weighed down with care, so does sad music. Harmonic and textural clarity go with happy music, while harmonic density and unresolved tension go with sad music, and again, these are experienced as resembling the outward-directed openness and enthusiasm with which happy people greet the world and the inward self-absorption and gloom that misery brings on.

Though I take this account to be the most credible of those considered in this section, it also faces objections. Some people deny experiencing the resemblances just mentioned, though they recognize the music's expressiveness. Also, this account replaces expressiveness as such with the presentation of expressive appearances, and it might be doubted that these are as compelling or valuable as music's expressiveness is usually thought to be. One option for addressing this last concern is to emphasize the role of the composer in the process. Whereas human appearances that have an expressive character without giving expression to an experienced emotion are thoughtlessly fallen into on most occasions, music's expressiveness is deliberately contrived by its composer. As such, it may play a role in a communicative act, and it is always appropriate to consider if the music tells us anything about the emotions whose expressive appearances it presents. The composer harnesses music's expressive potential and what she does with it is likely to be significant, whereas the sad aspect presented as an accident of nature by willow trees calls for little by way of response or appreciation.

6.5   The Emotional Response of the Audience to the Work of Art

We now consider the audience's emotional responses to artworks. There are a number of respects in which these might be problematic. Here the focus falls on three specific issues. People do not believe fictional worlds are actual, but if they do not believe them to exist, apparently they have no reason to respond emotionally to the characters, events, attitudes, and places they contain. Also, some works of art, such as tragedies, prompt a negative response, yet people seek them out and return to them. Third, why do people respond emotionally to music's expressiveness if the music is not the intentional object of their response? That is, why do people feel sad on hearing sad music if they are not sad *about* the music?

6.5.1 Responding to fictions

Most emotions involve commitments about and attitudes toward their intentional objects, including the belief that the object exists. To be frightened by a lion, I have to believe that it poses a threat and also, of course, that it exists. If I learn that the shadow that frightened me is made not by an intruder but by a tailor's dummy, my fear disappears. Many works of art present made-up stories and are known to do so by their audiences. Understanding that Anna Karenina exists only as a character in the fictional world of Tolstoy's novel, and, hence, that no such person threw herself under a train in reality, still we pity her. Even where a story fictionalizes events, settings, and people borrowed from the actual world, awareness of their reality is not a prerequisite for responding emotionally to them. For example, the plot of Thomas Pynchon's novel *Gravity's Rainbow* (1973) revolves around Germany's use at the close of World War II of bombs transported supersonically by rockets, but the reader need not know that this in fact occurred as a requirement for engaging with his story. In other words, our responses to the characters and events in fictions appear to be indifferent to our beliefs about those characters' existence, whereas this is not the case typically when we respond to what is (or might be, or will be) in the actual world. In other words, many of the emotions audiences have regarding what they know to be fictional stories do not seem to depend on whether they believe, as opposed merely to entertaining, what the story tells. How can sense be made of this?

A number of attempted solutions to this paradox plainly fail. It is not that we feel for some real substitute for the character in the fiction. Even if we feel pity for women who have been murdered by their jealous husbands, when we watch *Othello*, it is Desdemona, not these actual victims, who is the focus of our pity. And it is not that we forget the fictional status of the character. If we did, we should attempt to rescue Desdemona, not continue watching the play. As to the suggestion that we *suspend our disbelief* – or to use more modern jargon, that we *put off-line our belief in the non-existence of the character* – this probably is true but does not explain how the response survives given that, via this process, we do not replace our disbelief with the appropriate emotion-relevant beliefs.

A first possibility is that it is not true that emotions always involve cognitive attitudes, such as belief. Some emotional episodes are triggered automatically and thoughtlessly, probably because they occur under circumstances in which it is better to react reflexively than to reflect and then act on that basis later. The emotional reaction can be automatic because it is hard-wired by evolution or because of environmental conditioning, but in either case it circumvents the higher cognitive centers. As such, it is *non-rational*, not irrational.

Even if we take the general point, this line does not deal convincingly with the problem at issue. Not all emotions are cognitively complex or involve conscious judgment, but it is very plausible that responses to what are known to be fictions must be cognitively sophisticated. The business of imaginatively entering into the world of a fiction – for instance, of knowing which beliefs should be suspended and which should be entertained, so we appreciate that the carbon-based alien life-forms must nourish themselves, even if this is not discussed, while we are not surprised to learn they share a group mind – involves a deep familiarity with relevant conventions for fictional types and a subtle grasp of how and to what purpose they are used. The appropriate response will be one based on following elaborate physical, social, and interpersonal arrangements many of which may be unique to the world of the fiction in question. The emotional response to a fiction is founded on insight and understanding. Even if some kind or degree of brainless, gut reaction is involved, this must be subject to cognitive processing and evaluation before it could form part of an emotional response that is sensitive to a fiction as such.

Another proposal, made by Colin Radford, a British philosopher, is that the response is *irrational*, not non-rational. Without belief we have no reason to respond, yet we do. To soften the blow, we can remind ourselves that irrationality of this kind is all too human. It is apparent in phobias, where no amount of information about the harmlessness of the object of the phobia wipes away the dread of that object. And on a more mundane level, a golfer will issue verbal instructions to his golf ball and use body-language to try to affect its trajectory, though he knows that, once struck, its course cannot be guided by such means. We all sometimes address inanimate objects as if they might be swayed by threats or sweet reason, while we know perfectly well that this cannot be.

The views that emotional responses to fictional characters are non-rational or irrational must be inadequate if such responses are indicative of, or even required for, the sensitive appreciation of works of fiction. Usually, we take a person's emotional responses to fictions as revealing her comprehension of the story. She pities Anna Karenina and feels that her death is tragic because she recognizes Anna's circumstances and the significance of the social and personal pressures that draw her to her fate. But if this pity is non-rational or irrational, it comes unbidden, or anyway, independently of the reader's following with understanding what happens in the world of the fiction. Moreover, these theories are at odds with the idea that at least part of the value of fictional works comes from the way they contrive to lead us to new insights and understandings by stimulating our emotions and thereby involving us in the world of the work.

Any alternative account that saves the audience from the charge of non-rationality or irrationality would be preferable, then. Two theories that do so refer to the role of *make-belief* and *make-desire* in the experience of fiction. According to the first, make-belief can play an equivalent role to belief in securing an emotional response to its object. As Noël Carroll reminds us, simply imagining an event, such as having one's fingernails pulled out or finding oneself in the arms of the Hollywood star one most desires, can be sufficient to provoke an emotional reaction. Indeed, we often respond emotionally to future possibilities that may never be realized. As the seventeenth-century philosopher Thomas Hobbes put it, humans are *famished by future hunger*. Hope and dread are always forward-looking and never directed solely at what we believe to exist. Emotions do presuppose cognitive attitudes directed at their objects, but thoughts entertained without belief, not just beliefs, can supply these. By contrast, the second theory, put forward by the American philosopher Kendall L. Walton, accepts that the presence of a belief in the existence of its object is essential for something's being an emotion. According to his theory, the feelings produced by fictions are not emotions as such, though they may have much in common at the physiological and experiential level with emotions. He calls these responses *fictional emotions* (and their physio-logical accompaniments *quasi-emotions*), meaning not that they are merely imagined as opposed to vividly experienced but that they occur in the context of an engagement with the fiction that is based on make-belief rather than belief. So, we do not really pity Anna Karenina. What we feel is pity-in-a-fictional-context, which is similar to but is not a fully fledged emotion.

Both these positions explain why our responses do not issue in the usual object-directed actions, such as warning a character who appears to be unaware of the danger of her situation, because make-belief operates independently of the kind of practical reasoning that bridges the gap from belief and desire on the one side to action on the other. Make-belief and make-desire parallel belief and desire, and use much of the same brain architecture, but they cut the close ties that bind belief and desire to action. Also, both theories can explain why emotional responses tend to be more muted and transitory when they are directed at fictional, not real, characters. Fictions usually impress themselves on the imagination with less urgency and power than that with which reality impacts on belief.

Yet another view argues that we have the relevant beliefs even when we are dealing with fictions. According to the English philosopher Alex Neill, what we need to believe is that Anna Karenina suffers, and, as we know, she does suffer in the world of the story. In other words, *pity presupposes the belief that someone suffers but does not require the further belief that the suffering takes place in the actual world*. Just as my fear evaporates when I learn there is no threatening intruder, my fear for one of the characters in a movie also disappears when it is revealed in the film that the shadow of an apparent intruder is that of a tailor's dummy. It is not true, then, that the shadow poses a danger in the fictional world. But if the movie portrays a dangerous intruder, the situation is different. I can fear on behalf of inhabitants of the movie's fictional world, because it is true in the fiction that they can be harmed by dangerous intruders. Similarly, my desire that the characters be saved is genuine, though it is directed at a fictional world rather than the actual one.

My belief that I am outside the fictional world of the movie rules out the possibility that I am frightened for myself, because I know that the intruder in the fictional world cannot interact with this one, thereby posing a threat to me. Video arcade games are interactive, though, and then I can fear for myself to the extent that I am also a character in the fiction that is enacted.

If the response to a fiction involves ordinary belief and desire, why do we not act on our feelings? The answer is that we realize that usually we cannot. I can intervene only if I can become an inhabitant of the fictional world. In an interactive video game, I might set out to rescue one of the fictional characters, but in other cases I cannot enter the world of the fiction because I cannot become a character within it. I can jump to the stage and interpose myself between the *actors* who play Othello and Desdemona, thereby interrupting their performance, but nothing I do can make it true in the fictional world of the play that Desdemona is saved. This parallels the real-world case in which one pities the climbers trapped in a blizzard on the peak but does nothing to rescue them because one's doing so is not practically possible. And one can pity the fifteenth-century victims of the Spanish Inquisition, though there is nothing that can be done now about what happened to them. In these instances, that one does not act does not mean that one does not have the desires relevant to a response of pity. It indicates only that one knows one lacks the ability to intervene. But if the feelings evoked by fictions involve the same beliefs and desires, why are they less strong or persistent than ones occasioned by events in the actual world? In reply, it can be denied that there is a consistent difference of the kind that is assumed. Emotions differ greatly in their strength and duration. Sometimes a person feels pity for the victims of tragedy as the newsreader tells of another earthquake, plane crash, or famine, but her feeling is not always acute and may be soon forgotten. Meanwhile, the emotions she experiences in conjunction with art sometimes are intense, overwhelming, and life-changing. I wager that more tears are spilled in movies and operas than in front of television documentaries.

If it is true that people can be frightened not only for the characters in horror movies but for themselves, despite the gap they recognize between the fictional world and the one they occupy, the account just offered is not universally adequate. Indeed, perhaps it applies only to the emotion of pity, and not to some of the other emotional responses we may have to fictions. If so, this should not surprise us. There is no reason to assume one theory will cover all possible cases, especially given the lack of uniformity among emotions. It may be that one theory is best for some contexts and kinds of response, whereas another applies to others.

6.5.2 Responding to tragedies

Why do we seek out and return to artworks that are saddening or harrowing, such as tragedies and tales of terror? We have no duty to do so. Our interest in art usually is self-motivated and rewarding for its own sake. We enjoy art, and this includes tragedies. But how can it be that we actually enjoy the negative experiences to which such works give rise?

Some theorists respond by denying the unpleasantness of the response. One such is the eighteenth-century Scottish philosopher David Hume. He claims that the eloquence of the story *transforms* the experience into a positive one. It is not that the pleasure we take in the narrative or drama *compensates* for the grief its contents cause us, but that grief is *converted* to something that is not unpleasant to experience. Berys Gaut (another British philosopher, as it happens, but a contemporary one) takes a different line: what is unenjoyable about such experiences when we have them in real-world situations is not how they *feel* but the *actions and consequences* they lead to. In the case of art, where there are no consequences or behavioral responses called for, we can savor the experience alone. When we do so we find it is not unpleasant after all. Another alternative suggests that we are all *masochists*, and take pleasure in our own suffering. The fact is, though, that masochists are a pathological minority.

These various theories are unconvincing if the response is unpleasant, as it often seems undeniably to be. For most people, it is extremely harrowing to witness enactments of the crushing depression of Alban Berg's opera, *Wozzeck*, the blind inhumanity of war in the film *For King and Country* directed by Joseph Losey, the injustice of political oppression in Aldous Huxley's novel *Brave New World*, and the unredeemable murders, rapes, mutilations, tortures, and mayhem that are featured in works such as Shakespeare's *Titus Andronicus* and Bret Easton Ellis's novel *American Psycho*. If so, it is false that a comprehending, sensitive experience of such works is not unpleasant.

A similar objection applies to the suggestion that, because they lack consequences in the actual world, exposure to such fictions is not as negative as the real thing would be. That observation, if true, does not explain or justify why we knowingly attend such works. The experience of them is bad enough, even if worse ones are possible, and why do we pursue any negative experiences that we can choose to avoid? There is no shortage of entertaining comedies. Why take an interest in tragedies at all?

A plausible reply to this question argues that tragedies also provide experiences with positive value that outweigh and *compensate for* the negative ones. Hume was right to observe that we can take pleasure in the skill with which the story is crafted, and in following subtleties of the plot, the wit of allusions, and the rest. To the extent that the benefits are independent of the negative experience, however, compensatory explanations always are open to the objection previously given: namely, that we should always prefer works that provide the same kinds and degrees of good experiences without the drawback of accompanying negative ones, but we do not in fact do so.

A stronger position maintains that tragedies provide valuable, positive experiences that other artforms cannot, and that this is because *their negative aspects are an integral part of the larger whole that is good*. In terms of a familiar slogan, we cannot get the gain without the pain. We tolerate, or even welcome, the negative because it is a central element in a larger package that is good and that provides an overall positive experience.

Different stories can now be told about what benefits are organically connected to the negative experiences that are also involved. According to the ancient Greek philosopher, Aristotle, tragedies are valued for providing catharsis, in which feelings are purged by being released. If the full benefits of catharsis are achieved only with the purging of negative, not merely positive, emotions, negative experiences are unavoidable for the person seeking the benefits of emotional purification via elimination. A different account is presented by Susan Feagin, a contemporary American philosopher. She argues that the negative response provides the occasion for another, higher-order reaction that is positive. Sometimes a person reacts emotionally to her own emotions, as when she feels ashamed for feeling angry, say. In the case of tragedy, Feagin says, we reflect on and respond to the fact that we react negatively to what is evil, terrifying, and disgusting in the tragedy. That self-aware response is positive, because we are reassured that we have the right moral values, care about what matters, and answer pain and suffering with sensitivity and compassion. It is only by reacting negatively in the first instance that we can go on to arrive at the affirmation of our good character and moral rectitude.

The story need not be so elaborate. There is much to understand and appreciate in art. This can concern the detail of the contribution made by expressive, narrative, and other elements to its overall structure and unity, to the influences on it and the references it makes, to the creative techniques it displays, to its connections to the artist and the times in which it was made, and to lessons it teaches more generally about life and its vicissitudes, about human nature, about virtue and vice. Elements calling for negative responses can contribute vitally to all or any of these sources of aesthetic value. We will not harvest the richest rewards art has to offer if we always shun works that elicit unenjoyable feelings, or if we always close our eyes to or skip over the nasty bits, because the value runs all the way down to the treatment of details. Recognizing the value of the whole involves appreciating how it is formed from all the elements that comprise it or contribute to its being how it is.

There is a parallel here between art and life. A life lived to the full cannot avoid confrontation with pain, sorrow, and loss. The life led by a person who pursues only pleasure and shuns everything that might make her feel uncomfortable or unhappy will strike most others as shallow and unfulfilled. And eventually she will fail to keep the world at bay, and then may not be able to save herself. The deepest satisfactions come not from clinging to the small pleasures of the easy path but from mustering the grace and courage to face the challenges and difficulties that come the way of anyone willing to commit to occupations, associations, and values that foster love, dignity, respect, and the realization of human potential, both for themselves and others. And this applies to everything, not just the life-threatening or serious stuff. It applies to playing the guitar, to cooking, and to gardening, not only to getting married or to having a cancer operation. Why should we expect the rewards of art always to come faster and cheaper than those of life itself? Why would we be more inclined to duck the negative in art, given that the potential rewards are high, than we are to do the same when we strive to get on the sports team?

These last observations suggest we should question the assumption that it is pleasure, or pleasure alone, that motivates us to take an interest in art. Art is a deep source of satisfaction, undoubtedly, but that satisfaction is often of the kind that goes with overcoming challenges and difficulties, or with achieving understanding and knowledge. It may be a mistake to equate this with pleasure, especially if we think of pleasure in terms of sensuous delight, such as one might get from a cold beer on a hot day or from a fine cheese at the close of a meal. Given the way the world is, and art's connection to that, it would be silly to think the satisfaction we derive from art fits easily under the heading of pleasure, and not surprising, therefore, that we are prepared sometimes to face what is unpleasant in seeking the pay-off art can provide. These are matters to which we return in chapter 8.

6.5.3   Responding to the expressiveness of instrumental music and abstract art

Here is a further problem. When a person feels sad and shows it, her emotions can be powerfully evocative of emotions in others. They are likely to feel pity or compassion, to desire to help or comfort her, and so on. This reaction comes, of course, from our empathic realization that she suffers. Other things being equal, we will sympathize with her suffering and want it to end.

Now, there are two things to note about this common state of affairs. The response differs in its character from the emotional expression to which it is a reaction. Sometimes one emotion typically arouses a given other: usually sadness calls for sympathy, anger for fear. Sometimes a variety of responses is possible, as when a person's exuberant triumph makes her mother feel proud, her rival feel bitter, and her life-coach wish she could be less exaggerated in her reactions. Either way, we do not usually expect the reactive response to echo the emotion that is its object. (Obviously, though, this can happen; I might respond to your anger with my own.) The second point is that the responder typically must believe that the other person genuinely feels the emotion she seems to be expressing. I will sympathize with your sadness only if I think it is not pretended, and I will sympathize with Anna Karenina's sadness and despair only if I think it is true in the story that she experiences those feelings.

This is the puzzle: people find the expressiveness of instrumental musical pieces and other abstract artworks highly evocative of emotional responses, yet they do not believe or make believe that the work (or anything else) experiences the emotions that are presented. Moreover, the standard response in such cases is to mirror what the artwork expresses. Happy music tends to make people feel happy and sad music to make them sad. Can we explain the nature of this response without having to concede that it is aberrant and irrational?

The earlier discussion anticipated some possible replies. It could be denied, as Kivy does, that people ever act in the way just described. This view need not deny the propriety of every emotional response the audience might have. A listener might be sad about the performance because it is inept, or might be ravished by the music's beauty, or might admire the composer's skill in making it expressive as it is. These responses are all unproblematic, because the auditor has beliefs about the music that make them suitable. But where the relevant beliefs are absent, so too is the response, according to this position. If a person does not believe the music suffers the sadness presented in it, he never responds by feeling sad. The main problem for this theory is that so many listeners believe that sometimes they are moved by music's happiness or sadness to feel corresponding emotions.

An alternative holds that there is someone about whom I am sad in such cases, namely, the person whose feelings of sadness are given expression in the music. For the emotivist, this is the composer or performer. For the theorist who advocates that the music expresses the feelings of a person it is hypothesized as depicting, the listener is sad for the persona whose feelings of sadness are given expression in the music. Again, the problem is that many music lovers do not believe the music expresses the composer's feelings, or make believe that it expresses those of an imagined persona, before they respond to its expressiveness.

The arousalist approaches the issue this way: the music does evoke the response and it is on that basis we judge it to be sad. Arousal of the response does not require or involve the listener's believing or imagining that anyone experiences the emotion that is expressed. The listener is not sad *about* the music (or anything else), but she is saddened *by* the music, and the course of her feeling is controlled by and answerable to the music's progress, which she should track attentively. The hard part for arousalism now comes in explaining why an emotional response is evoked at all and what makes the response one of sadness or whatever, given that it is not directed to the usual objects for sadness and involves none of the beliefs that would usually motivate a sad response. If emotions cannot be individuated solely in terms of their feeling-tone, the arousalist may have no answer.

Here the theory according to which the listener's sad response echoes a sadness presented in the music's sound fares better, because it holds that the music already presents expressive appearances and the listener can recognize her own reaction as resonating with those. Still, that mirroring response is not *about* the music, even if it is *to* it, and the usual emotion-relevant beliefs are missing. At this stage one might appeal to the possibility that the listener's emotional response falls nearer the non-cognitive end of the scale, so the absence of the relevant beliefs does not prevent the emotion's occurrence. Not all emotions involve the cognitive attitudes of belief or make-belief. And this suggestion is plausible in light of psychologists' experiments showing that people can often be subject to a kind of expressive contagion or osmosis, in which they unthinkingly catch the expressive tone or mood of their surroundings. The same may happen when sad music, attended to as such, tends to make people feel sad. A person who does not react that way is not thereby cruel or callous, as he would be if he were unmoved by another's sadness. Nevertheless, it is natural enough to come without calculation or reflection to share the emotional ambience of one's environment.

This explains why the response is non-cognitive, why it mirrors its cause, and why it is not about anything (though it requires close attention throughout to the music and its expressiveness). One difficulty remains. Earlier it was suggested that the emotional response to art is far too sophisticated to be analyzed in terms of non-cognitive models of the emotion. That point was made, though, in discussing our reactions to complex narratives and the lives of the fictional characters who inhabit them. In the case of abstract art that presents the appearance of emotions but no semantic or symbolic content to go with this, a more basic reaction can be suitable. Besides, that primitive, initial response can always be subject to scrutiny, evaluation, and subsequent refinement. The problem was to explain how the objectless response could arise at all, not to justify it as always the most appropriate or sophisticated that can be given.

Questions

6.1 Is there an inconsistency in wishing both that Romeo and Juliet (the lovers) not die and that *Romeo and Juliet* (the play) be done as Shakespeare created it?

6.2 Is it irrational or non-rational to be moved by non-representational art expressive of sadness, since no one suffers the sadness it expresses?

6.3 Is it irrational or non-rational to pity people who are now dead and thereby are beyond suffering? Is it comparatively more or less rational to pity fictional characters?

6.4 Is the experience of horror movies pleasant?

6.5 Is it possible to be frightened of being harmed by a fictional character? Is it possible to fall in love with a fictional character, to be jealous of a fictional character, or to envy a fictional character her wealth and talents?

6.6 If a person listens to an expressive musical work and does not respond, must this mean she did not follow it with understanding? If a person listens to an expressive musical work with understanding and does not respond, would this show a moral defect? If a person watches *Othello* and does not respond, must this mean she did not follow it with understanding? If a person watches *Othello* with understanding, would she show a moral defect if she did not respond emotionally?

6.7 Can an artist create an expressive work without at some time having felt what it expresses? Can an artist create an expressive work without feeling what it expresses as part of the creative process? Can a performer create a plausible interpretation of an expressive work without at some time having felt what it expresses? Can a performer create a plausible interpretation of an expressive work without feeling what it expresses during the performance?

6.8 In what ways can it be easier and in what ways harder to learn what a fictional character feels than to learn what another person feels?

6.9 How can a person's emotional reactions to an artwork provide evidence for what she understands and appreciates, or does not understand and appreciate, about it? Does the answer to the last question depend on the nature of the artwork; for instance, on whether it is factual, fictional, or abstract?

Readings

A useful collection is *Emotion and the Arts*, edited by M. Hjort and S. Laver (Oxford: Oxford University Press, 1997). Among many relevant chapters, it contains Jerrold Levinson's "Emotion in Response to Art: A Survey of the Terrain" (pp. 20–34), which reviews several of the problems and theories discussed in this chapter. Peter Lamarque's views on the place of emotions in the appreciation of literature are outlined in "Tragedy and Moral Value," in *Art and its Messages*, edited by S. Davies (University Park: Pennsylvania State University Press, 1997), 59–69.

For an overview of theories of how emotions are expressed in music, see Stephen Davies, "Philosophical Perspectives on Music's Expressiveness," in *Themes in the Philosophy of Music* (Oxford: Oxford University Press, 2003), 169–91, which favors the position that music is expressive because we experience it as presenting appearances resembling those with which humans display their emotions, and Jerrold Levinson's "Musical Expressiveness," in *The Pleasures of Aesthetics* (Ithaca: Cornell University Press, 1996), 90–125, which prefers the "hypothetical persona" theory, according to which we hear the music as expressing the feelings of a person we imagine as the subject of the musical "narrative." Jenefer Robinson's "The Expression and Arousal of Emotion in Music," *JAAC* 52 (1994), 13–22, and her *Deeper than Reason: Emotion and its Role in Literature, Music, and Art* (Oxford: Oxford University Press, 2005), offer another variant of the "hypothetical persona" position.

For critical discussion of the theory that, for an artwork to be expressive, it must be a direct expression of an emotion experienced by the artist, see Alan Tormey's *The Concept of Expression* (Princeton: Princeton University Press, 1971), especially 97–124. Derek Matravers defends a sophisticated version of the arousal theory of musical expressiveness in his *Art and Emotion* (Oxford: Clarendon Press, 1998), 145–203.

Among the fullest accounts of literature and fiction, including discussion of many of the issues raised here, are *Truth, Fiction, and, Literature: A Philosophical Perspective* (Oxford: Clarendon Press, 1994) by Peter Lamarque and Stein Haugom Olsen, and *Mimesis as Make-Believe: On the Foundations of the Representational Arts* (Cambridge, MA: Harvard University Press, 1990) by Kendall L. Walton. A classic discussion of emotional responses to fictions is Walton's "Fearing Fictions," *Journal of Philosophy* 75 (1978), 5–27. Because they are not accompanied by the relevant beliefs, Walton denies that responses to fictions are full-blooded emotions. Among those who argue that belief is not necessary, because make-belief can replace it in playing the role of securing the emotion to its object, are Noël Carroll in *The Philosophy of Horror or Paradoxes of the Heart* (New York: Routledge, 1990), 60–88, and Lamarque in *Fictional Points of View* (Ithaca: Cornell University Press, 1996), 113–34. By contrast, Alex Neill thinks we do have the requisite beliefs, at least in the case of pitying a fictional character. See his "Fiction and the Emotions," *American Philosophical Quarterly* 30 (1993), 1–13. In this he disagrees with Colin Radford, who judges such responses to be normal but irrational. For the exchange of views, see Radford's "How Can We Be Moved by the Fate of Anna Karenina?," *Proceedings of the Aristotelian Society* supp. vol. 49 (1975), 67–80, and "Fiction, Pity, Fear, and Jealousy," *JAAC* 53 (1995), 71–5, and Neill's "Emotional Responses to Fiction: Reply to Radford," *JAAC* 53 (1995), 75–8. A fine summary of philosophers' theories on the rationality or otherwise of responding emotionally to fictional characters is presented by Berys Gaut in "Reason, Emotions, and Fictions," in *Imagination, Philosophy, and the Arts*, edited by M. Kieran and D. McIver Lopes (London: Routledge, 2003), 15–34.

David Hume's "Of Tragedy" is published in his *Essays Moral, Political, and Literary*, (1741–2), edited by E. F. Miller (revised edn., Indianapolis: Liberty Classics, 1987). Aristotle mentions the beneficial cathartic effects of tragedy in his *Poetics*, edited by D. W. Lucas (revised edn., Oxford: Clarendon Press, 1972). In "The Pleasures of Tragedy," *American Philosophical Quarterly* 20 (1983), 95–104, Susan Feagin argues that we respond positively to what is revealed of our character and values by our capacity to experience tragedies in a negative fashion. For a lively exchange on why we are attracted by works – in this case, horror stories – that we know are likely to induce negative responses, see Carroll's *The Philosophy of Horror*, especially 178–95, and his "Enjoying Horror Fictions: A Reply to Gaut,"

BJA 35 (1995), 67–72, and also Gaut's "The Paradox of Horror," *BJA* 33 (1993), 333–45 and "The Enjoyment Theory of Horror: A Response to Carroll," *BJA* 35 (1995), 284–9.

Peter Kivy argues that sad music does not tend to make people feel sad, in "Feeling the Musical Emotions," *BJA* 39 (1999), 1–13. For the contrary view, see Stephen Davies's *Musical Meaning and Expression* (Ithaca: Cornell University Press, 1994), 279–320. Jerrold Levinson considers why we can be drawn to music that makes us feel sad in "Music and Negative Emotion," in *Music, Art, and Metaphysics* (Ithaca: Cornell University Press, 1990), 306–35.

Chapter Seven

Pictorial Representation and the Visual Arts

The topic of this chapter is the nature of pictorial representation. As well as analyzing some theories of representation and discussing what is distinctive to art painting, we also reflect on similarities and differences between handmade pictures (paintings, drawings, etchings, prints etc.) and photographs.

Sometimes the notion of representation is applied rather broadly to paintings. They are occasionally described as representing what they express or what they conventionally symbolize. For example, it might be said of a picture both that it represents hope and that it represents peace as a dove. In addition, paintings are sometimes said to represent parts of their content, such as relations involving colors and forms, the flatness of a painting's surface, or the materiality of paint. If a yellow square seems to stand out against a brown ground in an abstract painting, the two-dimensional form is presented in a three-dimensional pictorial space. (Kasimir Malevich, the Russian exponent of the movement in twentieth-century abstract art called Suprematism, created pictures that feature such effects.) Some people regard such works as not only showing three-dimensionality but also as representing spatiality or spatial relations.

Even if we should adopt an inclusive account of pictorial representation, it can be argued that equating representation with expression, which was the topic of chapter 6, serves only to obscure important differences between them and that pictorial representation similarly should be distinguished from symbolism more generally. Also, when the viewer's attention is drawn to some perceptible effect, it is not always helpful to regard the work as representing what is noticed. Though I accept that some pictorial representations are not of familiar objects – as when Paul Klee "takes a line for a walk," to use his words – for convenience the discussion in this chapter will focus on the paradigm for *pictorial representation*: namely, that in which recognizable (though possibly fictional) items, events, or scenes are pictured. In other words, we will concentrate on what is sometimes called *figurative* representation.

Note that not all pictorial representations are artworks. Sketches showing police suspects, political cartoons, and drawn advertisements typically are not. Also, not all pictures are representational. However broadly we construe the notion of pictorial representation, some abstract paintings surely are to be regarded as not at all representational.

We begin with an analysis of representation in paintings. Though it is only partial, it indicates a basis for delineating the class of pictorial representations. That leaves the task of considering if there is a use or manner of depiction that distinguishes the artworks from the non-artworks within that class. This leads to discussions of painterly style and, in comparing paintings to photographs, of the role of intention and control within art.

7.1   The Experience of Representation

Only a very few paintings could be mistaken for their subjects, and then only for a short time provided it is possible to come close to the painted surface. Some paintings, often in the form of still lifes of food and drink, are called *trompe l'œil* pictures. Many of these were painted in the seventeenth century, especially in the Netherlands. The title is misleading in implying that their aim is to deceive the eye, which they rarely do for long. Instead, the primary purpose of such works is to display technical skill by the degree of realism they attain. To be appreciated, such works must be seen as difficult-to-make representations, not mistaken for their subjects. (Contemporary paintings that imitate the textureless continuity of photographic images, so that they do not look handmade, are similar. American artists famous for their photo-realistic style of painting include Richard Estes and Audrey Flack.) By contrast, the marks that do the representing in the majority of paintings are no less apparent than the subject that is pictured. Indeed, in works by Impressionists, such as Claude Monet, the represented subject *disappears* when one approaches too near the canvas. At close range, all one sees are different colored patches, splodges, and points of paint. Also, caricatures and line drawings of stick men are too unlike their subjects to be mistaken for them.

For these reasons, theories that regard pictorial representation on the model of *illusion* are not convincing. An acceptable account of representation must accommodate the viewer's awareness of the marked surface, of the work's subject, and of a connection between the two.

Figure 7.1   Two-Js face

Let me introduce the next theory of pictorial representation by asking you to look carefully at figure 7.1. This can be seen either as two uppercase Js or as a face. Some people have difficulty seeing the face. (To do so, view the bar of the top J as eyebrows and the hook as a nose. See the bar of the bottom J as the line of a mouth and the hook as a chin.) Indeed, if the Js in figure 7.1 occurred in handwritten words listed vertically – say,

Ian		ADVICE
Jack	*or*	ADJECTIVE
Jill		ENJOY
Ken		ENDURE

it is unlikely the face would be noticed. If you did not see the face earlier, the sudden awareness of the face as you reconfigure the elements in the perceptual field comes as the dawning of an aspect. You should now be able to shift at will between seeing figure 7.1 as a face or as two vertically aligned capital Js. This phenomenon is called *aspect perception* or *seeing as*. A common suggestion holds that pictorial representation rests on the viewer's seeing the marked surface of the painting *as* what the painting pictures; that is, the surface of the painting presents the visual aspect of its subject.

There are several problems with this account. Many very realistic pictures do not require the kind of imaginative effort that was just described. With them, it is not clear that the painted surface can be seen independently of or prior to recognizing what is represented. Also, the subjects of such pictures are rarely ambiguous in the way that the examples typically used to illustrate aspect perception are. In addition, the experience of perceiving one aspect of a figure excludes, while it lasts, the recognition of other aspects. When a person sees lines and marks as a schematic face she does not see them as letters, and when she sees the same lines and marks as letters she does not see the face. With the vast majority of representational paintings, however, the viewer is *simultaneously* aware of the picture's subject and of its marked surface.

In an attempt to remedy such difficulties, the British philosopher Richard Wollheim proposes that representation involves not seeing *as* but seeing *in*. We see the picture's subject *in* the painted surface and are simultaneously aware of both. Wollheim refers to the twofoldness of the experience as characteristic of representations.

Whether Wollheim's terminological finesse maps a genuine difference corresponding to two, distinct perceptual modes is disputable, though. And it can be doubted that all awareness of pictorial representation is twofold, though much is. (As mentioned above, some artists display their prowess by achieving a realism that removes the viewer's simultaneous awareness of the work's surface. Wollheim denies that skillful *trompe l'œil* pictures are representations at all, but that saves his theory at the cost of making the notion of pictorial representation unacceptably narrow.) Finally, even if Wollheim's account is correct as far as it goes, it does not yet address the further requirement listed above: that the theory account for the *connection* between our twofold awareness of the picture's subject and of the surface in which this is seen.

A different theory is offered by Kendall L. Walton, who suggests that a person viewing a representational picture makes believe that his seeing of it is a seeing of what it represents. He imagines of his looking at the designed surface of the picture that it is a looking at the picture's subject.

Like the others, this hypothesis faces objections. As already noted, no acts of imagination or make-believe seem to be involved in perceiving the subjects of many realistic paintings. What is more, it is hard to understand how such imaginings could succeed without the collaboration of the picture, such that its subject is perceptible in it. In other words, this account seems to presuppose that (rather than explain how) we can recognize a picture's subject. As a result, it looks as if Walton's theory requires the support of a view like Wollheim's. But Walton does try to explain how the viewer connects the painted surface to the work's subject;

namely, via imagining certain things about the perceptual acts that are undertaken.

Suppose we harness Wollheim's and Walton's analyses together, do we get a theory of pictorial representation that will run? This is doubtful. Neither theory seems consistent with the way we experience the representational character of highly realistic pictures. And for the remainder of cases, though these theories explain what it is like to see representational art as representational, and the possible role of make-belief in bringing about that perception, they do not explain how representation works. They analyze the *experience* of representation but not its *basis* in a connection between actual subjects in the real world and representations of them.

7.2 Representation and Resemblance

How do we recognize what pictures represent? It is likely we do so by using the same perceptual and cognitive modules and processes that govern the recognition of their actual subjects. We are evolved visually to identify items in our environment. When we do so, our brains "interpret" an image reflected on the curved surface of the retina into a visual representation of a three-dimensional world populated with objects. And we are evolved visually to re-identify items in our environment, though they are presented to us at different times from different perspectives, either continuously as we move with respect to them, or at temporally separated moments. So, if we can recognize a man in full face, we will probably also be able to recognize him in profile.

Our recognitional capacities often rest on our ability to compare what is before us with what we have seen previously. This process of comparison does not usually involve occurrent perceptual memory. I do not recognize a leaf as lime green by matching its color to a mental color chart that I hold in my mind's eye as I examine the leaf. (How could I be sure of the mental chart's accuracy? By imaging a second chart to compare it to?) The cognitive procedures on which we base our recognitions are usually nonconscious and most are such that they cannot be brought to consciousness if we try. Despite their inaccessibility, one conscious outcome of these processes is that we experience similarities and resemblances between things we identify as the same or as of the same kind.

If we ordinarily recognize things on the basis of similarities between their occurrences or kinds, and if the same underlying cognitive processes are involved in recognizing the subjects of representational pictures as are involved in recognizing those subjects themselves, it is plausible to suggest that pictures represent their subjects by resembling them in relevant visual respects. Indeed, this conclusion might seem so obvious that it could be taken for granted earlier. It might have been assumed (though Wollheim himself does not do so) that we see the picture's subject in the painting because the painting presents a visual aspect recognized as of the subject on the basis of its resemblance to that subject. Despite its initial plausibility, the suggestion that pictorial representations are under-pinned by resemblances – identified as such by courtesy of our naturally evolved perceptual systems – needs to be treated with caution, as I now explain.

To begin, representation uses some conventions that clearly do not rely on resemblance. For instance, shading might be shown by hatched lines and a car might be trailed by "speed lines" to show that it is moving quickly. Also, a painter might represent a historical figure, Moses say, though the face with which Moses is depicted is not the one he actually had. In that case, the ability to recognize the real Moses would not transfer automat-ically to seeing that Moses is represented in the picture. Furthermore, we can appreciate what is represented in pictures that use systems of projec-tion that do not mimic what the eye sees. Modes of projection can be partial and highly stylized, as in caricatures and drawings of stick men. They can mix points of view. (Notice that the two-Js face simultaneously shows the eyes from the front and the nose and chin in profile. A similar effect can be seen in some ancient Egyptian and south-east Asian art. Cubism in the early twentieth century took the mixing and fragmentation of perspectives and points of view to the extreme.) Systems for showing spatial dispositions can differ from the now standard central-vanishing-point perspective. For instance, architects' plans often use isometric projections, and flat scrolls can show 360-degree dioramic views. Under other systems, the size and location of what is shown are not to be interpreted perspectivally. The order of frames and scenes in cartoons and scroll paintings shows temporal succession rather than spatial location (recall figure 3.1, the Balinese picture). Meanwhile, the size of characters in Byzantine paintings indicates their religious or other rank rather than their height. Some of these systems are capable of conveying more visual information than can be communicated using methods of projection that mimic the way light from actual objects strikes the eye at a given moment. For example, they might show the appearance of an item relative to a variety of simultaneously adopted viewpoints and thereby reveal more of its appearance than is displayed by using fine-grained perspectival natural-ism relative to a fixed viewing point. So, the departure from what is "natural" and biologically based is not always accompanied by a loss of visual information or acuity. In sum, art can represent the world in more ways than we can see it with our unaided eyes. To that extent, an adequate account of representation must go beyond "naturally" perceived resem-blances and standards of realism set only by reference to "normal" conditions of perception.

I observed earlier that, when we recognize things, we often experience them as similar to their prior occurrences or to others of the kinds in which they are members. According to the Canadian philosopher Dominic McIver Lopes, rather than taking these perceived resemblances as the basis for the recognitions they accompany, they are likely to be an experiential outcome of those recognitions. In other words, it may be because a picture is recognized as representing a dog that we experience what it pictures as resembling a dog, not vice versa. Consider again the two-Js face in figure 7.1. If you saw the face without prompting, did you do so as a result of noticing a resemblance between the hook of the bottom J and a chin, or did the hook resemble a chin only when the face was recognized as such? One way of making the point would be to suggest that it is only after a work's contents are clarified in terms of its style, genre, and so on, that the viewer is in a position to know where and what kinds of resemblances to look for. How a painting's style interacts with and shapes its content, including what it represents, is explored below.

These caveats do not demonstrate that appeal to visual resemblances will play no role in a successful account of pictorial representation. The recognition of gestalts or patterns might involve the noticing of similar-ities. Even if we do not recognize a stick man drawing as of a man by noticing resemblances between individual lines and individual body parts, still we might make the identification on the basis of a similarity perceived between the overall disposition of the various lines and marks and a schematized abstraction of the human form. What is clear, though, is that it is wrong to think resemblance answers all our questions, even all our fundamental questions, or that it is self-explanatory. Resemblance cannot possibly suffice as the only basic element in a theory of depiction. But some sort of resemblance (between outline shapes, for example, as is argued by the English philosopher Robert Hopkins) might be as basic as anything else.

7.3   Representation: Culture and Biology, Again

If the biology and psychology of perception alone determine how pictorial representation works, we would expect to find only one system of representation globally in use, but we do not. And if natural resemblances are what underpin representation, we would expect to find the representational systems of all times and cultures to be equally transparent to their pictured subjects, but we do not. These observations suggest – and who would deny it? – that human representational systems are shaped by cultural factors and contingencies. This admission invites a return to the sort of question posed in chapter 1: are human schemata for pictorial representation entirely and arbitrarily conventional or are they significantly channeled and constrained by fundamentally biological systems, even as they are tweaked and titillated by culture?

The American philosopher Nelson Goodman argues for the first option. He holds that systems of pictorial representation are as culturally arbitrary as are linguistic ones. As symbol systems, schemata for pictorial representation have formal characteristics that distinguish them from schemata for linguistic description, but they do not differ in their cultural arbitrariness. If some systems of representation seem more natural than others, this is only because we are more habituated to them. In other words, there is nothing to choose in terms of pictorial realism between a picture of the village mayor that resembles him and one created under different rules of projection with the result that it looks like the village idiot. The resemblances we perceive in the first picture are based solely on our inculcation into the pictorial symbol system it employs. Goodman thinks that, were we to reject this system in favor of the second, once we were used to it we would experience the second picture as resembling the mayor.

If some systems of pictorial representation are more easily mastered, applied, and interpreted by a great many people than others are, there is good reason to assume that the differences between them are not merely a function of our familiarity with them. In a relevant sense of the term, the user-friendly systems are more *natural* than the alternatives. In that case, they are not as arbitrary as Goodman maintains.

The empirical evidence appears to count against Goodman. Very young children seem to recognize some pictures effortlessly and without prior training. And the contents of movies and TV shows seem to be accessible to people of all cultures without special training in how they are to be looked at. This is not to say that one system of projection trumps all. (I listed above some of the ways systems of pictorial representation can, without loss of realism, go beyond the perspectival system that most closely mimics the effects of ordinary vision. And most of these systems can be learned very quickly by people who are not initially familiar with them.) It does suggest, however, that systems of projection resulting in portraits of the mayor that look like the village idiot are not on a par with those in which he is recognized more readily. Within systems that generate realistic images, if we can recognize the subject of one picture we can almost always recognize the different subjects of other pictures in the same system. But even if we know the rules of the system of representation in which a portrait of the mayor looks like the village idiot, we will have to work from scratch to determine what is actually represented by a second picture that seems to present the appearance of the town policewoman.

Perhaps the most plausible account of pictorial representation is one that acknowledges the following: there is a biological basis for our general recognitional capacities. These same capacities are intimately involved in recognizing representations, both as the pictures they are and as the subjects they show. The cognitive processes that underlie these capacities (whatever they are) explain how representation works, but not necessarily how representations are made. Whatever role is played within representation by the biological character of our evolved perceptual systems, those perceptual systems tolerate considerable flexibility in the representational schemata over which visual recognition functions. And, in turn, this flexibility provides scope for cultural variation and creativity as regards the systems of pictorial representation that a given culture favors.

7.4   Art versus Non-Art: A Matter of Style

We have reviewed the main contenders among theories of pictorial representation and the issues they face. Such representations are ubiquitous, and many of them have no pretension to be artworks: the newspaper, for example, might show sketches of scenes observed in courtrooms and furniture advertisements in the form of line drawings. It is worthwhile, then, to consider what distinguishes pictorial representations that are artworks from those that are not. Of course, the borderline between the two is hazy and disputed, and we do not wish to revisit the question of art's definition, so the search here will be for typical indicators of difference, even if some artwork representations lack the relevant features while some non-artwork representations possess them.

An appealing but unsatisfactory suggestion is that artwork representations are commonly less realistic than their non-art counterparts, since the artworks are less concerned with conveying information about what they represent than are the non-artworks. The view is unsatisfactory because many non-artwork representations reject realism. The newspaper probably also contains political caricatures and comic strips, and the women wearing the clothes in the drawn fashion advertisements may be impossibly slim and long-legged. Besides, for the 500 years leading up to the close of the nineteenth century, Western art paintings were obsessed with perspectival verisimilitude and naturalism, not least because they were intended accurately to report religious stories, important events, or the wealth and appearance of those who commissioned them as portraits. (Abstraction was more prominent in the art of Muslim cultures because of religious prohibitions on picturing God and the human form generally.) Since the time of ancient Greece, when Apelles painted a horse so realistically that real horses neighed at it and birds were deceived into pecking at grapes painted by Zeuxis, artists have striven after and been praised for achieving realism in their works. Reflecting this, there has been a strong tradition in the West of celebrating the virtuosity of painters possessing the techniques and skills to capture the insubstantiality of soap bubbles or dust motes in the air, the texture of crushed velvet, the complex pattern of sunlight filtered through lace, the forms and colors of a bowl of fruit, and so on.

Despite its manifest falsity, the idea that artworks are less concerned with realism than are other pictorial representations has appeal, I claim. Because not far from it lies an important idea: even when they aim at realism, artwork paintings are often no less concerned with the manner in which they represent their subjects than in those subjects themselves. And this is something on which the viewer needs to reflect, because artists often aim at finding original ways of bringing style, medium, and subject-matter into mutual interaction. By contrast, non-artwork representations usually employ standardized or stereotypical styles that do not function to attract attention away from their pictured subjects. It is as if they are supposed to be experienced as pure content. To put the same point in a different way, the appreciator of an artwork painting must always be open to consideration of how it is painted, whereas the appropriate response to a non-artwork representation typically concentrates on the message to the exclusion of the piece's medium and style.

To highlight this difference, philosophers argue that *style* plays a role in artworks that it does not play in other pictorial representations. Some, such as Arthur C. Danto and Jenefer Robinson, deny that non-artwork representations possess any style. This seems wrong to me. Commercial designers are very aware of the styles they use, and some forms of commercial drawing, such as advertisements for high fashion, are highly stylized. What distinguishes art from non-art representations is not the absence of style in the latter but contrasts in the functions their styles play. In non-art representations, the spectator is not always expected to take note of the style and how this affects what the work communicates. With art, this concern should be central, as I explain further below. Before we get to that, some more general comments on the notion of style are in order.

Styles are apparent through an artist's use of particular themes or subjects, techniques and methods, media, colors, and design. As this list makes clear, style and content are not separate and opposed but, rather, interactive. A style is recognized as a *signature* or *grammar* across a body of works. For example, J. M. W. Turner in his later work scraped, smeared, and blurred his oils to create atmospheric seascapes and landscapes showing indistinct or foggy backlit scenes. More than other artists of the mid-nineteenth century, he painted light itself. Styles can be individual (Vincent Van Gogh's style, Pablo Picasso's neoclassical phase), or belong to schools or movements (Impressionism, Cubism, Abstract Expressionism), or characterize whole eras (fifteenth-century Venetian, eighteenth-century French Royal Academic).

The significance of style for representation is illustrated in the description by the art theorist E. H. Gombrich of Piet Mondrian's *Broadway Boogie-Woogie*. This painting is in Mondrian's mature style, which features matt-textured arrays of vertical and horizontal lines (usually black) framing color fields (typically white, sometimes in blue, yellow, or red, but always with a limited range of primary colors). With its restricted formal and color options, the style is severe, ascetic. *Broadway Boogie-Woogie* (of 1942–3) is much more "busy" in its formal complexity and use of color than most, however. Despite its apparently restrained and structured appearance, in the context of Mondrian's personal style the work can be seen as representational (recalling a Manhattan street grid) and abandoned, with a jazzy rhythm.

Another, different case is the use of vivid, unrealistic colors by Van Gogh (in works such as *The Night Café in Arles* and André Derain (for instance, *Effects of Sunlight on Water*). Whereas it is common for many painters to use colors to exemplify the colors of the work's subject, in the styles of Van Gogh and Derain color plays more an expressive than a representational role. A viewer familiar with their styles appreciates that the paintings' colors are not the colors of their subjects, and that they indicate a mood or psychological attitude toward what is represented.

The contrasting styles of different artists are also relevant to comparisons of their works, as is illustrated by the following. The twentieth-century British artist Henry Moore represented the human form in rounded, smooth-surfaced sculptures with Junoesque proportions. By contrast, his Swiss contemporary Alberto Giacometti made human representations that are roughly textured and rake-like in their vertical elongation. Suppose that Moore had set out to cast a bronze of a starving child, while Giacometti had represented an obese adult. Chances are that Moore's statue would have had objectively fatter proportions than Giacometti's. Yet, to be appreciated, these works would have to be seen in relation to their respective artist's oeuvre and the style exemplified there. Viewed in those terms, the person Moore's work represents genuinely is emaciated, whereas Giacometti's subject is porcine.

To return to ideas emphasized in chapter 3, an artist's style (as displayed in her oeuvre) is among the contextual factors that affect the content of her latest work. Either she continues in the same style, which then determines what kinds of features of the work are significant, or she repudiates it, in which case what is important is the overturning of what previously were norms in her work.

Reverting now to the earlier discussion, which invited a comparison between artworks and non-artworks as regards their representational character, the point is not that only the former display pictorial style. Non-artistic pictorial representations often possess their own style. This style may be generic – the advertisements in the newspaper tend to adhere to a familiar and widely adopted manner of drawing. Their style may also be individual, however. The comic strips created by Charles Schultz, for instance, have a readily recognizable style. (That it is possible to mimic, forge, and parody his cartoons is evidence for this, I claim.) Commercial designers are sensitive, I am sure, to every stylistic nuance of their work and to the impact of these subtleties on consumers' responses, but that does not mean their use of pictorial style is intended to become the focus of attention. When inspecting furniture advertisements, the target audience is supposed to examine the merchandise, not admire the manner of drawing. Sometimes, so familiar and unoriginal is its use, the style is supposed to be invisible, as if the drawing is transparent to its subject and thereby shows it just as it is. At other times the viewer can be expected to notice the piece's style, which may be intended to be emblematic of the product's classiness or to serve more simply to promote the goods. Either way, the style is supposed to make the piece's subject more appealing or credible. While non-artworks have and use styles, the appropriate focus for them is on their content, and on their style only insofar as this makes the spectator more receptive to their subject.

Most artwork pictures use the style they display in ways that have artistically significant outcomes for the work as a whole. Style serves to develop the work's motif or theme rather than simply to make its subject salient. And this use of style frequently is not formulaic or straightforward but instead aims at originality, depth, and seriousness. Artwork pictures invite consideration not only of what is represented but also of the means and manner of representation, because these all affect each other, and that interaction, rather than the depicted subject, is the locus of the work's meaning. Accordingly, the viewer should take account of its style in calculating what the work is about and what it achieves.

How do artworks invite us to consider their style? One way of doing so is by representing another style, as Pop Art does. For example, Roy Lichtenstein creates works that represent themselves as having the style of frames in comics. Comics have the same style, of course, but they do not represent or refer to that style as they use it, which is what Lichtenstein does. (Notice what happens when transmission goes in the opposite direction. When commercial works take from artworks – tea-towels with Leonardo's *Mona Lisa*, Impressionist landscapes on the lids of cake tins – it is mainly the *image* of the artwork they take. They peel off the content, leaving many marks of individual style behind, fixed in the painted surface of the work.) Another way of attracting attention is to juxtapose different styles in an unintegrated fashion within a single work. Pablo Picasso's *Les Demoiselles d'Avignon*, in which "primitive" and proto-Cubist distortions of the faces and bodies are set alongside more orthodox modes of showing them, graphically exemplifies the upheavals and crises confronting the artist of the time when faced with the final collapse of centuries of European commitment to pictorial naturalism.

The style of most artworks is not highlighted in so dramatic a fashion. Nevertheless, consideration of its style is always likely to be relevant to appreciating an artwork's identity and content, because most artists try to achieve something beyond merely the representation of a work's subject, and their style defines the limits on, while providing the means for, their proposed solution to whatever problem a given work addresses. Georges

Seurat aimed to find a way of painting – the juxtaposition of small points of primary colors – that illustrated and vindicated scientific theories of color vision, not merely to show Sunday strollers on the island of La Grande Jatte in his painting of that name. Claude Monet's interest was in picturing light and shade, not just in capturing the likeness of a haystack. For many artists, the issue is one about reconciling formal energies and balances with the content that is to be shown. For example, the painter of a group portrait might aim to create a work that treats all figures equally but interestingly, thereby avoiding a single focal point within the work. In all cases, the artist's individual style constrains her options, yet, if she is successful, she is so because she finds the necessary resources within the repertoire of her style. In art, styles problematize both what paintings are about and what they represent.

Given that a work's style typically is displayed in the gap between, on the one hand, the marks, textures, and strokes of its painted surface and, on the other, the way its subject would appear in actuality when perceived from the given point (or points) of view, any move toward illusionism leads to the effacement of style. In other words, in those rare cases where the painting is so realistic that the spectator is unaware of its marked surface, she ceases to be experientially aware of its style as she focuses on what it pictures. Yet this does not show the irrelevance of style to the appreciation of photo-realist or *trompe l'œil* artwork paintings. Instead, it emphasizes how the fullest experience of such works must lead the viewer to their surface, however transparent this might at first seem to be. Such works draw attention to their style not as one fold of a twofold experience of which the other fold involves simultaneous awareness of the subject that is pictured, but by forcing the percipient to consider the surface independently of looking in it for what it represents. (That is why highly realistic works were used earlier as counterexamples to Wollheim's claim that representations always involve a twofold, simultaneous awareness of the painted surface and of the subject represented in the painting.)

The claim, by the way, is not that a work's style always contributes positively to what the artist brings off. Many journeyman artists work within well-established, widely shared styles, and they deal with issues in the reconciliation of medium and message by following solutions worked through by others. And some "primitive" or "outsider" artists seem to have little style or technique, yet achieve striking effects despite this. Also, where an artist has developed an individual style, this is not inevitably a source of artistic value. He might cleave to it to the point of self-caricature, so that it cries for attention but then adds nothing to what is pictured.

(Marc Chagall's works have been criticized on these grounds.) The claim is this: consideration of the style of an artwork painting is always potentially relevant to its appreciation. And where style is minimized or played down, that itself can be a factor to be pondered for its significance in working out what the artist tried to do and how she set about doing it. Non-artwork representations are in a style, but this is not supposed to attract attention to itself or to serve the artistic function of problematizing the work's subject.

Before closing this section I want to draw attention to the views of two philosophers – Richard Wollheim and Arthur C. Danto – who subscribe to the idea suggested above, namely, that artwork pictures are to be distinguished from non-artwork pictures by reference to the role played by the use of stylistic features within them. They both make the argument by observing that artworks, as well as showing their subjects, express an attitude toward those subjects, with the works' styles playing a crucial role in effecting these acts of expression. Other philosophers to present ideas on the same wavelength and to emphasize the interaction between a work's style and its represented content are Kendall L. Walton, Jenefer Robinson, and James D. Carney.

Despite these initial similarities, there are differences between the views Wollheim and Danto propose. Wollheim's account is largely psychological, in that he characterizes an artwork's style in terms of the mental state of its artist, the way this causes her to mark the surface, and the mental state this produces in the sensitive and informed spectator. In his view, the work's style is not so much a list of salient features but a psychological reality expressed through the way the artist creates the painting. In the artist, this psychological process is directed at achieving a "fit" between what the painting asserts or expresses and the cultural moment in which it is located. There are limits to what a work can assert or express, if that is to be accessible to its audience, given the artist's oeuvre and the history of art to that point, though works that are understandable when first they are created remain so for later audiences. The viewer's task is to consider the artist's style with a view to discovering what kind of "fit" she was trying to achieve.

Danto argues for similar views as regards the way the history of art's creation and reception affects what it is possible for an artist to bring off at a given historical-cum-cultural location. Indeed, his account of artistic style is historical rather than psychologistic and intentionalistic. He characterizes a work's style in terms of its public features taken in relation to the artist's unselfconscious use of these and other elements over time. This is necessary because, as a style emerges, it is possible that neither the artist nor the art critics of the time will be aware of it. As the relevant elements come to be taken up in the artist's subsequent works, their stylistic significance at the point of their emergence can be established. The artist's use of style is typically no more calculated than other expressions of her personality through her behavior. (If it becomes deliberate, style is reduced to mannerism. The process of forging or copying an artwork transfers its content but leaves behind every indication of its style, Danto thinks.) What distinguishes artwork representations from their non-artwork counterparts is their style. (Only art-paintings display the painter's style, Danto thinks.) In art, styles have significance not only in achieving representation but also in expressing some thought about what is pictured or the manner of picturing it. If a colorblind, novice painter (who is unaware of Van Gogh's work) paints something that looks like *The Night Café in Arles*, the distorted perspectives, naive technique for showing the irradiation of light from the lamps, and the unnaturally vivid colors might all be signs that the work is poor. Within Van Gogh's paintings, however, they are stylistic devices expressing the artist's view of the scene. They show both what is seen and a way of seeing it: the café as it appears when filtered through the prism of an emotionally fraught mind. And the spectator's job, according to Danto, is to grasp the "metaphor" – the transfiguration of reality brought about by the interaction of medium and content under the control of style – that lies at the heart of each artwork.

These accounts of the significance of style in artwork paintings are not beyond criticism, of course. I suspect that Wollheim is wrong to think that decisions regarding matters of style are always conscious and intended, and that Danto is mistaken to suggest they never are. It is not clear that style becomes mannerism whenever it is aware of itself, or that duplicates never transmit signs of technique and at least some elements of style. In the early twentieth century, Han Van Meegeren forged works after the style of Jan Vermeer, a seventeenth-century Dutch painter. He was successful in fooling the experts because he reconstructed the style, not just the subject matter, of religious works that Vermeer might have painted. Admittedly, he "quoted" Vermeer's style, rather than expressing his own, but he also developed the style to a point where, when the forgeries were exposed, people wondered why experts saw them as consistent with Vermeer's works. If quotations or copies can preserve the sense and tone of the original, they must preserve at least some aspects of its style.

Despite these quibbles, Wollheim's and Danto's general claims – that the appreciation of style is central to our understanding of art pictures, because such works are to be considered not only for the what they convey about their subjects' appearance but also for the attitude and moods they express toward this – surely is correct.

7.5 Representation in Photographs and Paintings

So far in this chapter we have reviewed theories of pictorial representation and considered what is distinctive about art pictures. In this and the following section, we trace a similar trajectory in discussing photographs. To present the contrast between photography and painting as starkly as possible, I will assume for this initial discussion that the photographs in question are taken with a foolproof camera and printed mechanically. In other words, the camera does not provide its user with options or choices (except where to point it and when to take the picture), and the resulting prints are generated chemically or electronically by machines. As well as learning about photography, the comparison should add to our understanding of representation in paintings.

Photographs (of the type we are considering) differ from paintings in the way in which they relate to their subjects. An automated, causal process takes the place in photography of the intentional path that is crucial in pictorial representation. Whereas a painting that depicts X must be intended to do so, once the foolproof camera is pointed and triggered, what it photographs is determined by what is in front of its lens.

Already, these opening assertions need to be clarified and qualified. A painter might intend to picture *Jim* but end up representing *John*, because he mistakes *John* for *Jim*. If pictorial representation is necessarily intentional (which some philosophers deny), care is needed in specifying the content of the relevant intention. For example, it might best be understood as the intention to paint what the artist points to as her subject, which covers the case just described in which the artist paints what she targets though not what she believes herself to be painting. And on the other side of the ledger, it looks as if photographers' intentions can be relevant to what their pictures depict. Admittedly, if I intend to photograph the Taj Mahal but only my thumb shows in the print, the photograph is of my thumb, not the Taj Mahal. But consider this different case: I photograph my brother dressed in a toga and, by titling the work appropriately, offer it as a representation of Julius Caesar. If the painter can use her brother as a model and capture his likeness, yet make her work depict Julius Caesar by titling it so, it is hard to see why the photographer cannot do the same. (I think stills of Ben Kingsley used to advertise Richard

Attenborough's epic movie *Gandhi* represent the actor as the Indian leader Mahatma Gandhi.) So, when it is said that what is in front of the lens determines what is pictured, *what is pictured* must be understood as referring to the causally responsible item or event, not the things or events that might be (also) represented intentionally via the further use or titling of the photograph.

With these caveats in mind, we can consider what is implied by the fact that automated causal processes are responsible in photography for outcomes that, for painted representations, depend on intentions and decisions made by the artist. Here are some: a painting's appearance is dictated by its painter. Even for a painting that achieves the highest level of naturalism and realism, we can infer how the world is from the way the painting looks only by assuming that the painter has certain beliefs and intentions. We have to know that she is skilled, that she sincerely intends to represent how she perceives the world, that her eyesight is not defective, and so on. By contrast, the appearance of the image in the photograph does not depend on the beliefs and attributes of the person who activates the shutter. Indeed, the camera works the same even if it is fired mechanically; for instance, whenever a sensor detects motion. In considering if the photograph accurately shows how the world is, we check the reliability of the causal mechanisms, not the sincerity of the photographer. We can learn both from paintings and from photographs how the world looks, but the paths of inference must take different routes.

If the appropriate intentions are necessary for pictorial representation, while they play no such role in photographic picturing, it follows that pictorial representation is distinct from photographic picturing (as it is done by the foolproof camera). There are two ways we could respond to this. We might decide that there are (at least) two modes of visual representation, the pictorial and the photographic. Or we might choose to deny that photographs are representations of their subjects. I now consider and reject one argument for the second position.

Because of the mechanical nature of the kinds of photographs we are discussing, it might be argued that they provide visual access to their subjects. Just as, when I look at someone through binoculars, I see her, when I look at a photograph I really see the person it is of. Photographs are prosthetic aids assisting perception, and so are to be classed alongside telescopes, periscopes, mirrors, and spectacles. The argument now can be developed: when I see someone through binoculars, I see her, *not a visual representation of her.* Similarly, when I see someone through a photograph, I see her, not a representation. (The philosopher Kendall L. Walton analyzes the nature of automatic photographs in the fashion described here.) According to this conclusion, the difference between painted representations and photographs are such that the latter do not qualify as visual representations.

What makes for transparency in photographs, so that we see *through* them to their subjects, is the mechanical process of image capture and reproduction, plus the iconic similarity of their visual pattern with what would be seen of their subjects from the point of view of the camera's lens. Together, these guarantee the counterfactual dependence of the appearance of the photograph on that of its subject. In other words, had the subject looked differently, the photograph would have also differed correspondingly. (By contrast, grossly over- or under-exposed pictures are indifferent in their appearance to possible changes in or substitutions of their subjects, and therefore fail to show what they are of.) Aspects of our reactions to photographs are also indicative of their transparency. For instance, they seem natural and, when they generate perceptual errors or illusions (as when the train-tracks seem to meet at the horizon), these are of the same kind as those to which ordinary perception is vulnerable.

Admittedly, the transparency of photographs is something we must learn about and become experienced in interpreting. We need the opportunity to compare photographs with their subjects, and we need to know that a photograph has been produced via an appropriate mechanism and process. For example, if fast-moving things have come out as blurs in the past, while other things in the picture have been in focus (so the blur was not a result of hand shake), and if a given photo is blurred in that way, we can know it is a picture of a fast-moving object.

In photography, a chemical process mediates between the exposure of the film and the production of a print; or, if the process is digitized, the mediation is electronic. As a result, viewing photographs differs from some cases of "aided" vision, such as looking down an optical microscope. But it is continuous with other cases that we accept as involving indirect seeing. For example, the pictures received by a television are compressed and coded for transmission, being decoded by the television. Yet, despite the mediation of the electronic processes involved in encoding and decoding the signal, we can honestly claim to see the President speak when we watch a live broadcast of the event.

7.6   Photographic Representation

Is there a possible alternative to the view just sketched, according to which we see a photograph's subject through it? Yes, there is a plausible rival. It maintains that what we perceive in a photograph is not the person photographed but a *trace* she has left. Because of the way it is produced, we can learn a great deal about the appearance of the source from the appearance of the trace. Nevertheless, in viewing her photographic image, we are not viewing the person photographed. (Similarly, when regarding a footprint, we do not see the foot that made it.) In this view, the systematic dependence of the one appearance on the other, plus iconicity in their forms, is *not* sufficient for transparency. Photographs are representations of their sources, though they are not of exactly the same kind as paintings.

How are we to adjudicate between these rival theories? There is a series of cases from direct perception in the presence of an object, through various modes of mediated perception, to ones where what is perceived is plainly not the object but, rather, signs left in its wake by its passing. Somewhere along the way, one stops seeing the object. These two theories disagree where in the series that occurs. That is a disagreement of substance. One way of probing the arguments is by considering imaginary cases and testing the limits of analogies. If the optical center of our brain were connected to that of another person, would we see what they do? What if our optical centers were connected to a computer that was itself connected to a camera? Does a photograph stand to its source more as a thermometer does to heat than as a person stands to her reflection in a distorting mirror?

Rather than attempting to answer these questions, we will take a different path. The issue we are considering, remember, is whether photographs should be counted as visual representations of what they are of. We moved to the argument that photographs are transparently of their subjects because this seemed to count against the suggestion that they represent those subjects. When we see someone through our spectacles, we see her, not a representation. But I will try to show that photographs are unlike spectacles in this respect. Even if photographs are transparent to their subjects, this does not show that they are not also representations of their subjects. The argument works this way: realistic representational paintings are transparent in the same kind of way that photographs are (or are alleged to be). Since the transparency of paintings does not count against our regarding them as paradigms of visual representation, the similar transparency of photographs must be consistent with treating them also as representations.

Let us characterize a *realistic* painting as follows: it is based on some actual person, thing, event, etc., and this subject can be reliably identified on the basis of the painting. If it is a portrait, we could use it to recognize the sitter. If the painting is of something with many actual (or possible) instances that share the same appearance, a paperclip say, we could use the painting to identify items of the same kind, if not the particular paperclip that served as a model. This is to say, we can tell what the subject of a realistic painting looked like when it was represented, even if we have never had perceptual contact with that subject. A realistic painting provides this information because its appearance is iconic with and counterfactually dependent on the appearance of its subject. If the subject had looked different, so would have the painting. Of course, we can make the requisite inferences from the appearance of the painting to the appearance of what was painted only if we know about the artist's skills and intentions and the conventions (of perspective, or whatever else is relevant) that are used, and can compare realistic paintings sometimes with their subjects, but it was also conceded for photographs that we need to know about the process of production and have experience of comparing the photographs with their subjects if we are to take them transparently. Additionally, we are liable to make perceptual errors with respect to realistic paintings that are similar to many of those made with ordinary vision (and with photographs).

Transparency depends, among other things, on the responsiveness of the image to perceptual features of its subject. For photographs, the relevant guarantee is provided by the mechanical efficiency of the process by which the image is recorded and transmitted. For paintings, we depend on the intentions, skill, and sincerity of the artist. Artists can be no less reliable in capturing an image than can a mechanical process, and, as viewers, we need be no less confident in their ability to do this, especially where we can sometimes compare a painting to its subject. If photographs are transparent to their subjects, so too are realistic paintings. That is why, in past ages, miniature portraits successfully played the role now usually taken by photographs.

Here is the point: if I paint my brother wearing a toga and title the work *Julius Caesar*, it matches my brother, who can be recognized in it, and it *represents* Julius Caesar, just as the corresponding photograph would do. And if I paint my brother and title the work *My Brother*, it both matches and represents him. When realistic paintings are transparent, this plainly does not count against their also being representations of their subjects. Such paintings are among our paradigms of pictorial representation. In that case, the similar transparency of photographs should not count against their also being representations of their subjects. Admittedly, the one mode of representation is largely intentional, where the other accords a fairly central place for mechanical processes. Yet the basis for transparency is crucially the same: namely, there is iconicity between the appearance of relevant parts of the painting/photograph and the appearance of its subject and there is a counterfactual dependence of the appearance of the painting/ photograph on the appearance of what it is of.

What of the earlier observations, that we see a person through spectacles, and not (also) a representation of her? If they are both transparent to their subjects, what distinguishes spectacles from photographs such that the latter produce representations where the former do not? Here is a suggestion: a representation captures the likeness of its subject at a particular place and time. What one sees of its subject as one continues to regard a photograph/painting is unaffected by subsequent changes to that subject (though what one sees may be affected by the ravages of time on the painting/photograph). This guarantees the separation of the painting/ photograph from what it is of. Separateness is generally considered to be necessary for representation; a representation is distinct from what it represents. By contrast, when I (continue to) contemplate my brother through my spectacles, what I see at every moment reflects his ongoing appearance, including changes to this. There is a constant dependence between what I see through my glasses and the ongoing appearance of my brother. This is the hallmark of direct seeing. So there is a difference between directly seeing something and seeing it (as it was at some past moment and place) in a representation, even if the representation is transparent to its subject (as it was at that time and place).

7.7 Photography as an Art

According to the preceding, even photographs generated by foolproof cameras and automated processes of developing or digitizing involve the representation of their subjects. At the same time, the method or basis of representation is not like that for paintings. So, we are back to the earlier suggestion: that representation comes in at least two species, the pictorial and the photographic. Whereas the relevant intentions (or use of conventions) are necessary for representation in paintings, the equivalent condition for photographic depiction requires an appropriate causal process linking what is in front of the camera to what appears on the print.

This outcome may seem innocuous. There could be a sting in the tail, however. It has been argued, most notably by the British philosopher Roger Scruton, that photography is artistically inferior to painting, because when causal mechanisms replace intentions much that is central to artistic value is lost along the way. The argument is like this: art paintings show not only what is represented but also a manner of representing that reveals how the painter thought about his subject (as we noted in discussing style in an earlier section). They express the view of the artist on his subject. The expressive character of the painting depends on the artist's control over what is shown and its detail. The painter can use her imagination; she need not confine herself to representing only what exists. Art paintings are valuable in themselves, not solely for the sake of the visual information they convey. By contrast, photographs are of interest only as surrogates for what they picture. They can only picture what exists. Because of the mechanical nature of the medium, photographers lack control over the detail of their work. As a result, photographs show only the *location* of the camera in relation to its subject, not an artistically interesting *point of view* on that subject. Photographs simply record the appearance of their subjects and that is the sole source of their value.

Almost every point made here seems false on inspection. To begin with, the comparison seems to be between art paintings and snaps taken with the foolproof camera, and it is not surprising if photography comes off worse in that comparison. We should recall, however, that only some painted or drawn representations are offered as art (as was discussed). The others are valued as surrogates, not for the interest of the representational perspectives they display or for the manner in which their subject, medium, and style interact. So, if we are talking of artistic merit, we should compare art paintings with art photographs, and put aside the holiday snaps along with the drawn advertisements, textbook illustrations, miniature locket portraits, and the like.

At the same time, we need to put aside the foolproof camera and consider how photographers aiming to create works with a claim to art-status control the detail of what finds its way to the print. Indeed, we might distinguish art photography from snapping by observing how the former expects the photographer to subvert or bypass the roles played by automatic, causal mechanisms in the latter.

Some photographic artists work directly on unexposed film, without using cameras at all. When the photographer does use a camera, it is likely to be one giving her a number of options. For example, she can set the length of the lens (which affects magnification and perspective), the focal aperture (which affects depth of field), the focus (which affects the clarity of parts of the image), the speed and number of exposures per print (which also affects clarity and depth of field, the quality of exposure, and the way movement is shown), and the use of filters (which may affect color, clarity, or perspective). She selects her film – color or black and white, its speed (which can affect the graininess of the print), and its brand (which can affect color balance under conditions of mechanical development). As well, she chooses what to film and how to frame it. She can often pose the subject, arrange the setting, and organize the lighting of the scene. Once the picture is taken, she can control and manipulate the image that is generated. This might be done, for example, by adopting non-standard materials, timings, or methods in the use of developing and fixing chemicals, by applying different techniques to different parts of the image, or by "blow brushing" or otherwise altering the image before it is fixed. In the case of digital images, a huge variety of editing options are available, of course. The nature of the final image is also affected by her decisions about the medium on which the image is to be displayed. For instance, she chooses the quality or kind of paper on which the photo is printed. And the print, when it is made, might not yet be the finished artwork. She might use it as the raw material for mosaics, collages, picture-sculptures, and the like.

When we allow the photographer the tools that permit her to exercise her art, the resulting photographs are far from the transparent ones discussed earlier. Indeed, the contemporary photographer's editorial control over digitized images surely comes close to eliminating the difference between photographers and painters. And even where the art photographer adopts a more traditional approach to shooting and processing her films, the evidence suggests she has sufficient control over the photographic medium to express herself and her thoughts toward her subjects. In other words, art photographers, like art painters, can have an individual style and, through its use, can express thoughts and feelings regarding the subjects of their works. Appropriately then, when it comes to art photographs, spectators are just as interested in the manner of photographic depiction for the light this sheds on the photographer's attitude to her subject as in what is shown. We should not underestimate the artistic effects that are within the photographer's power, just because her methods and materials differ from the painter's.

What of the claim that photographers are restricted to shooting what exists, whereas painters are not? It is true that the artist need not work only "from life", and can produce what are sometimes called "genre" paintings – portrayals that are of imagined people or scenes. It is also true that the photograph shows some aspect of the appearance of what was in front of the lens, so long as commercially standard techniques for focus, exposure, lighting, and development are followed. But this is not a significant limitation if, as was suggested earlier, a photographer can represent Julius Caesar (or Sherlock Holmes, or some entirely original fiction) by photographing her brother. Live theater and movies rely on actors, but are not regarded as artistically limited for doing so. And in live theater and movies, the audience views real performers along with the fictional characters they portray, yet we do not deny these genres art-status on this basis. In that case, why should the negative judgment be applied to photographs?

As it happens, Scruton denies that a person can represent Julius Caesar by photographing her brother. Instead of a *photographic representation* of Venus (to use his example), we get a *photograph of a representation* of Venus, he claims. His point cannot be that the photographer poses, dresses, and lights his subject, because the painter does the same. It must be that, insofar as the photographer does anything artful, it happens exclusively at this preliminary stage, so that the act of photography merely records or reports a prior act of representation. But this is false if the photographer controls how the representation appears through the use of the photographic techniques described previously. We do not regard Orson Welles's movie *Citizen Kane* as a documentary film of a staged representation, and that is because so much of the art in this movie depends on editorial decisions about what is filmed, how it is filmed, how it is edited, and so on. It seems likely anything true of movies will be true also of photographs, because they share many techniques and possibilities in common. If movies can represent fictions, so too can photographs, and if movies qualify as artful representations by virtue of the cinematic skills and techniques employed in transforming what happens in the studio into a film, so too can photographs. Compared to films (and literature and drama), photographs are limited in their capacity to convey narratives, but so too are art paintings. They make up for this (as also do art paintings) by their power to present a still image that is available for detailed inspection, not only in respect of what it represents and to its layers of symbolic content, but also with regard to what it displays of the photographer's view on these. This perspective is revealed through the treatment of both medium and content and their mutual interaction with distinctive elements of the photographer's or genre's style. And even if our interest in the photograph always acknowledges its subject, this is no different from our appreciation of realistic paintings, where we must also recognize the subject in order to consider its treatment in terms of the artist's style and techniques.

It is worth noting that art photographers sometimes exploit the naive expectation that photographs accurately show what is in front of the lens by producing works showing impossible or startling scenes, thereby jolting the spectator into considering how the image has been manipulated and drawing attention to the photograph's artistic features. Jerry Uelsmann, an American expert in photomontage, uses darkroom editing to seamlessly blend images into surreal scenes from nature – trees with human faces and the like. Another photographer, Zeke Berman, creates and photographs still-life objects and arrangements that often play with illusions of perspective. *Goblet Portraits* (1978), at first shows silhouetted goblets on display shelves, until one notices that the picture is composed of mirrored profiles of faces.

In chapter 3 I described ways in which a work's art-historical location can affect its identity and contents. Among other matters, what a work means can depend on when and how it was done. The same applies in photography. A contemporary photographic artist can, if she chooses, return to the foolproof camera and take snaps that look as if they might be by a tourist on holiday. Her work, unlike the tourist's, borrows its style and idiom. In this way it takes on a significance the tourist's could not possess, because her photos invite the viewer to take into account the sophisticated photographic manipulations she has rejected. Similarly, the camera-clicking image appropriator distances her work from the images she collects, even where they are art photographs. In chapter 3 I mentioned the work of Sherrie Levine, who photographs the photographs of male artists, and I observed that her works make an art-political point that is absent from the works she co-opts, this being one about how women get to be hung in galleries only via art made by men. Another aspect of her work is pertinent to the current discussion: when she photographs the photographs of others, she represents not the *subjects* they photographed but the *photographs* they produced. Though her works look like theirs, hers embody an importantly different artistic content that is in no way impugned by those aspects of photography that may be automated or mechanical.

7.8 Moving Images

As we have already noted, much of what is written above about photographs can be applied to movies. The striking difference, of course, is that movies contain or represent movement, whereas photographs freeze the action or events of a time-slice. Even if a photograph shows movement in its subject, the image does not move its boundaries or within its boundaries. By contrast, movies not only represent the movement of their filmed subjects, they do so with moving images. Yet is the movement of the image merely apparent or actual?

The issue is not whether viewers in the cinema mistakenly believe they are really present at the events portrayed in the film. That does not happen here, any more than it happens in the theater, with photographs, or with paintings and sculptures. And the issue is not whether the film can successfully represent the movements of the subjects or characters in it, or continuous changes in the point or field of view (in tracking, panning, and dolly shots). It does. Instead, the question concerns the images on the screen and asks if the appearance of movement they present is real or illusory. The misperception, if there is one, is like that generated by the Müller–Lyer illusion (see figure 7.4), in which one line appears to be longer than another, parallel line, though they are the same length. And just as the line continues to look longer even when it has been proved not to be, so the illusion of movement in film survives the audience's awareness (or discovery) that this appearance of movement is deceptive.

Figure 7.4   The Müller–Lyer Illusion

Movement requires some continuously existing item that changes its location over time. First it is here, and, later, the same thing, which exists throughout, is elsewhere. A paradigm instance would be that of a material item that is spatially displaced, such as an apple that falls from a tree. Nevertheless, images are candidates for movement, though they lack substantiality. The light of a flashlight can move across the surface of a wall, changing shape as it does so; or a person can be dogged by her shadow as she walks through the sunny park. These cases differ from that of the movie, however, because the movie involves the projection of discrete, discontinuous images, each separated by a moment of black, at the rate of 24 per second. So, even if some images can move, it remains to decide whether those in movies do so.

The difficulty in claiming that the images move on the cinema screen comes from their lack of continuity, which becomes apparent if the film is slowed. Here are two analogous cases: on freeways, warning lights some- times are configured as two pairs, one above the other. When the bottom pair switches off, the top pair comes on. The appearance is of a single pair of lights that jumps up and down. Yet it is proper to resist the idea that this apparent movement is actual, because there is no continuous pair that changes its location, but two alternating pairs instead. Similarly, cartoon flipbooks create the impression of movement, but again we should deny that the movement is actual, because each page of the book presents a discrete cartoon image that differs from the ones that follow it. Intuition suggests that movies are similar, because they are constituted by successively screened, but detached, images. Because of the physiology of human perception, we cannot help seeing the appearance of movement, so long as the projection rate is maintained. Yet knowing (or learning) how the appearance is achieved, we should regard the movement of the images (and equally, that of the field or point of view) as illusory.

It might be objected that the identity of an item can survive temporal discontinuities, and hence that movement in it can do so also. As it traverses the night sky, a spotlight sometimes lights the underside of clouds and at others it is lost in the deep dark of space. And a person's shadow might be eclipsed as the rays of the sun are blocked by trees she passes. If we are inclined to think of the spot of light as continuing a single movement or the shadow as continuous (and continuously moving), though they come and go, why not the same for movie images?

Here is a possible answer: if it were not for externally caused interruptions, there would be seamless continuity in the existence of both the light of the lamp and of the shadow. But in the case of the movie, there are no externally caused interruptions. The light of the movie projector is blocked by dark gaps between the individual film frames, with the result that the screen is black some 24 times per second. The gappiness of the film is built into its nature, because the gaps define and separate the individual frames. The regular, short periods of darkness are not the result of external interruptions to what otherwise would be a continuous process. Instead, they are a part of the film that is shown, as becomes apparent if the projector slows. The appearance of continuity is a side-effect of human optical and brain physiology, not a reflection of genuine continuity within the movie's images. The seamless continuity of the movie's showing is merely apparent, therefore.

As illusions go, this one is benign, since few are fooled into believing that the images of movies are like those cast by shadow-puppets. It is also a fortunate illusion, because it makes cinema possible. Our make-believe engagement with the world of the film is not inhibited, of course, by the recognition that we are subject to a trick played on us by our senses. Among the thoughts we entertain without belief as we watch a movie is that the images we witness are continuous, not gappy. Indeed, we imagine of them that they are continuous because we imagine they are the images of people and things that exist continuously in the world of the film.

Questions

7.1 If we can plainly recognize the subjects of the paintings of other cultures or of ancient times, does that show that pictorial representation relies on universal, natural principles? If you think the answer is *Yes*, why did artists struggle for so long before solving the problem of linear perspective? Could we expect to recognize the subjects of pictures painted by Martians? If you think the answer is *No*, why do children seem to understand pictures more readily than they learn language?

7.2 Are there principles of representation for instrumental music without accompanying words analogous to those for representation in paintings or photographs? Are only sounds represented in music, or can emotions, thoughts, personalities, and the like be musically represented? Can music represent a painting?

7.3 Can you see President Kennedy shot if the event happened before you were born? Do you see the 100-meter run at the Olympics if you watch a live TV broadcast? Do you see the race if it is a replay, or if the replay is interrupted by advertisements, or if it is shown in slow motion?

7.4 If the optic center of your brain were connected to a camera, could you see? Would it make any difference to the answer if you could not control the camera and had no idea where it was?

7.5 How do the possibilities of digital editing affect our view of the nature of photographs and of paintings?

7.6 Does the stock market index really go up and down? Do musical themes move up and down?

7.7 If a painting shows as part of its content another painting, does it represent the painting, what that painting represents, or both? Is the story different if one photograph includes the image of another?

Readings

A useful collection covering many of the topics of this chapter is *The Philosophy of the Visual Arts*, edited by P. Alperson (New York: Oxford University Press, 1992).

A sophisticated version of the illusionary account of representation is presented by E. H. Gombrich in *Art and Illusion* (5th edn., Oxford: Phaidon, 1977). The classic discussion of "seeing as" is by Ludwig Wittgenstein in *Philosophical Investigations*, translated by G. E. M. Anscombe (3rd edn., Oxford: Blackwell, 1968), 193–214. Representation has been widely analyzed in such terms. "Seeing-in" is contrasted with "seeing-as" by Richard Wollheim in "Seeing-As, Seeing-In and Pictorial Representation," in *Art and its Objects* (2nd edn., Cambridge: Cambridge University Press, 1980), 205–26, and in *Painting as an Art* (Princeton: Princeton University Press, 1987), ch. 2. Also see his "On Pictorial Representation," *JAAC* 56 (1998), 217–26. Wollheim regards the artist's intention as a crucial determinant of what (if anything) a painting represents, and he sees interpretation as directed to retrieving the artist's intention from the painting. Kendall L. Walton's discussion of representation is in *Mimesis and Make-Believe: On the Foundations of the Representational Arts* (Cambridge, MA: Harvard University Press, 1990), ch. 8. He holds that we make believe of our seeing the picture that it is a seeing of the picture's subject. Two chapters by Malcolm Budd also are relevant: "On Looking at a Picture," in *Psychoanalysis, Mind and Art*, edited by J. Hopkins and A. Saville (Oxford: Blackwell, 1992), 259–80, and "How Pictures Look," in *Virtues and Taste: Essays on Politics, Ethics, and Aesthetics*, edited by D. Knowles and J. Skorupski (Oxford: Blackwell, 1993), 154–75, as is "Depiction, Vision and Convention," *American Philosophical Quarterly* 9 (1972), 243–50, by Patrick Maynard.

The most notorious example of a theory of depiction that rejects the centrality of perceptual experience is by Nelson Goodman in *Languages of Art* (New York: Bobbs-Merrill, 1968), especially 1–10, 34–43. Goodman regards pictorial representations as forms of symbolic denotation no less arbitrary than language. He denies that the resemblance experienced between a realistic picture and what it depicts should figure in the analysis of pictorial representation. The recognition of such resemblances is simply a result of the viewer's familiarity with the pictorial symbol system that is used.

Three book-length discussions presenting closely argued theories of pictorial representation are Flint Schier's *Deeper into Pictures* (Cambridge: Cambridge University Press, 1987), Dominic McIver Lopes's *Understanding*

Pictures (Oxford: Clarendon Press, 1996), and Robert Hopkins's *Picture, Image and Experience* (Cambridge: Cambridge University Press, 1998). Schier maintains that our ability to interpret pictures depends solely on a general competence with respect to the system of representation plus the ability to recognize what is represented were we to see it in the flesh. Contrary to Goodman's thesis, recognizing representations does not require resort to semantic or syntactic rules relating the picture's parts to its subject. Lopes is an anti-intentionalist who regards representation as involving the re-creation of perceptual aspects of a subject according to the strictures of a symbol system. Though he regards pictorial representation as perceptual, he is skeptical of resemblance-based accounts of it. He also argues against privileging the "Alberti rules of three-dimensional perspective" that duplicate ordinary perceptual experiences. Other representational symbol-systems – ones with inverted, curvilinear, and split-image perspectives – are no less legitimate or information-preserving. Lopes, like Schier, stresses the manner in which pictures engage the capacities we have for recognizing things face to face. Hopkins, by contrast, provides a resemblance-based account: pictures look like what they represent because they show their subject's outline shape, which is the silhouette plus all inner planes or surfaces that it projects when viewed from a given point (or points) of view, and sometimes also its color and tone. In *Depiction* (Cambridge, MA: Yale University Press, 1998), the art historian Michael Podro considers the interaction between medium and content in the works of a number of artists.

A collection on the subject of style in art is *The Concept of Style*, edited by B. Lang, (revised edn., Ithaca: Cornell University Press, 1989). Among other chapters, this contains Richard Wollheim's "Pictorial Style: Two Views" (pp. 183–202). Other relevant works by Wollheim include "On the Question 'Why Painting is an Art?'," *Proceedings of the 8th International Wittgenstein Symposium* 10 (1983), 101–6, and *Painting as an Art*, chs. 1 and 2. For critical discussion of Wollheim's equation of style with psychological dispositions rather than with sets of properties uncovered in paintings by art historians, see James D. Carney's "Individual Style," *JAAC* 49 (1991), 15–22. Arthur C. Danto adopts the theory that styles are elements viewed for their significance in the set of an artist's work in "Narrative and Style," *JAAC* 49 (1991), 201–9. His account of the stylistic mode that is distinctive to artworks is found in chs. 6 and 7 of *The Transfiguration of the Commonplace* (Cambridge, MA: Harvard University Press, 1981). For discussion of the anti-intentionalism apparent in Danto's discussion of style, see Noël Carroll's "Danto, Style, and Intention," *JAAC* 53 (1995), 251–7. Meanwhile,

Kendall L. Walton prefers the view that artistic style is an aspect of the actions with which an artwork is produced, rather than (solely) a property of the work. See his "Style and the Products of the Processes of Art," in *The Concept of Style*, 72–103. In "Style and Significance in Art History and Art Criticism," *JAAC* 40 (1981), 6–14, Jenefer Robinson argues there is a mutual dependence between a work's represented content and its style. She regards non-artwork diagrams as being in no style, which is an opinion Danto also holds. E. H. Gombrich's remarks on style (and Mondrian's *Broadway Boogie-Woogie*) are found in chapter 11 of *Art and Illusion*.

Kendall L. Walton argues for the transparency of some photographs – ones taken with the foolproof camera and developed mechanically – in "Transparent Pictures: On the Nature of Photographic Realism," *Critical Inquiry* 11 (1984), 246–77, and "Looking Again Through Photographs," *Critical Inquiry* 12 (1986), 801–8. Among his critics are Edwin Martin in "On Seeing Walton's Great-Grandfather," *Critical Inquiry* 12 (1986), 796–800, and Nigel Warburton in "Seeing Through 'Seeing Through Photographs',", *Ratio* new series 1 (1988), 64–74. Also relevant is section iv of John Dilworth's "Internal Versus External Representation," *JAAC* 62 (2004), 23–36. Roger Scruton's attack on photography's credentials as an artform is found in "Photography and Representation," *Critical Inquiry* 7 (1981), 577–603. Among the many who defend photography against his criticisms are Joel Snyder (see "Photography and Ontology," *Grazer Philosophische Studien* 19 (1983), 21–34) and Robert Wicks (see "Photography as a Representational Art," *BJA* 29 (1989), 1–9). The cultural commentator Susan Sontag characterizes the contents of photographs as traces in *On Photography* (New York: Farrar, Straus & Giroux, 1977), as well as describing how photographers control the images they produce. A philosopher's discussion of art photographs is given by Barbara E. Savedoff in *Transforming Images: How Photography Complicates the Picture* (Ithaca: Cornell University Press, 2000). Also relevant is Nigel Warburton's "Individual Style in Photographic Art," *BJA* 36 (1996), 389–97.

The question *Do movies move?* is considered in: Noël Carroll's "Defining the Moving Image," in *Theorizing the Moving Image* (Cambridge: Cambridge University Press, 1996), 49–74; Gregory Currie's "Film, Reality, and Illusion," *Post-Theory: Reconstructing Film Studies*, edited by D. Bordwell and N. Carroll (Madison: University of Wisconsin Press, 1996), 325–44; and Andrew Kania's "The Illusion of Realism in Films," *BJA* 42 (2002), 243–58.

Chapter Eight
The Value of Art

This chapter is concerned with the value and evaluation of art. Not every philosopher would agree that at least some art is valuable. Plato, for one, is deeply suspicious of art. He regards it merely as copying the appearance of reality, and he views the appearance of reality as a misleading approximation of reality's true nature, which is a realm of abstract forms. Accordingly, his account of art is negative: it is an unreliable source of truth. Moreover, art's power to work on the emotions, thereby subverting reason, makes it liable to confuse us, he thinks. (We could perhaps reply to Plato's concerns by denying that reality has a hidden nature and, anyway, by questioning if art can be valuable only by representing reality's inner essence.) Most philosophers have a more positive attitude to art's value. More widely, an interest in the arts is considered to be a good thing and many artworks are regarded as of considerable merit.

Philosophers differ over whether the value of art is intrinsic or extrinsic. According to the first view, art is valuable in and for its own sake, while the latter view maintains that art is valuable because it is a means to independently specifiable effects that are valuable. The first position maintains that the goodness of an artwork resides exclusively in, say, its beauty, while the second holds that art is good because through it we can be educated about what is important in life, for example. The nineteenth-century Russian novelist Leo Tolstoy advocated this last view. He denied that art is valuable for its beauty. He believed, instead, that it is valuable only where it serves morality or religion, which are valuable independently of their connection with art. He concluded that good art must promote the equality and fellowship of all people in a universally accessible way, and he condemned Shakespeare's works, as well as many of his own, for failing to do this.

It seems odd to suggest that art can be valuable independently of the way we experience it. Even if we believe that an uninhabited beautiful world would be better than an uninhabited ugly one, still we think in terms of what they would be like were we to come across them. Perhaps for this reason, many philosophers maintain that art is valuable because the experience to which it gives rise is valuable, either because that experience is itself intrinsically valuable, as pleasure is, or because the experience is extrinsically valuable in its turn. Some of these philosophers deny that this always entails that the value of art is extrinsic, however. If the experience is intimately bound up with the artwork that is its cause, so that it cannot be described except by characterizing the qualities of the artwork that give rise to it, and if the value of the experience is intrinsic to it, then the value of the artwork is also intrinsic, they would maintain. If we value the work for the pleasure its contemplation yields, and if this pleasure just is the pleasure of apprehending and understanding the artwork's pleasure-making features, then the artwork is not merely an incidental means to a valuable effect that could exist, or retain its value, independently of is connection with the artwork. Let us accept, then, that a theorist who maintains that art is good only if it produces an intrinsically valuable aesthetic experience when it is contemplated for its own sake thereby regards the value of art as intrinsic.

As we have just seen, Tolstoy regarded art's value as exclusively extrinsic. For him, the value of art derives entirely from the value of the moral or religious message it conveys. Other philosophers think the value of art is exclusively intrinsic. For example, aesthetic formalists consider the value of art to be confined solely to its structural unity and integrity. They need not deny that artworks have qualities valuable for purposes other than the contemplation of their forms. A copy of Shakespeare's plays may be useful for propping the door open, and we can learn from Hans Holbein's portraits of Henry VIII and his retinue how the English aristocracy dressed in the 1530s. But, so the claim goes, the works are not valuable as *art* for having such uses; instead, they are valuable as a weighty object and as a historical document. As art, their value is solely intrinsic.

Though some philosophers opt for one position to the exclusion of the other, as we have just noted, it is plausible to think that art might have both intrinsic and extrinsic value. It can be a source of pleasurable experience, which we accepted above as a form of intrinsic value, and it can provide information that is useful for helping us to navigate and comprehend the wider world. To meet the objection raised above – that the extrinsic value of an artwork is never among its virtues *as an artwork* – it is necessary to show that art, identified and appreciated as art, is a source of extrinsic, as well as intrinsic, value. That demonstration follows later, when the educative value of art is explored.

In illustrating claims about the intrinsic value of art, I have so far referred mainly to theorists who talk about the value of art's aesthetic properties, or the value of aesthetic experience. Some of these authors use the term *aesthetic* as a general term covering all that is appreciable in art, but others take a more restricted view, regarding aesthetic properties as objective features perceived in the artwork when it is approached for its own sake and without regard to its origin and its intended or possible functions. In chapter 3 I distinguished the aesthetic, specified in this narrow way, from the artistic. Artistic properties, such as symbolism and allusion, are art-relevant features of the work that depend on relations between its immediate content and matters external to its borders. I also argued that identifying artworks and their content depends on awareness of their artistic, as well as aesthetic, properties. In line with this, I now propose that the evaluation of an artwork should take account of both its aesthetic and artistic properties. I will refer to the complex composite of these assessments as the work's *artistic* value or as its value *as a work of art*.

One further point should be clarified. Some people regard the concept of art as essentially evaluative. Tolstoy was one such. Only good art qualifies as art, he thought. If the artist intends something to be art but fails in the attempt to make it good, the result is a *non*-artwork, not a *bad* artwork. By this approach, defining art and analyzing what makes art valuable are related like the sides of a coin. By contrast, aesthetic functionalism – which was outlined in chapter 2 as the view that something is art if it is intended to provide the person who contemplates it for its own sake with an aesthetic experience of significant magnitude on the basis of an appreciation of its aesthetic features – allows for the possibility that something qualifies as art despite being an aesthetic failure, because its artist intended it to be better than it turned out to be. But aesthetic functionalism does propose a connection between the analysis of art's value and the project of definition, because the intention mentioned in the definition is to be understood as the intention to create a work with sufficient aesthetic value to warrant an aesthetic experience of significant magnitude. Most other definitions proposed for art differ by denying that there is an essential connection between art's nature and its value. For example, the definition offered by the institutional theory – something is an artwork if it is an artifact of a kind created by an artist to be presented to an artworld public – treats the classification of art as descriptive, not evaluative. Descriptive theories allow for the possibility of bad art that is produced without any failure in the execution of the artist's intentions. Of course, proponents of descriptive definitions do not deny that much art is valuable and that its value is of extreme importance. Their point is that the tasks of defining art's nature and of analyzing its value do not impinge upon each other. Unless we agree with Tolstoy's extreme position, which denies art-status to all but the greatest works (and then characterizes their greatness as depending solely on the correctness of their moral or religious message), we can allow that the discussion of artistic value can proceed without first settling how art is to be defined, or whether it can be.

8.1   Evaluation and Functionality

One way in which we evaluate humanly designed items is in terms of how well they perform their function. A good X is an X that successfully does what Xs are made to do. A good car is one that provides efficient transport for small numbers of people. There may be many different aspects to an account of the item's purpose or function. In evaluating a car, we are likely to consider its purchase price, fuel economy, speed, safety, handling, comfort, maintenance and insurance costs, and so on. As well as a primary function, the item may have secondary ones. Cars can be used as status symbols, for instance. The item can be evaluated in terms of any of its actual or possible functions. For this reason, the function governing the evaluation should be specified. Where no function is indicated, usually we are to assume the evaluation is directed to the item's primary function.

As humanly made items, artworks can be evaluated in functional terms. A good artwork will be one that does the job for which we make such things. What job is that? Some approaches that seem initially attractive are unsatisfactory. One of these identifies the function of art as being to provide a rewarding artistic or aesthetic experience when contemplated for its own sake.

This specification of art's function may be applicable to high Western art of recent centuries, though it remains to spell out what is worthwhile about the experience in question. It does tend to beg the question against the possibility of art that is intended to be practically useful, and not to be contemplated solely for its own sake. For example, it is prejudiced against the idea that art can primarily serve domestic, religious, political, or other ritual functions, and it thereby excludes much of what might deserve the title of art in small-scale non-Western cultures or women's work. Is there a way of modifying the account of artistic value to accommodate such items? A common strategy for doing so identifies a secondary artistic or aesthetic function that is independent of their primary, practical function. If the primary function of religious art is the affirmation of faith and the glorification of God, a piece of religious art will be good if it achieves these results, but that will not be relevant to its *artistic* value, according to this view. To evaluate religious art from an artistic point of view, we should disregard its primary religious function and focus on its artistic and aesthetic merits, such as its emotional expressiveness, assuming that it is intended, secondarily, for contemplation in such terms. Because the secondary function is conceived as separable from the primary one, it is possible that such a work is a failure as *religious* art while being a success as religious *art*, or vice versa.

Items are sometimes decorated in aesthetically pleasing ways that clearly are regarded as incidental or irrelevant to their primary functions. These might be appropriately assessed for their success in meeting secondary artistic or aesthetic goals. But, no less often, items are made to possess artistic or aesthetic features that are linked to the pursuit of their primary practical functions. Indeed, it is just such works that have the strongest claim to being art. For them, the proposal sketched above is unsatisfactory. It detaches the artfulness of such pieces from their usefulness and their most prominent design features, whereas we would expect these all to harmonize in a mutually supportive fashion when such pieces genuinely deserve the title of art. Moreover, the makers of the kinds of items we are considering plainly do not separate artistic considerations from practical ones. The Balinese, for instance, make elaborate offerings to please their gods and ancestors. These offerings take the form of dances, statues, intricately sculpted tributes of food and flowers, and so on. The Balinese assume that, for the offerings to be efficacious in pleasing the gods and ancestors, their artistic or aesthetic elements must be integrated into their design. Moreover, though they intend their offerings to be enjoyed by the human as well as the divine audience, they do not regard them as for disinterested contemplation, even as a secondary use. There is no reason to think similar attitudes are not also common in other societies.

In light of this, a better idea might be that something is a work of art if its artistic and aesthetic features contribute significantly to its primary function. In this approach, the goodness or badness of a work of art is measured in terms of the extent and success with which this contribution is made. The virtue of the account is that it remains open about the range of art's primary functions. Some art could have the primary function of producing a rewarding appreciative experience via the contemplation of its artistic and aesthetic elements, but other art could have other functions, such as affirming religious faith and glorifying God. The artistic judgment of a religious work does focus on its artistic and aesthetic attributes, then, but it considers these in relation to the primary purpose fulfilled by such artworks. A religious artwork is good when evaluated from the artistic point of view if its artistic and aesthetic properties, recognized and appreciated as such, produce an experience that vitalizes the convictions of believers and exalts God.

8.2   Rules, Universality, and Objectivity in Artistic Evaluation

Is the value of art regulated by rules? Are there any practical principles that can be guaranteed to produce a good artwork if the artist follows them successfully? Many philosophers, dating back to the eighteenth century and earlier, have thought not.

Here is an argument that supports their doubts. The value of an artwork depends on the nature of its aesthetic and artistic properties – its formal unity, semantic complexity, expressive subtlety, and so on – and, as was explained in chapter 3, they depend in turn on the combination of that artwork's base properties. (The bases for aesthetic features are located in the work and may include, for example, the disposition of paint, words, notes, and the like. The bases for artistic features include relations to matters outside the work, such as the artist's intentions or conventions of symbolization, and so on.) A painting is not good if it is garish and it may be garish because of the vivid shade of purple that dominates it. The value of art would be rule-governed only if there were systematic general principles specifying what artistic and aesthetic qualities depend on what base properties. Such principles do not appear to exist. The same base properties contribute to the goodness of some works and the badness of others, and no base property is common to all good artworks or all bad artworks. The vivid shade of purple that is garish in one work may make another vibrant. The repetition of elements and patterns that unifies one work may be boring in a different piece.

If we examine matters more closely, the success of this argument might be questioned. In chapter 3, I suggested that artworks are to be interpreted in terms of their genre, period, and other contextual factors, since these affect their identity and content. The same should apply to evaluations of art. And it may be that, when we apply this restriction, the significance of given properties becomes more orderly. In realistic landscapes, perhaps the given shade of purple is always garish, whereas in surrealist paintings it is always vibrant. It is not clear how far we can take this observation, however, and in what follows I accept for the sake of further argument that the relation between a work's aesthetic or artistic properties and its base properties is not tightly regimented and for that reason cannot be encapsulated in rules or formulas.

If there are no rules governing the production of artistic merit and disvalue, it follows that judgments of value in art are not logically deducible. In other words, it is never possible to prove that an artwork must be good or bad by appealing to descriptions of its base properties. It does not follow, however, that judgments about an artwork's value cannot be universal and objective. If they are universal but not rule-governed, the facts they reflect are unique singularities. Such facts cannot be established by reason, but perhaps they can be directly perceived or intuited. Artistic judgments then would be true when they accurately report the work's value. They would also be objective, because this value resides in the work, independently of what the judges judge. And they would be universal if everyone – or, at least, every expert who experiences the artwork and has the time to return to it and think about it – arrives at the same, true judgment of its value. (I assume that experts are those with experience of relevantly similar works, familiarity with the art practices and traditions from which the work emerges, and with a track record of making judgments that other experts find convincing. Many art lovers could qualify as experts.)

The ideas just presented have a long and distinguished philosophical pedigree. The proposal that artistic value is not rule-governed was accepted, for example, both by David Hume in the mid-eighteenth century and by Immanuel Kant some forty years later. They also held that judgments of artistic value can be universal. Hume outlined the characteristics of the "true judge" who can detect artistic value and its source within the work: such a person requires, as well as good sensory capacities and attention to detail, relevant knowledge or sensibilities, an unprejudiced attitude, and a great deal of practice. Hume held that art of high merit will pass the *test of time* and become universally acknowledged, though he also allowed that an element of subjective preference is always involved in artistic judgments. Kant, for his part, distinguished aesthetics from ethics on the ground that, while both allow for universal, objective judgments, aesthetic value is not governed by general, practical principles. As a result, there is no method or rule for the production of great art; it must be created through acts of genius. True aesthetic judgments demand universal assent, he thought.

The thesis that artistic judgments are universal and objective can be challenged in at least two ways. First, even if they are universal across, say, Anglo-American contemporary culture, they might not be objective. Cultural relativists are liable to argue, for example, that the coincidence in opinions is a result of common indoctrination, not of perceived facts. It could have been otherwise in that we could have been taught to disvalue these qualities and to value quite different ones. As possible evidence for their position, relativists can rightly point to the fact that our artistic judgments are not independent of the processes by which we learn about and enter the culture in which we live. We are taught how to appreciate artworks by other people. Also, such appreciation often depends in part on common knowledge each person acquires as a member of a culture or subculture.

The suggestion that measures of artistic value are cultural constructions and that there is no trans-cultural standard for what is meritorious in art, as against an alternative by which at least some art is great precisely because it touches important aspects of our common humanity and thereby transcends differences in cultures and eras, recalls the disagreement that was the focus of chapter 1. This is not the place to rehearse the nature versus nurture debate, or to review cross-cultural studies of artistic and aesthetic evaluations. Needless to say, the debate is too complex and interpreting the studies is too difficult for us to expect quick or easy answers. I am doubtful, though, that full-blooded cultural relativism will prove attractive. There is much that is common to the experience of human beings. We all eat and sleep, work and play. We share many desires, needs, and vulnerabilities, whether we live in the town or country, beach or forest, in Manhattan, Marrakesh, or Manila. Themes reflecting this common ground – love and friendship, mating and parenting, peace and war, ritual and religion, birth and death – have an abiding importance and attraction. Moreover, we are interested in and can follow how these matters are tackled and played out in cultures, periods, and circumstances very different from our own. Art often addresses these themes and is significant and valuable for doing so. It also provides respite from the demands of life, and that too answers a universal need. So, it seems likely that some measures of artistic or aesthetic merit will be valid across the spread of cultures, though it seems equally likely that other dimensions of artistic or aesthetic goodness will be culturally localized.

Even if we reject the claim that artistic judgments are totally relative to the ideologies of the societies in which they are made, consideration of a second objection may make us reluctant to embrace the idea that such judgments are objectively true. This objection draws attention to the apparent absence of high agreement in the evaluations of experts, choose them as you may. In other words, such judgments lack the universality that is claimed for them. As the American philosopher Alan H. Goldman argues, if not even the decisions of experts coincide, there must be an ineradicable and significant element of personal preference expressed in such evaluations. They are relative not only to features of what is judged but also to each judge's predilections, and thereby are not objective or universal.

If it is true that there are no general rules for artistic value from which reliable judgments can be deduced and also true that a personal element enters into them, still it does not follow that such judgments are no more than unsupported expressions of idiosyncratic preferences. Certainly, it follows that there is no logical guarantee that we can correctly identify the value of art from *generalizations* about what people in fact value, but that does not show that we cannot critically examine *particular* evaluations and the reasons offered for them in the hope of placing our own judgments on a firmer basis. The subjective facet included within such evaluations is not always hidden and can be assessed for its influence. And where it is present, it is not always dominant or decisive. Anyway, though it can steer the judgment, it cannot legitimately ignore or misrepresent facts about the work that may be relevant to its evaluation. The subjective element in such evaluations should not lead us automatically to reject their integrity, then, but it should encourage us to seek second and third opinions, which is how we often greet the fallible judgments of experts on topics in predominantly fact-based disciplines such as medicine. The fallibility of medical experts does not lead us to regard all medicine as quackery, or to deny that there are objective facts about medical conditions and whether or not they are present in particular patients. And the fallibility of medical specialists does not compel us automatically to the conclusion that their judgments are no more reliable than those of GPs, or that GPs are not better placed to recognize signs of health and illness than are most members of the medically untutored public. Similarly, there is no reason to assume that the fallibility of judgments about art and the personal element they involve means that all opinions are equally worthy, or that there are no objective facts of artistic value applying to particular cases.

8.3   The Purpose and Form of Artistic Evaluation

When we consider the purpose to which artistic evaluations are put, their departures from ideals of impersonal objectivity do not look to be fatal flaws.

Typically, we are interested in determining the value things have not exclusively in order to record that knowledge but also to direct preferences and guide actions, either our own or those of others. The match with preferences is not perfect. It is not contradictory to say *I judge that bad but I like it* or *I judge that good but I don't like it*. Nevertheless, a person's evaluations are generally coercive, if not determinative, of her choices and inclinations.

Evaluations are comparative. They rank things against each other. Those who must decide what to buy, or to give the prize to, or to perform, or to hang in the gallery might be committed to choosing the best, but many others are more interested in good/better and bad/worse than in best and worst. This second group of art appreciators is not out to decide a winner that will exclude all its competitors, because its members recognize that there can be many instances of the good and that these can complement each other without competing. This is evident in their practices and dispositions. They like to return to good art if they can, but not too quickly or too often. They also value variety and novelty, so they make time for encounters with new works. They are always looking for more good works. In doing so, they rely on their experience or the evaluations of others they trust when they must select among many works that are unfamiliar.

We judge within a terrain shaped by our settled dispositions. We would not normally ask ourselves which is better, James Joyce's novel *Ulysses* or a chocolate cake. This is not because we cannot find respects of comparison – the cake is easier to digest – but because we do not see them as rivals. The same goes for artworks. Most people do not usually consider if Shakespeare's tragedy, *King Lear*, is better than *The Haywain*, a painting by John Constable. These works need not be in direct competition if there is room in our lives for both theater and painting.

There is a question about temporal priority: Which should I see first? This might be settled by circumstances or by reference to personal inclination. Perhaps I choose to see the movie because today is its last showing and I can play the recording of the symphony at any time. Or perhaps I decide I am not in the mood for a harrowing tragedy and so choose a light comedy. These judgments of temporal order may have the appearance of value judgments but they are not always so. In deciding which work to put first in time, I need not also be ranking them for quality.

Given all this, it is not difficult to see the usefulness of experts' evaluations, even if they always contain a subjective aspect. Such evaluations can provide reliable but not infallible advice about the objective value artworks possess, which is helpful because we do not have an unlimited amount of time for art. But on the other hand, a person can make a fair amount of time if she chooses, so she can always sample widely and test the opinions of others. What is more, because she is likely to be interested in locating a fairly wide range of good artworks, and because what will appeal at any moment can vary with her mood and inclination, more rigid, exclusive, or narrower modes of evaluation would be counterproductive. It would be misguided, therefore, to complain that evaluation in art falls short of some ideal standard of objectivity when, in fact, the evaluative practice typically provides the kind of guidance – an eclectic, varied blend of objective assessment leavened with personal tastes – that perfectly suits our interest in art.

8.4   What Is Rewarding about the Experience of Art?

So far I have supposed that the source of art's value lies in the rewardingness of the experience to which it gives rise when it is appreciated. Different views on what is worthwhile about this experience are considered in what follows. At the most general level, two contrasting positions each have their defenders. According to the first, the value of art and of the experience it engenders depends on an approach that treats art as belonging to an autonomous realm, separate from the ordinary, practical world. The second, by contrast, sees art as a source for knowledge and skills that are valuable for their real-world usefulness. The first sees the value of art as intrinsic, the second as extrinsic.

8.4.1   Value and pleasure

Why do people interest themselves in art? What do they get out of it? The answer seems obvious. Pleasure. They do not usually attend to art as a matter of duty owed to others, or as an exercise in self-discipline, but for pleasure taken in understanding and appreciating it.

One objection to this view maintains that we value art as an end in itself, for its own sake, and not merely as a means to other things. A person who seeks pleasure from art uses it merely as a means, and is not, therefore, a true art lover. But this objection is misconceived. It wrongly assumes that the pleasure taken in art is separable from the process of attending to art and appreciating it, as if the pleasure is a bodily sensation that might be induced also by things other than art. The pleasure is not separable from the artwork that is its cause, however. This kind of pleasure is not produced merely by exposure to art. It requires and arises out of the person's active perceptual and cognitive involvement with the artwork that is its focus. As I have stressed in earlier chapters, this engagement is concerned with determining the work's identity and content, so that the work can be recognized and appreciated in its particularity. If this process yields pleasure, that pleasure is taken in the artwork, not incidentally derived from it. Generally, it is the kind of pleasure or satisfaction that goes with understanding, not some sensuous glow or visceral thrill that happens merely to accompany the experience of art.

Though the former objection fails, there are other reasons for being wary of accounts that tie the experience of art too closely to the pleasure of the experience that it produces. One of these was discussed in chapter 6: art can be a source of negative emotions of sadness, horror, and pity. We can also note that a fair amount of art turns out, when understood, to be boringly average and not a source of special delight. Moreover, people do not always expect to derive pleasure from their experience of art. For instance, they might be curious about the latest avant-garde offerings, though they do not anticipate finding these to be enjoyable.

Several lines of reply are available. We might sort higher, cognitive levels of enjoyment from lower, emotionally negative ones they encompass. We might note that it is the prediction of pleasure that draws us to much art, even if that anticipation sometimes is unfulfilled. And where the person does not expect to find pleasure in the given work, we might describe her as seeking a derivative pleasure; for example, by confirming the breadth of her connoisseurship or the sensitivity of her taste.

The idea that we are motivated by pleasure whenever we are not driven by duty or self-discipline is vulnerable to over-extension, though, with a corresponding dilution in its explanatory power. With a bit of ingenuity, we could respond to any counterexample by identifying a potential pleasure lurking in the background. But the temptation to take the account in that direction should be resisted. It might be more convincing to accept that our interest in art can be motivated by curiosity, or habit, or by many other considerations that pay no regard, directly or indirectly, to a pleasurable pay-off.

Even if the pursuit of pleasure is not the sole reason why we interest ourselves in art, it might yet be thought to be a primary motivator. The hedonist continues: some people attend to art out of curiosity, or to pass the exam in their art appreciation class, or for the knowledge they obtain, and their experiences could be pleasure-free, but in fact they would be in the minority. Fancy arguments aside, most art gives pleasure in being understood and appreciated, and if particular pieces do not, this is a reason for not seeking them out in the future. Most people enjoy and value art, importantly if not exclusively, for the pleasure it gives them.

The critic of artistic hedonism can persist, however. Pleasure is too puny and one-dimensional to measure art's human significance. Our experience of art is demeaned and trivialized by suggesting it is primarily motivated by a desire for pleasure. Most of us love some kind of art, if not always of the high and serious kind, and love is a passion that is diminished when it is confused with enjoyment or pleasure. We love others, such as our friends or children, for themselves, not for the sake of experiences of pleasure. Love often gives rise to pleasure, but that is not its goal. (Love often gives rise to difficulties and pain, too, and that is something we expect from it as much as we expect pleasure.) To suggest that a mother is interested primarily in her children as a source of pleasure for herself would be insulting in most cases. The art lover, like other lovers, is not out for herself but is devoted to the object of her passion, which may be frustrating or irritating as often as it is delightful. The art lover, like other lovers, assigns priority to interests that go beyond the sphere of the self, narrowly construed. Under the influence of love, a person's sense of her identity changes and expands, so that the relationship becomes central to her conception of herself. Something similar is true of the art lover. For her, art is not merely an optional accompaniment to life but becomes integral to its fabric and her place in the world. Making or appreciating art is for her a mode of existence and self-realization.

Art can take on this role as a result of transformative experiences of individual pieces on particular occasions. A person might undergo a kind of epiphany on reading William Faulkner's novel *The Sound and the Fury* or on seeing Steven Spielberg's movie *Schindler's List*. As she is aware, the work has changed her outlook on life. But like many other things that turn out to be important, art can also creep up on a person, just by being around all the time. Repetition and exposure turn to habit. These more gentle influences can be no less life-shaping than the abrupt, dramatic ones.

Here is the point: to suggest that we interest ourselves in art for the pleasure we get from the experience is odd, like saying we eat food for the pleasure we get from the experience. Though this might be the reason given for eating a specific food on a given occasion, and though the consumption of food is regularly pleasurable, the claim is peculiar because it fails to make clear that eating is a necessity, not something we choose to do only for the sake of an incidental reward. Similarly, it would be puzzling to suggest a person values her left arm for the pleasure of having it. No doubt she would be very unhappy to lose it, but this is because she regards it as making an important contribution to her proper functioning, not as a means to pleasure. In general, it would be strange to ask a person if she is the way she is because of the pleasure she gets from being like that. This is why, if a person's relation to art has become part of her identity and selfhood – which is the norm, not the exception – the suggestion that she seeks pleasure from art, even if often true, does not come near to indicating the extensiveness of its role in her life.

Do these observations support those who think the making and consumption of art is an evolved behavior over those who think art is a creation of Enlightenment and modern age Europe?

Ethologists who explain human behavior with reference to biological evolution are vulnerable to the criticisms leveled previously against the idea that art is valued for the pleasure it provides, because they too claim that art is a source of intrinsic pleasure and that this is evidence for its being an adaptive behavior. They make the same observation about other behaviors that clearly are adaptive, such as the drive toward reproduction. So their error, if it is one, is general, not confined solely to what they say about art. They are guilty of expressing their view more crudely than they should, as are all those who equate what is naturally good with what is pleasurable. Instead of talking of pleasure, they should insist that selected behaviors are self-motivating and a source of fulfillment and satisfaction, even when they are not always pleasant. And they should continue: even where evolved behaviors lead to considerable pleasure, they are not always driven solely or mainly by this goal, because they are self-propelling. (One might say they are instinctual, except that appeals to this notion are no less confused in their explanatory significance than are ones about pleasure.) It is open, then, for the evolutionary theorist to revise her claims about the role of pleasure in accounting for art's value. There is no doubt that art plays a vital role in people's lives and is a source of deep rewards and satisfactions.

That is sufficient to ground the view that making and appreciating art is an adaptive behavior, without having to resort to more dubious claims about pleasure. But now, suitably revised, is the evolutionary theorist better positioned than her rivals to explain why art has this central role?

We pursue many activities with a passion so deep that they come to define our identities, attitudes, relationships, and values. Sometimes these rivers of passion might be fed from biological springs and result in behaviors with a universal, long lineage because they enhance survival and reproduction. In other cases, though, similarly strong passions are temporary, local, and fueled by cultural ephemera. People are frequently committed to the latest transient fads and fashions and also build their identities around their relationships to those. Where the universality and longevity of what is to count as art is disputed, the fact that art usually plays a self-defining role in people's lives does not favor the views of the evolutionist over those of the cultural relativist.

If anything, we are evolved to find significance and satisfaction in both work and play, especially where these are engaged in with full-hearted enthusiasm. As a result, art can take on a self-defining importance for the individual, but it does so along with many other things. Making, growing, tending, relating, reasoning, feeling, and all else are likely to be no less important. In other words, if any evolutionary account is supported, it is the one according to which art is a spin-off from more general human dispositions – ones that lead us to find meaning and fulfillment in many of life's aspects – rather than a specific target of evolutionary forces.

8.4.2   Art and education

Alongside the view that art is intrinsically valuable as a source of pleasure, there is an equally distinguished tradition that sees art as educative. To take just one example, R. G. Collingwood suggests art should be thought of not as product or artifact but as an act or process of expression through which the artist clarifies her inchoate emotions and states of mind. As such it is a source of self-knowledge, and not only for the artist because, through the work's communication, the community reproduces a similar process and thereby comes to a new understanding of itself.

Collingwood may be right as far as he goes, but it seems clear that art's educative potential reaches further than he describes. Art can be a source of propositional knowledge, of perceptual information, and of imaginary or vicarious experiential insight. We learn from it that things are or could be so-and-so, and what this would be like to experience or achieve. And we can transfer this knowledge to the actual world. As well, art can refine our perceptual and discriminatory skills, enhance our imagination, and shape or change our attitudes and values. For example, through art we might better recognize signs of stress or emotion in others, empathize more deeply with them, absorb more effectively their points of view, and be more sensitive and sympathetic to their feelings, more aware of our own prejudices, and so on. These skills and resources can then be applied in our transactions in the actual world. Art is extrinsically valuable because it has such educative powers.

Objections to this account of art's value come in many varieties. A first denies that we learn anything about the actual world from art. This view, call it the *fictional worlds objection*, stresses art's fictive nature. It notes that most literary works and many paintings create fictional worlds, rather than describing the actual one. They may be based on fact, of course, and they presuppose many similarities between their worlds and the actual one. Nevertheless, they involve a story-telling, not a fact-relating, mode of address. They *mimic* assertion and reference. As a result, they call not for belief but for imaginative engagement.

The fictional worlds objection continues: in stories with an explicitly indicated narrator, sometimes she reflects on the story and seemingly connects it to the actual world. She says: *Impulsive Dave's fate should be a lesson to us all: think before you act!* This appearance is misleading, however. The narrator is distinguishing her world from the world of the story she tells, and is relating information from the world of the story to her world. Her world may be the "actual" one from her point of view, but from the reader's, her world is part of the fiction as a whole. Within that fiction, her world contains another, that of the story she tells. In other words, the fiction contains nested worlds. Though information learned from one of these might be applied in another, the connection is made between worlds internal to the fiction, not between the fiction and the real world in which the reader resides. Accordingly, fictional works of art should not be understood as *directly* describing the actual world, even if they ape assertion and other forms of informative discourse. That is why it is a mistake to infer the beliefs and attitudes of the actual author from what is expressed in her work. Also, if the fiction sets out self-consciously to be instructive, the reader should understand that it is about the fictional world, not the actual one, that she will be educated.

Here are some responses: it is plain that much art is intended to represent or depict the actual world; consider portrait and landscape painting, for example. Tales relating history can be given poetic form without being fictionalized; not all literature or poetry is fictional. In general, functional art is tied to the real world, for it is there that it achieves its consequences. Religious art, for instance, is supposed to provide a route to the experience of God in this world. Arguments to the effect that art is insulated from reality apply only to some kinds and typically assume without argument that only the most abstruse and sophisticated forms of Western art qualify as such.

What is more, assertion can be achieved even in the fictive mode. To understand how, compare fictional utterance with quotation. If a person quotes another, usually she *mentions* what the other said without *affirming* it as her own view. We should not infer that she agrees with what she quotes. Sometimes, however, she does assert what she quotes and this can be apparent to her audience. She says *To thine own self be true*, quoting Polonius from *Hamlet*, and *means* it. Fictional artworks that appropriate the form of ordinary utterance are like quotations. Usually they tell the story without affirming what they relate. Just as quotation can be used to generate assertion indirectly, however, so too can fictional utterance within works of art. This is most evident when authors make obvious the didactic nature of sections of their fictions. For example, where they wax lyrical about the joys of gardening, or pronounce in a heartfelt way about the moral bankruptcy of politicians. These passages often can be reasonably interpreted as making indirect assertions about the actual world, as well as making observations within the fictional context about what is true in that world. Appreciating the real-world assertoric character of these authorial pronouncements does not involve the reader in ignoring or overlooking the fictional character of the relevant works.

A second objection to the view that art has educative value draws attention to the fact that abstract works, including purely instrumental musical pieces, present no semantic or representational content as such and, therefore, cannot comment on the actual world. Indeed, the undeniable value of abstract art might depend on its separateness from reality. It creates a space in which the appreciator can put aside all worldly concerns.

Again, the objection is not convincing. It is not true that abstract art is without content, since it can be expressive of emotion. It can be about the emotions expressed in it, given that it is designed by the artist to take the expressive form it does. In addition, we can learn from abstract (and all other) art important facts about what humans can achieve, because we see exemplified in it the skills, attributes, and talents that went into its creation. We learn from this art about the manual, imaginative, and intellectual feats of which our fellows are capable.

The defender of art's autonomy and isolation from the world could adopt a third line of objection, which was anticipated earlier in this chapter: she concedes that we can learn about the world from art but claims this is possible only where we adopt an inappropriate attitude to the work. For example, instead of appreciating a fictional novel for itself, as art, we approach it as ordinary, informational discourse. And here is a further point: when we abstract from the story's specific detail, what we learn often is banal in its generality – crime does not pay, pride comes before a fall, murdering your father and marrying your mother is unlikely to make for a happy life in the long run. Besides, if we are to learn from a fiction, we must discriminate the ways in which its worlds are like the actual one and the ways in which they are not, which can be done only in terms of knowledge of the actual world we already possess. The result very often is not new knowledge about the actual world so much as recognition of the story's verisimilitude.

Here are replies to these new points. Learning about the actual world frequently involves imaginatively considering "fictional" scenarios about what might happen in the future or could have happened in the past. We might ask: what would have happened if Hitler had won World War II, or what can prevent global warming? The same imaginative processes and simulations are also activated by fictional works of art. Indeed, we might watch a movie based on the idea that Hitler did win World War II or one addressing ways of halting climate change. The process of deriving knowledge about the actual world is similar in either case. So, the person who engages with a work of art does not have to mistake it for, or pretend that it is, factual discourse before she can take information from it. She remains aware of it as a fiction and as a work of art throughout.

What one learns from art might be indifferent to its being art – as when old paintings are studied to see the agricultural implements used at the time – but often this is not the case. Indeed, learning from the work can be intimately bound up with recognizing and understanding it for the artwork it is. To follow Tolstoy's *Anna Karenina*, the reader must come to appreciate how the heroine can be led to suicide by the events of her life, and it is precisely that understanding that might translate to the real world. We learn through example, mimicry, and experience, as well as by explicit instruction, and artworks provide the opportunity for us not only to observe how fictional characters grapple with and perhaps learn from their situations, but also to imaginatively rehearse our response to equivalent, possibly future, circumstances. It is true that we need to bring beliefs, values, and sensitivities from the real world to our appreciation of the novel, but it is no less true that through appreciating the fiction we may develop, reorganize, and refine them. Fictions can represent complex situations in concrete detail and thereby bring to life ideas and emotions we may previously have grasped only in schematic, abstracted forms.

Moreover, by how they structure and juxtapose the elements in the stories they convey, fictions can bring out morally significant or otherwise important connections and patterns we might never notice under similar, real-world conditions. Indeed, they are especially suited to achieving this result, being crafted by skilled observers of human nature who can control and highlight through their use of fine detail particular aspects of the events they describe, thereby gently steering the reader toward new, subtle understandings. Also, the reader can become transfixed by the world of the story without facing the demands and problems that go with interacting with that world. Fictions have a special power, then, and it can make them potent educators. Their seductiveness is a source of both value and danger, depending on whether the work correctly informs or misleads the reader about what is involved in experiencing or responding to the states of affairs it describes.

The educative power of a fictional artwork does not depend on its being treated as something other than an artwork; for example, merely as ordinary informative discourse. The reverse is the case. The very features that allow it to perform an educative function do so most effectively when they are appreciated in ways that make apparent their artistic value. What is fictionally presented and the means by which it is presented contribute together to the work's artistic and to its educative value, so intimately are these two linked.

As observed earlier, if it works, this last argument clears the way for the suggestion that art can possess both intrinsic and extrinsic value.

8.5   Messages through Art

So far we have been considering the possibility that fictional artworks can convey claims about the actual world, and that part of their value can lie in what we learn from them or in how we are otherwise positively altered by them. There is another case to consider, though. The artwork assumes as background certain ideas and values that its audience does not share. For instance, it might presuppose that the earth is flat or that some women are witches who truck with the devil. When these presuppositions are widely held in the artist's culture, she might be unconscious of them and, anyway, would not regard them as part of the work's message. Nevertheless, her work can be understood only by an audience that recognizes (and perhaps also imaginatively adopts) these same assumptions. As I emphasized in chapters 3 and 4, determining the identity and content of works of art requires that they be approached in light of relevant facts about the broader social conditions and beliefs in the artist's society, as well as the piece's art-historical setting.

If the ideas, values, attitudes, or points of view presumed by the work are not ones taken for granted by the current audience, the fact that the work mandates that they be accepted (or imaginatively adopted) brings them to that audience's attention. In this way, the audience can learn from an artwork about attitudes held by its creator, or more widely within the society in which it was generated, because they are betrayed in the work. The author did not aim to convey them and their communication is obviously not an intended purpose of the story, yet they come across to the audience's members – indeed, they may do so quite vividly if they disagree with them. Like the product of any action, works of art can be symptomatic of the attitudes and values of their creator and of other of the circumstances of creation. Sometimes these are referred to as messages conveyed *through*, rather than *in*, art.

Feminist philosophers have drawn attention to how works that are not blatantly misogynist manage to convey the sexist presuppositions that underpin them. In movies, the viewer is called upon to adopt a *male gaze*, with female actors presented as passive, dependent, sexual objects whose function is to validate the hero, while males are portrayed as powerful and active. Women are depicted as prostitutes or as dutiful mates, and as sexually available in either role. Those who assert their independence and autonomy from the patriarchal paradigms are punished, often with death, while "good girls" are shown as finding fulfillment in the servitude of marriage and motherhood. Other artforms also express gender bias in their treatment of women and relationships. Paintings of female nudes show them in ways that presume the heterosexist interests and attitudes of a male viewer. In operas, women are frequently charac-terized as irrational slaves to passion, or, if they are willful and independ-ent, they die from disease or are murdered. In pornographic works, women are depicted as meaning *yes* when they say *no* and as insatiably desiring physical subjection and domination as well as meaningless sexual intercourse with strangers.

Not surprisingly, women can feel excluded from the intended audience and thereby alienated from engagement with such works. Though they might imaginatively take on the cognitive and emotional profile a work assumes in its audience, they resist doing so. They are liable to interpret the work *against the grain*; that is, by drawing out and criticizing the objectionable attitudes it exposes in the artist and his times. In the process, the work is faulted. It fails as art because it presumes to say something universally true and thereby to attract a global audience, yet it does neither.

The concerns of feminist philosophers about art have their counterparts in other areas of social deprivation and prejudice — race, class, religion, sexual orientation, animal ethics, and environmentalism. But those who would defend the autonomy of art insist that it should not be valued positively or negatively for its treatment of such issues. They deny that it is fair to assess the attitudes of past societies by present moral standards. More importantly, they object to what they see as the inappropriate application of moral values in the evaluation of art. They deny that the artistic merits of an artwork are ever dulled by its immoral content, or that its artistic faults can be redeemed by the rightness of its ethical vision. Are advocates for art's autonomy right to insist that artistic and moral values are never connected?

8.6   The Relation between Artistic and Moral Values

As described earlier, Tolstoy derived the value of good art directly from that of morality and religion. I have argued that he was wrong to do so. Art has its own forms of value, both intrinsic and extrinsic. Nevertheless, it is plain that artistic and moral values intersect. For example, a person's recognition of the moral virtues and vices of the characters in a story, and of the attitude projected in the work toward these, is indicative of her understanding of the work, and hence counts toward the reliability of her assessment of its value. (A similar point was made in chapter 6, where it was suggested that a person's emotional reaction to a work of art can reveal her comprehension of it.) As well as intersecting in this way, do moral and artistic values interact? In particular, does immorality in a work's production or content ever compromise its artistic value?

Immoral actions can be associated with the creation and presentation of artworks without affecting the identity and content of those works. A film producer might cheat the cast and crew of their wages at the end of the shoot, or a statue might be stolen. The agents of these acts can be blamed, but their immorality is not relevant to the artistic evaluation of the film or statue. A different case is that in which, when a forgery is detected, the judgment of the work is revised. This can be appropriate, as was explained in chapter 3, because originals and copies do not necessarily share the same art-relevant properties. Note, however, that what matters here is not the immorality of deliberate deception, but rather the correction of misinformation about the work's origins. The same kind of reconsideration is appropriate when the misidentification of the work is innocent or accidental. It is not the immorality of forgery, therefore, that prompts the review of the judgment about the forged work. Instead, the piece's true identity and content are uncovered, and this leads to reconsideration of the work in light of this new information.

Some immoral actions that do not affect the identity and content of works, or distort their audiences' perceptions of these, can influence how an artwork is approached, even if they should not affect how it should be evaluated as a work of art. If we learn that the painter murdered his model shortly after he finished her portrait, we may find that it is no longer possible to accept the calm innocence of the painting's appearance at face value. That same experience might occur, however, if she was killed not by the painter but by her deranged lover. And for that matter, if the painter had simply dropped dead of old age as he finished the work, awareness of this is likely to structure or filter the viewer's experience of the piece. These examples show how knowledge of contextual features not relevant to the work's identity and content can sometimes inhibit, color, or skew our consideration of the work, even if they should not count in its artistic evaluation. The point is not about immorality as such. The effect is no different when it is hard to put from one's mind the current monetary worth of the painting by Claude Monet that is before one, though its price is neither an artistic merit nor a deficit in the painting.

In other cases, the immorality is central to the artwork's identity and content. It can be created to have this content, it can inherit it through the process of production, or it can receive it through the manner in which it is instanced. An example of the first is a fictional story featuring rape, torture, murder, and cannibalism; an example of the second is a movie recording real acts of rape, murder, and the like, instead of fictional representations of such acts; while the third is illustrated by a performer who cheats her audience, as when a classical musician mimes to a CD at what is represented as a live performance. The question addressed here asks whether ethical features should bear on a work's artistic value. More particularly, the focus is on whether the immorality of an artwork's or a performance's content should count as an artistic, not just a moral, fault.

8.7   Should a Work's Immorality Undermine its Claims to Artistic Merit?

Three answers to the above question should be considered. The first defends the autonomy of art by arguing that the immorality of an artwork's content is never relevant to its artistic evaluation. One reason why we might be tempted to take this line is out of fear of the effects of moral censorship on the freedom of artists to express themselves, and on the freedom of their publics to choose without restraint what art they wish to engage with. Such worries are real enough, but the issue here is whether there are *any* moral limits on what can be done in the name of good art, and the answer that will be advocated is *Yes*. The second, also extreme, view maintains that immorality in art is always an artistic defect. Counter-examples showing why this position should be rejected are offered below. The theory I favor is the third, which maintains that immorality in art is sometimes an artistic defect and sometimes not.

Consider cases in which immorality is represented or described in a fiction. A novel features torture and cannibalism, let us say. A crucial first point is that the work also expresses a point of view on what it depicts. Immoral acts might be described in a fashion that exposes their dreadful consequences and the kind of vicious or corrupted mentality that causes them. In other words, the fiction might present a morally appropriate attitude to the immorality it contains, this being one a morally sensitive audience will share. For example, the film *The Accused*, directed by Jonathan Kaplan, portrays gang rape as horrifying and callous, and Shakespeare's *Macbeth* shows murder to be soul-destroying for those who commit it. In these cases the depiction of immorality does not mar the work's artistic achievement. Indeed, the work might be better if its description of immorality is skillfully played off against the point of view it adopts toward that immorality. Immorality in a work's content does not automatically score against its value as art.

In other cases, the work might adopt a neutral moral stance with respect to immoralities it presents. Perhaps they are incidental to the main storyline, serving only to establish a mood or ambience. Or perhaps the work assumes a matter-of-fact *this is how the world is* stance to what it depicts, or, at least, does not explicitly condemn or moralize about what it describes. Again, it is not obvious that the depiction of immorality counts as an artistic defect. Indeed, if the work's artistic merit depends on the interest and complexity of its narrative structure, and if that derives from the immorality it presents – as might occur if it records, say, how betrayal can lead to revenge that provokes retaliation, and so on, in a complex spiral of mutual degeneration – then its portrayal of immorality adds to its artistic value.

Yet more interesting are genres, such as action movies, westerns, and crime dramas, in which immorality is sometimes treated with benign toleration when it is perpetrated by the heroes as they pursue their private vision of justice. They aggressively eliminate their enemies with a ruthless disregard for the law and for the suffering their actions will cause, and the work projects a point of view on this that is approving. What is more, as an audience we are supposed to empathize with the heroes and enjoy the death and havoc they cause so recklessly. This is another case in which the representation of immorality is supposed not to be an artistic defect. Yet how can that be, since such works endorse immorality and surely therefore betray a diseased taste and sensibility?

It is important to recognize the special conventions that govern works of this kind. In them, brawling men break chairs over each other's heads, or get thrown through glass windows, without getting seriously hurt. These are sure signs that some concerns applying in the real world should be held in abeyance in considering the work's fictional world. The henchmen of evil frequently are two-dimensional cutouts; they are not seen to suffer from their wounds or their violent, untimely deaths, and if they have parents, wives, and children, these are not shown to endure consequent grief, pain, misery, or deprivation. Meanwhile, the pace of the story constantly drives the audience's attention past the last explosion to the next danger. It is not appropriate, in following such works, to dwell too long over the fate of these "bit" players. Within the narratives of these genres, they are dispensable, cardboard extras at best, or vermin at worst, and in neither case are they fully human. In enjoying the action and overlooking the heroes' immorality, the audience is responding in a way appropriate to the genre, so long as all agree that the heroes' cause has natural or rough justice on its side. The conventions for this kind of work reveal its fictional world as differing from the real one in ways that blunt the immorality of the heroes' actions and the pain of the consequences of those actions. Given an audience at home with the relevant conventions and keen to be entertained, it would not be appropriate for them to judge the works' artistic merits negatively. And while a case might be made for regarding such genres as artistically limited because of the immorality they endorse, it would be prudish to see this as outweighing their positive artistic values, especially given the widespread toleration in other contexts of sports, pastimes, and entertainments that are genuinely violent and harmful.

Conventions of the kind just described can also be exploited and subverted in more sophisticated pieces. For example, a work could begin in the style of a James Bond movie but stop suddenly to focus on the death of someone who in that genre should be a minion – on how he got there and what his death meant to others – thereby turning him into a human, rounded character. Works on this wavelength are Tom Stoppard's play *Rosencrantz and Guildenstern Are Dead* and the western movie directed by Howard Hawks, *Red River*. A similar kind of sophistication would be apparent in a work that gradually reveals the heroes' sense of justice as perverse and that ends by showing them as no less evil than the villains.

It is different, though, when immorality, portrayed in all its brutal detail and destructive ramifications, is presented in a manner that glorifies it. The celebration of evil – that is, the relishful depiction of unmitigated iniquity and the suffering to which it leads – corrodes the work's artistic value. Again, however, a subtler approach is possible. The work could elicit sympathy for an evil character, while letting it be known that he is evil, before showing him at his worst. Such a work challenges the audience by drawing them into contradictory responses. Something like this happens in Jonathan Demme's movie *Silence of the Lambs*.

If we can make believe of action thrillers that they depict a different moral universe without also seeing this as an artistic defect, why can we not do the same for works in which evil and its consequences are savored? Why do we resist entertaining, even though we do not believe it, the suggestion that rape, torture, murder, and cannibalism, say, are good and are to be praised in the world of the fiction? The answer lies in differences between what the two kinds of fiction – the action thriller versus the piece that revels in the depiction of malevolence and anguish – require their audiences to imagine. It is because the spectator shares the action thriller's overall moral vision regarding the course of natural justice that she is prepared to suspend some of her other moral principles, namely, ones according full humanity to others, including barely glimpsed strangers, or counting all the predictable bad consequences of an action, including ones not on immediate display. Nothing like that happens in the work celebrating rape, torture, murder, and cannibalism, where there is no basis for sympathy with the overall moral vision that is presented and where the humanity of those affected and the length of their suffering are emphasized.

In fact, the spectator is liable to show a kind of conceptual incapacity, not merely moral resistance, to making believe what the evil work mandates, as Kendall L. Walton points out. This is a matter of the definition of the relevant terms, as it were. To cut up un-anaesthetized people slowly causes them pain and suffering. To be aware of, yet indifferent to, the suffering of others is to be callous; to enjoy that suffering is to be cruel. Cruelty and callousness are vices. To be vicious is to be immoral. So cutting up people for no good reason, while being aware of yet indifferent to their suffering, or while enjoying it, is immoral. We can make believe a world in which the language is such that the word *good* means what we mean by the word *bad*. We can also imagine a world in which the inhabitants are mistaken about the moral significance of their actions because they are misguided about what is true in that world. For example, they wrongly believe that some races are not human and do not feel pain. But, unlike these cases, what the spectator of the problematic fiction is called on to imagine is close to conceptual incoherence. She is to make believe that pain is intrinsically good in the world of the fiction, although the experience of it there is just as it is in the actual world, or that it is moral to be vicious and immoral to be virtuous in the fictional world, though the same concepts apply there as in this one. It is one thing to imagine that characters depicted as less than fully human do not really suffer, or that consequences have no moral weight if their representation is assiduously avoided, but quite another to make believe that what is a paradigm of evil action is both accurately represented and an archetype of good action.

How does the artistic defect emerge? The artist presents the work with the intention that it elicits particular effects from its audience. If she miscalculates, the work is an artistic failure. When we focus sincerely on the work in the desire to engage with it, yet we can only laugh when we should cry, find ourselves drawn irresistibly to cheer the baddies, and cannot find the interest to care whether girl ever finds boy again, though we know at every point what reaction is expected and intended, the work is an artistic flop. A work that looks for the audience's sympathetic approval and alienates them instead, because it is both morally repulsive and incoherent in what it requires them to suppose, is not an artistic success.

In a similar fashion, the morally virtuous content of a story can sometimes contribute to its artistic value and sometimes count against it. An example of the first would be one in which the positive morality endorsed in the work is presented in a way that furthers the story in an artistically constructive fashion. It makes it more unified, psychologically revealing, complex and subtle in the balance of characters, say. (This is to be distinguished from the case in which the audience approves of a story and finds it successful simply on the grounds that they strongly share the moral perspective it puts forward.) And the positive moral stance of a story can be an artistic defect where it shapes the story in an inappropriate fashion. For example, the story conveys moral outrage disproportionate to the wrongful acts it describes, thereby revealing a lack of toleration, compassion, or insight into its subject matter.

8.8 Morality in Documentaries and Fictions

As was mentioned in chapter 7, film can have the interesting property of representing a fiction and matching a slice of reality simultaneously. This is relevant to the current discussion.

Consider a documentary maker. She manages to film the crash of a helicopter and later uses the footage in a documentary about air disasters. No moral problems. The situation is different, obviously, if she sabotages the helicopter in order to film the crash. If we were then judging the resulting documentary artistically, two considerations would come into play. First, she violates a convention of the genre. Despite all the art and editing that go into them, documentaries are meant to *document*, to record what is presented as the central facts. (This is not to deny that they can contain simulations. Audiences are supposed to be able to distinguish re-enactments from the events they portray.) Manipulating the outcome in certain ways – causing the helicopter to crash, say, or digitally editing together photographs taken at different times and venues – counts as cheating. One option, then, is to say that the work is an artistic failure because it does not qualify for the genre in which it presents itself. To return to a similar case mentioned earlier, we might say the classical musician who mimes to a recording at what is advertised as a live performance thereby fails to create a performance, so the outcome is an artistic as well as a moral failure.

Alternatively, we could argue that the major artistic defect is like that just discussed, in that an audience aware of how the expected convention is violated will respond to the film of the helicopter in a fashion that is at odds with the audience uptake the work is intended to achieve. The reaction will be a moral *yuck*, not *oohs* and *aahs* of fearful horror. But in that case also, the immorality that leads to the violation of the work's conventions produces an artistic demerit, because the intended audience will not be capable of responding as the work requires.

Now consider a work represented as a fiction. As fortune has it, the movie director catches the accidental crash of a helicopter in which many are killed. The script calls for scenes of just such an event. The director decides to save the costly simulation and inserts footage of the real crash. There does seem to be a moral problem here, where there is not in the appropriate use of the same footage in a documentary. Fiction movies involve a convention (and also a legal requirement, no doubt) somewhat the reverse of documentaries – directors are to manipulate what is filmed so that real actors and others do *not* suffer the injuries and actions that are depicted. (This convention is so well known that filmmakers do not add a line to the credits saying *No actors were injured in the making of this film*, even if they do insert the equivalent disclaimer about non-human animals.) The director who uses the film of the actual helicopter crash abuses the relevant convention. And as well as that artistic black mark, there is likely to be another of the kind described previously: the audience cringes at the moral insensitivity and disrespect being shown, when another reaction should be forthcoming if the work is to be an artistic success. The director's miscalculation undermines the movie's quality as an artwork.

Pornography relies for some of its effects on the potential ambiguity between fictional movies and documentaries. It is defended on the ground that it presents a fictional world using actors who give informed consent to their participation. (The last claim could be challenged in many cases, especially given the coercive power of money in a world in which many are destitute and deprived.) Yet it is frequently designed to come across in a documentary style and to establish that the acts filmed are actual, not merely simulated. In other words, it does everything it can from within the fictive mode to make assertions about the real world, and those assertions are degrading to and abusive of women. These moral faults also become artistic or aesthetic ones when pornography manipulates its audience by deliberately fudging the line between movie fiction and documentary fact. An artistically successful work must respect its audience by providing the space they need to reach an appropriate judgment of the work. Cheaply controlling, emotionally oppressive works fail both morally and artistically on this count.

A new moral consideration of artistic relevance was just introduced: the audience is to be respected. Ways of engaging their interest and sympathy that undermine their chances of appreciating the work for what it is are both morally and artistically suspect.

These final observations lead us to one of the most notorious cases, that of Leni Riefenstahl's *Triumph of the Will*, a documentary about the Nuremberg rallies of Hitler's National Socialists in 1934. In her film, Hitler is represented as an eloquent, visionary savior and hero who is loved by and unites the German folk, to whom he will bring fulfillment and self-respect. This depiction is largely an artifact of the cinematic mastery evident throughout the film, as Riefenstahl skillfully blends stunning, beautiful, forceful images and symbols. (To a modern audience, the pace of editing is likely to seem drearily slow, however.) It is hard to deny that the artistic technique displayed in the film is of the highest order, yet many people now are repulsed by Riefenstahl's glorification of ideas and values that led only a few years later to Hitler's barbaric, racist rule.

If there is an artistic fault with this work, it lies in its commitment to image over truth, given that it presents itself as a documentary. It tries too hard to persuade, to sell its message. It is too complicit with what it purports to report. A defender might suggest that it is no more at fault than most party political broadcasts, while it is more artful than most. It is an advertisement, not a documentary. A critic could respond that the proper reaction to political propaganda of any kind should be skepticism and discomfort. To the extent that propaganda does what it can to prevent such results, as it must if it is to be persuasive, it is inevitably at odds with its own nature. It does not show the sincerity, honesty, and self-awareness that are found in great art. As a genre, it cannot lend itself to artistic achievements of significance. If Riefenstahl's film seems to do so, this is only because it is careful to pretend to be more than a political advertisement.

Questions

8.1 Leo Tolstoy thought true art should project moral values and should better society. Being merely beautiful and a source of pleasure are purposes too trivial for it. What do you think of this view?

8.2 Many novels, including James Joyce's *Ulysses*, D. H. Lawrence's *Lady Chatterley's Lover*, and Hubert Selby Jr.'s *Last Exit to Brooklyn*, were banned for their nonjudgmental attitude to the immorality they describe. Should we ever ban or censor art and, if so, on what grounds? Is the artistic merit of the work relevant to whether it should be banned?

8.3 How important is art to the way people conceive of themselves? Is it more or less important than other things, such as relationships, religion, race, and fashion?

8.4 Can art be beautiful and immoral? Can it be morally perfect yet ugly? Are there any kinds of moral messages or sensitivities that only art can teach? Are there any that art can teach better than other routes to moral knowledge or skills?

8.5 Western artists have often chosen to paint scenes with a sexual, sometimes violent, content. There are more depictions of the naked Susannah at her bath, being spied on by the elders, than is justified by the relative insignificance of this story in the Old Testament. Similarly, there are numerous depictions of the rape of the Sabine women and of harem scenes. Do the male heterosexist points of view and sexist attitudes presumed by such works undermine their beauty or value?

8.6 When aesthetically judging the Roman Coliseum and the pyramids of Central America, is it relevant to recall they were designed as places for human sacrifice?

8.7 Many movies, such as Woody Allen's *Zelig* and Philip Kaufman's *The Unbearable Lightness of Being*, make use of historical footage of actual events in the fictions they create. Sometimes this is indicated in the credits, sometimes not. How might the use of such clips be morally or artistically relevant to an assessment of such films?

8.8 How far can a documentary maker go in editing her work for the sake of making it artistically pleasing?

8.9 Is it the vision presented in *Triumph of the Will* that is corrupt, or is it the reality that lay behind that vision and contradicted it? Could the work be artistically redeemed by arguing for the second view?

8.10 Gunther von Hagens, a German artist, plasticizes human cadavers. He displays his plastinates in a manner showing the internal organs. For instance, he has created sections through the body that can be pulled out, like drawers, to show the muscles and viscera inside. In another case he made a plastinate of a smoker's jet-black lung. Eduardo Kac, an Argentinian-born artist, has taken iridescent genes from jellyfish and planted them in a rabbit fetus to produce a rabbit that glows green under blue light. Artists at the University of Western Australia have created *Fish and Chips*, a work involving neurons from a fish's eye grown over a silicon chip and kept alive by a bath of nutrients. When the neurons are triggered (as when someone in their field of view moves) electronic impulses activate mechanical devices that draw lines on paper. Does "biological" art raise special ethical considerations, and how are they to be addressed?

Readings

Plato's negative characterization of art as a bad copy of a copy of the underlying structure of reality is in book 10 of the *Republic*. See *Republic 10*, translated with commentary by S. Halliwell (Warminster: Aris & Phillips, 1988). Leo Tolstoy's views on the connection between art and morality are set out in the title essay of *What Is Art? and Essays on Art*, translated by A. Maude (Oxford: Oxford University Press, 1930). David Hume's discussion of the "ideal judge" is found in "Of the Standard of Taste," in *Essays Moral, Political, and Literary* (1741–2), edited by E. F. Miller (revised edn., Indianapolis: Liberty Classics, 1987), 226–49. R. G. Collingwood considers art as a form of expression that provides the artist with knowledge of the nature of his or her emotions in *The Principles of Art* (London: Oxford University Press, 1938), ch. 6.

Wide-ranging (and conflicting) accounts of art's value have been offered. Monroe C. Beardsley, in *Aesthetics* (New York: Harcourt Brace & World, 1958), 571–83, suggests that art is valuable if it provides an aesthetic experience of great magnitude, and that such experiences are valuable in turn because of their instrumental effects, such as refining perception and discrimination, fostering mutual sympathy and understanding, and relieving tensions and destructive impulses. Nelson Goodman, in *Languages of Art* (New York: Bobbs-Merrill, 1968), ch. 6, describes the value of art as primarily cognitive. In *Evaluating Art* (Philadelphia: Temple University Press, 1988), George Dickie reviews many theories as well as outlining his own account of how judgments comparing artworks can be made. He maintains that some aesthetic properties just are intrinsically, not instrumentally, valuable, though he allows also for cognitive and other values. Dickie's position is expanded and clarified in *Art and Value* (Oxford: Blackwell, 2001). Alan H. Goldman sees the value of art as consisting in the experience produced through total engagement with the work and the exercise of our faculties, not in terms of knowledge artworks convey. There is an element of subjective preference in artistic judgments, he holds, though the evaluations of experts are useful. See his *Aesthetic Value* (Boulder, CO: Westview Press, 1995). Malcolm Budd, in *The Values of Art: Pictures, Poetry, and Music* (London: Penguin Press, 1995), regards the experience of art as valuable in itself, though this experience has cognitive as well as aesthetic aspects. Though the various arts involve different kinds of values, comparisons across the arts are sometimes possible.

R. A. Sharpe insists that art is not appropriately valued for the pleasure its appreciation yields in "The Empiricist Theory of Artistic Value," *JAAC* 58 (2000), 321–32. Among his targets is Jerrold Levinson's "Pleasure and the Value of Works of Art," in *The Pleasures of Aesthetics* (Ithaca: Cornell University Press, 1996), 11–24. A relevant collection on the topic is *Pleasure, Preference and Value: Studies in Philosophical Aesthetics*, edited by E. Schaper (Cambridge: Cambridge University Press, 1983).

Two collections exploring the connection between art and ethics are *Aesthetics and Ethics*, edited by J. Levinson (Cambridge: Cambridge University Press, 1998) and *Art and its Messages*, edited by S. Davies (University Park: Pennsylvania State University Press, 1997). Among many valuable essays, the former includes Berys Gaut's "The Ethical Criticism of Art" (pp. 182–203) and Mary Devereaux's discussion of Riefenstahl's filmic glorification of Hitler in "Beauty and Evil: The Case of Leni Riefenstahl's *Triumph of the Will*" (pp. 227–56). The latter contains debate on the artistic relevance of messages presented in and through art by Jerrold Levinson in "Messages in Art" (pp. 70–83) and by David Novitz in "Messages 'In' and Messages 'Through' Art" (pp. 84–8).

Excellent overviews on the relation between ethics and art are provided by Noël Carroll in "Art and Ethical Criticism: An Overview of Recent Directions of Research," *Ethics* 110 (2000), 350–87, and "The Wheel of Virtue: Art, Literature, and Moral Knowledge," *JAAC* 60 (2002), 3–26. Among many relevant readings are: R. W. Beardsmore, *Art and Morality* (London: Macmillan, 1971); Martha Nussbaum, *Love's Knowledge: Essays on*

Philosophy and Literature (Oxford: Oxford University Press, 1990); Marcia M. Eaton, *Aesthetics and the Good Life* (Cranbury: Associated University Presses, 1989); and Peter Lamarque and Stein Haugom Olsen, *Truth, Fiction, and Literature: A Philosophical Perspective* (Oxford: Clarendon Press, 1994), 386–97. In "Morals in Fiction and Fictional Morality," *Proceedings of the Aristotelian Society* supp. vol. 68 (1994), 27–50, Kendall L. Walton argues that the audience is liable to show a kind of conceptual incapacity, not only moral resistance, to imagining what immoral works require.

Collections on feminist aesthetics include *Aesthetics in Feminist Perspective*, edited by H. Hein and C. Korsmeyer (Bloomington: Indiana University Press, 1993), and *Feminism and Tradition in Aesthetics*, edited by P. Z. Brand and C. Korsmeyer (University Park: Pennsylvania State University Press, 1995). Also relevant is *Beauty Matters*, edited by P. Z. Brand (Bloomington: University of Indiana Press, 2000), and Carolyn Korsmeyer's *Gender and Aesthetics: An Introduction* (New York: Routledge, 2004). For the application of feminist theory to movies, see Laura Mulvey's "Visual Pleasure and Narrative Cinema," in *Film Theory and Criticism*, edited by G. Mast and M. Cohen (3rd edn., Oxford: Oxford University Press, 1985), 803–16, and Mary Devereaux's "Oppressive Texts, Resisting Readers and the Gendered Spectator: The 'New' Aesthetics," *JAAC* 48 (1990), 337–44. For a critical examination of these views, see Cynthia A. Freeland's "Feminist Frameworks for Horror Films," in *Post-Theory: Reconstructing Film Studies*, edited by D. Bordwell and N. Carroll (Madison: University of Wisconsin Press, 1996), 195–218, and Noël Carroll's "The Image of Women in Film: A Defense of a Paradigm," *JAAC* 48 (1990), 349–60.

Art is discussed from the perspective of critical race theory by literary and cultural critic Henry Louis Gates Jr. in *Loose Canons: Notes on the Culture Wars* (Oxford: Oxford University Press, 1992), art historian Ann Gibson in *Abstract Expressionism: Other Politics* (Cambridge, MA: Yale University Press, 1997), and cultural commentator and poet Amiri Baraka (with his wife) in *The Music: Reflections on Jazz and Blues* (New York: Morrow, 1987), especially "The Great Music Robbery."

Index

Printed and bound by CPI Group (UK) Ltd, Croydon, CR0 4YY